Joshua R. Giddings
and the Tactics
of Radical Politics

◄§ ℈►

JOSHUA

R. GIDDINGS

AND THE TACTICS OF RADICAL POLITICS

JAMES BREWER STEWART

The Press of Case Western Reserve University
Cleveland and London • 1970

This book has been brought to publication by a grant from the William and Françoise Barstow Foundations in The New York Community Trust.

To Dottie

CONTENTS

PREFACE

During his twenty-six-year participation in the nineteenth century's antislavery crusade Joshua R. Giddings constantly faced a
choice familiar to Americans of every generation who have been
eager for drastic reform of their society. Realizing that the behavior
of Americans denied self-professed national values, Giddings was
forced to make a tactical decision—either to try to improve institutions gradually or to call for the overthrow of the entire political
structure as a prelude to a new beginning.

The American people proclaimed the virtues of freedom while
practicing and excusing slavery. They celebrated the high moral
nature of American government, yet they relied on legislation by
the majority to protect and promote the practice of enslavement
and racial discrimination. Even the Capitol in Washington, symbolic repository of American liberty under law, was surrounded
by slave pens and auction blocks.

To some antislavery partisans like William Lloyd Garrison all
attempts to reform the political system from within amounted to
morally debilitating compromises, only forestalling the day of
emancipation. Joshua Giddings, however, spent his years in Congress trying to achieve what Garrison deemed impossible, a fusion
of morality and conventional politics for the building of a more
humane society. By committing himself to this combination of
means and ends, Giddings based his career upon the bipolar tensions of conviction and political expediency. He was convinced
that by moral agitation he could persuade his fellow representatives to act upon fixed Christian principle, and he refused to be
deterred as he found himself repeatedly dismayed and misled by

the calculating attitudes and compromising actions of his associates.

Despite all the pitfalls of pragmatism inherent in his position, Giddings spoke out courageously in the House of Representatives from 1838 to 1859, hoping to mobilize American politics against the Southern labor system. And while his sectional activities made him a political pariah for much of his career and a maverick for all of it, no Northern political figure did more to channel opinion and move institutions against slavery. All the while, Giddings remained a capable guardian of his own integrity, never letting his desire to work within the system make him accept that system's compromises.

By assuming the role of Congress' moral catalyst, Joshua Giddings enjoyed a successful career as a practitioner of radical politics, a liaison transmitting the moral perceptions of true revolutionaries like Garrison to the thoroughly institutionalized politicians of ante-bellum America. Without the vital link which Giddings helped to create between traditional representative government and the root-and-branch activist, much of America's moral impetus for constructive change would have been without effect in the halls of Congress. For this reason alone, Joshua Giddings' activities take on larger significance to our own generation, which is faced with moral and social crises every bit as pressing as the slavery question was.

In reconstructing Giddings' career I have been assisted by many individuals who have given generously of their time and talents, helping to expand this biography's meaning, while pointing out the wrong-headedness and technical errors of the author. Not to recognize such aid would constitute a grave academic sin.

Mr. David Larson, of the Ohio Historical Society, as well as Mrs. Alene Lowe White and Mr. Kermit Pike of the Western Reserve Historical Society, assisted greatly by procuring documents vital to this study. So did Mr. Dan Beame of Freiburger Library, Case Western Reserve University. My debt to my father, Mr. Richard H. Stewart, is both academic and pecuniary, for his exacting criticism of parts of this manuscript accompanied his help in defraying the costs of photoduplication and typing. My brother, Henry A. Stewart, made it clear that an undergraduate can suggest important changes in a historical monograph.

Bertram Wyatt-Brown of Case Western Reserve University played an instrumental role during every phase of the writing of this book. In the research stages he suggested sources and offered essential interpretive suggestions. In the writing and rewriting stages he waded through every page, pointing out flaws of all sorts while offering indispensable advice and friendly, trenchant criticism. Robert Huhn Jones, also of Case Western Reserve University, worked his way line by line through the first draft, making constructive and justified destructive criticisms whenever appropriate. I am greatly indebted to both James M. McPherson of Princeton University, who also read the entire manuscript and graciously offered many important suggestions for revision, and to Louis Filler of Antioch College. Charles Crowe of the University of Georgia was instrumental in guiding my interests toward anti-slavery issues, and for this service I express my gratitude. My appreciation is also extended to the Adams Manuscript Trust for permission to cite and quote from the papers of John Quincy Adams and Charles Francis Adams.

An especially warm thanks is extended to my wife, Dorothy C. Stewart, who helped me uncomplainingly as the spectre of Joshua Giddings haunted my day-to-day life. She read every word of what follows, criticized style with utter frankness, and took blunt exception when she thought me wrong. Usually, she was right. All this was done with enthusiasm, and it is to her that my work is dedicated.

After exploiting the talents of so many people, it must be made absolutely clear that any errors, factual or otherwise, are entirely of my own making. To claim otherwise would constitute "guilt by association."

March 1969   J.B.S.

Explanation of Abbreviations in Notes

LAG   Laura Ann Giddings
LMG   Lura Maria Giddings
LWG   Laura Waters Giddings

Joshua R. Giddings
and the Tactics
of Radical Politics

•❧ ❧•

Chapter 1

THE
DYNAMICS OF
AMBITION

◄◊►

1795-1837

Joshua Giddings usually spent his evenings quietly and alone. Through his window he often watched small boats inching up and down the Potomac River, while across the street he could see the Capitol parks, filled with evergreens and dormant flowerbeds crisscrossed with neatly kept gravel paths.[1] The atmosphere was ideal for personal stock-taking, especially so because his unpopular antislavery opinions made few congressional colleagues wish to converse with him.

In 1840, with two-thirds of his life behind him, Giddings was only beginning his most productive and difficult years in the House of Representatives. Already he had begun playing a unique part in his nation's history as a radical, a maverick who stood on the periphery of politics. His position was very unusual, but the contradictions within it were those which many Americans would one day share with him. He was a politician publicizing an issue which eventually caused the nation's structure of

3

government to collapse into violence. That issue was slavery. Most congressmen either condoned or participated in a practice he could not abide—the owning of other human beings. Yet he relied on congressional action as the only way for the nation to correct the evils of bondage. Giddings perceived deep defects in American society demanding immediate remedy. Nevertheless he upheld a federal system not susceptible to rapid change, which avoided or compromised pressing questions.

In December, 1840, the dilemmas of the antislavery-reformer-turned-politician could be terribly confusing. But as Giddings looked out of his window he enjoyed a considerable sense of self-fulfillment. Once, instead of espousing radical programs, he had carefully held only "correct" ideas, acceptable to powerful men. Throughout his earlier life he had courted esteem, not the national ostracism he now suffered so willingly. Behind him lay a thirty-year struggle for material goals—money, status, and respect. Once, his ambition had nearly cost him a lifetime's work and even his personal equilibrium. Now he held different values and felt little anxiety about his difficult station. With complete honesty he could write: "While young, I lived for the purpose of *ambition,* of distinction and honors. . . . [Now] I expect no higher honors for *myself.*" [2] Late in life his self-centeredness had capitulated to a desire to recast the nation in a better mold. Joshua Giddings now wished only to awaken the nation to the sins of slavery. Though a maverick, his choices and actions would reflect, and add to, the agonies of the generation which witnessed the Civil War.

Joshua Giddings never spoke of his Puritan heritage; genealogy meant little to him after the poverty and instability of his childhood. It impressed him not at all that the first of his forebears had set foot in America in 1635 or that later generations had mingled blood lines with families which were to boast such luminaries as Rufus Choate and Nathaniel Hawthorne. All that mattered was that one Giddings named Joshua had moved with his wife from his native Connecticut to Bradford County, Pennsylvania, and had begun to farm. From this union Joshua Reed

4

Giddings, the fifth of a long Puritan line to bear this name, was born on August 6, 1795.[3]

Gidding's childhood was one of hard work and little stability, for the family was large and he was the last of seven children. Six weeks after his youngest son's birth, father Giddings packed up his family and moved to Canandaigua, New York. Ten more uneventful years of farming followed, during which the Giddingses fared no better than they had in Bradford County. While the farmers of Canandaigua were busily founding schools, Joshua was not even exposed to the rudiments of education; at age ten he could barely recite the alphabet. Then in 1805 Giddings' father, well beyond his middle years, decided once again to make a fresh start, this time in Ohio's Western Reserve.[4]

The elder Giddings' decision was typical for New Englanders who were down on their luck. A few intrepid souls, mostly from Connecticut, had by the turn of the century established several small communities in this part of northeastern Ohio. These pockets of civilization, set in dense forests filled with Indians, became attractive to disgruntled New Englanders. Joshua Giddings' father was one of the earliest to move to the Reserve, but thousands like him soon followed.

Pioneering agreed with young Giddings. By the time he had reached eighteen he had grown into a robust, two-hundred-pound youth of over six feet two inches, with an open, heavy-featured face and curly, thick blond hair, characteristics which changed little over the years. Homestead chores made him an expert with axes and horses, while teenage roughhousing gave him a reputation as an unbeatable wrestler.[5]

But if frontier living benefited Giddings physically, it left him far behind in education. He arrived in Wayne, Ohio, before anyone had built a schoolhouse, and the constant demands of the livestock ruled out full-time study elsewhere. As late as 1812 the farm was not a profitable venture, and Giddings' help was constantly needed at home. His father compounded problems with some ill-advised land speculation. Giddings, however, obtained a copy of Lindley Murray's *Grammar* and taught himself

5

the rudiments of reading and writing. After a while he was devouring every pamphlet and newspaper that fell into his hands.[6] Self-study did not make Giddings an accomplished man of letters, however, and throughout his life he would fill his correspondence with misspellings and incomplete sentences. But such diligence went far beyond the needs of his nondescript farm upbringing because Giddings wanted, more than anything else, to avoid his father's mediocrity and improvidence.

Upon returning home after six months of service in the War of 1812, he found the homestead threatened with crisis. His father's speculative debts had finally resulted in bankruptcy, and the family decided to start over in the nearby town of Williamsfield.[7] It was Giddings' fourth home in eighteen years. All the while he had watched his father proceed from one failure to another.

In 1814 young Giddings accepted a part-time teaching position at the local grammar school and practiced self-improvement despite the homestead's need of his strong arm. While keeping a bare lesson ahead of his unlettered students of English and mathematics, he sought out a minister in nearby Trumbull County to tutor him in Latin.[8] Academic training supplied Giddings with some mental skills useful to an ambitious young man. Success, however, required special training, and in 1818 he decided to study law. He was destined to follow his choice to the pinnacle of success, then through a deep personal crisis, and finally to antislavery politics and Congress.

Elisha Whittlesey of Canfield, Ohio, embodied many qualities which Giddings wished to emulate. To many in the Reserve who imported their attitudes from Connecticut, Whittlesey represented the best characteristics of conservative New England Federalism. His impeccable personal life, legal reputation, and credit rating qualified him as a member of that high class of men whose principled judgment should prevail on major questions of the day. Graduates of Whittlesey's law office, usually destined for success as attorneys, were also fully equipped with the contracts and views requisite for entry into the social elite.[9] Giddings applied to read law and Whittlesey assented. His parents fretted

6

about his having to borrow from his brothers to begin this new venture, but they finally relented. In September, 1818, Giddings set off on foot to Canfield carrying two changes of clothing, seventeen dollars, and an insatiable desire to make himself a respected member of the community.[10]

Giddings throve in the two years of Whittlesey's challenging program. The regimen began before sunrise and continued long into the evening. He quickly discovered that within the pages of Coke and Blackstone lay not only the "road to honor and fame" but also a subject matter which was intrinsically fascinating. Investigating the masses of cases and precedents, Giddings recalled, was "the greatest pleasure of my life. . . ." [11] In 1819 he added to his responsibilities by suddenly marrying Laura Waters, a local school teacher. She, like himself, was bred from upright but poor Connecticut stock. The details of the couple's courtship and their personal relationship are unclear, for none of Laura Giddings' letters are to be found. Apparently she partook of all the stolid virtues of a good nineteenth-century wife, for she devoted herself to child rearing, religion, and sewing. She showed no interest in Giddings' two main interests, law and politics,[12] but her attitude never disturbed him, for he later inflicted political news upon her incessantly. Actually, it was the pleasures of the stable, well-run household which Laura created that continually endeared her to Giddings. After he had begun his long career in Congress, it took him several years to adjust to his long absences from the family circle. In 1820 the couple's first son, Comfort Pease Giddings, was born. The family grew rapidly, with the birth in 1822 of a second boy, Joseph, and the arrival of a daughter, Lura Maria, three years later.

Despite the added burdens of domestic responsibility, Giddings passed the bar examination, but only after his questioners had satisfied their fears that the applicant's humble origins in no way compromised his attitudes on matters of politics and morals. Giddings opened a small law office and set out to prove his theory that "the only thing that will ever raise you to fame and distinction is . . . to labor[,] constantly and unceasingly." [13] His

7

practice, however, failed to keep pace with family needs and his own aspirations. The first year in isolated Williamsfield proved fruitless. Jefferson, the county seat, seemed a far more likely place to find clients, and in late June, 1822, Giddings found quarters there. He opened a new law office and Jefferson became his permanent home.[14]

Superficially, Jefferson hardly looked like a promising place for Giddings to achieve his aims. The town was small, already overshadowed by the nearby port of Ashtabula on the shores of Lake Erie. During the 1820's Jefferson contained none of the large houses, elm-lined streets, and well-kept lawns which by the 1850's marked it as a notable example of refined living in the Western Reserve. Instead, the streets were largely mud bogs and the most numerous buildings were unimproved log cabins. Only a few yards from the town limits lay deep forests and small farms.[15]

Nevertheless, the citizens of Jefferson, like everyone else in the Reserve, were struggling to reproduce in their town an exact replica of the older Connecticut society which they had left behind. Very quickly the "best people" of Jefferson had identified themselves by becoming active in the Congregationalist church, founding a chapter of the American Bible Society, organizing a local debating club, and establishing a Masonic lodge. Typical of the Federalist penchant for blending elitism with detached social concern was the American Colonization Society, in which Elisha Whittlesey held important standing. By the late 1820's Jefferson had its own high-minded colonization group, dedicated to solving the problems of slavery by gradual, compensated manumission and the founding of a Negro state in Africa.[16]

Giddings hoped most of all to join in these activities, all of which were signs of social acceptance, but in order to realize this goal he first had to make a reputation in law. Again, the environment of Jefferson offered unusual possibilities, for the county court house attracted a steady supply of clients and cases. Attorneys would often sit on the front steps and contract for prosecutions and defenses as litigants walked into the building.[17]

Besides being located in the center of legal activity, Giddings found a second asset worth exploiting, the patronage of Elisha Whittlesey. Giddings' ambition and his eagerness to endorse Whittlesey's own ideas had impressed the older man from the first. The two lawyers quickly formed a close friendship.[18] Moreover, in 1822 each discovered that he could be useful to the other, for both were beginning new careers. While Giddings was struggling to establish his practice, Whittlesey resolved to run for the United States Congress.[19]

The harmonious interplay of self-interest was obvious. Whittlesey, a legal chieftain, offered Giddings contacts, advice, and influence. The wide-awake attorney, on the other hand, could serve as a local political observer and liaison, for he mingled with editors, judges, and lawyers, and such men made up the most politically powerful segments of Reserve society. A tacit agreement to exchange services was in full operation by 1823,[20] and both men's careers prospered as sponsorship from Washington assured political services from Jefferson. Whittlesey, with Giddings' help, not only retained his seat for eleven years but quietly used his acumen to build a machine which left a lasting impression upon party politics in Ohio.

If Whittlesey engineered his ascent subtly, Giddings often relied on the sensational as he created a legal reputation for himself. His specialty became criminal and maritime law, and after a series of successful prosecutions and defenses his practice grew rapidly. By 1826, he had risen high enough to serve a term in the Ohio House of Representatives. He found the experience boring, however, and deemed the political process infected with much wasted motion and log rolling.[21] One day he was to change his mind about the value of public office, but for the moment he was anxious to get on with his regular practice.

His eagerness paid handsome rewards. In 1827 a spectacular malpractice suit, pitting the classic poor widow against one of Ohio's most respected physicians, assured Giddings his goal of pre-eminence. Whittlesey aided Giddings by arranging for distinguished medical men from Washington to testify for the prosecu-

9

tion. Giddings, who had attached the poor widow's estate, repaid his old teacher by splitting the fees with him. In 1831, after four years of exhaustive appeals, the State Supreme Court found the rich doctor guilty.[22] Hard labor and Whittlesey's patronage had brought Giddings to the threshold of success. His law practice soon became the largest in the Reserve, and family finances were hardly strained by the addition, in 1834, of a third son named, quite appropriately, Grotius.[23]

Business came across Giddings' desk in such volume that he decided to take on a partner. His choice was colorful, competent, Benjamin F. Wade, in whom Giddings found a congenial associate. Wade's origins matched Giddings' for their obscurity, and he was certainly Giddings' equal in ambition. As a youth Wade had spent several years with a work gang, digging the Ohio extension of the Erie Canal. He too had read law with Elisha Whittlesey and was determined to make himself a person of public esteem. Not surprisingly, Giddings and Wade grew to be close friends who shared similar interests and generally agreed about politics and law. Their professional talents also complimented each other nicely. Giddings, never sure of fine legalisms but an expert courtroom rhetorician, took charge of the actual trials, while Wade, whose mastery of technical detail was complete but who turned beet-red whenever confronted by an audience, drew up all the briefs. The firm soon had no equal in the Reserve.[24]

With legal success came the distinction which Giddings had long craved. By 1828 he belonged to the Jefferson Debating Club and the Colonization Society. He now spent many leisure hours in conversation with men whose views were highly respected. The local Masonic Lodge, impressed with his credentials and powerful sponsors, allowed Giddings to join the society in the mid-1820's. In 1830 the Ohio Grand Lodge, located in Columbus, elected him "Grand Warden" of the state organization. Citizens of Jefferson also recognized Giddings as an upstanding supporter of the Congregational church, for he now held the office of elder. In addition, he was president of the Bible Society, and both positions required that he maintain and perpetuate strict Chris-

10

tian principles of piety and social behavior. For perhaps the first time in his life Giddings could feel secure. Occasionally he scanned the newspapers and laughed at the "political squabbles that are going on in every part of the country." He even boasted mildly to Elisha Whittlesey, "I am as contented, I believe[,] and enjoy myself as well as my neighbors do." [25]

Moods of complacency, however, were fleeting, and his easy dismissal of politics a momentary aberration. Despite Giddings' prosperity, neither his beliefs nor his temperament left room for extended self-congratulation. Though he had attained his clearly defined goals, he still felt that there was simply no point at which a man could justly cease working toward higher levels of achievement. Success in the law dictated that he turn toward other challenging horizons, for *"ambition, professional ambition,"* he believed, was the "principal ingredient in the moral qualities ... of any moral man." [26]

How much of this ethic Giddings drew from the conservative creeds of his social circle, and to what extent he created it to live in peace with himself, can never be known. Nevertheless, it is clear that by 1830 he had become emotionally unsuited to placid living. He languished to the point of physical pain when released from the tension of difficult tasks, a complaint which he called "hypochondria." Once while in New York City on business, he grumbled about the laziness of his associates. "Nothing," he complained, "is to be done with them except between ten o'clock & 3. . . . I have had the hypo. till all was blue." [27] Incessant mental engagement was the only palliative, and the law practice by itself no longer sufficed. Giddings became engaged in politics, and again Whittlesey's sponsorship proved crucial to his aspirations.

From the first, Whittlesey had carried his Federalist convictions into politics and had developed a strong distaste for Andrew Jackson's rising party. Keenly aware of the Reserve's political temper and economic interests, he had adopted the National Republican party, with its programs of using federal power to stimulate the

11

national economy. Reserve farmers depended on roads, canals, and well-maintained harbors in order to ship their grain and dairy produce to market. Henry Clay's "American System" promised federal help in such projects, while laissez-faire Jacksonianism always seemed to stand athwart the Reserve's economic progress.[28]

Giddings agreed wholeheartedly with Whittlesey in these matters, as did nearly all Reserve voters, and he also shared his mentor's deep revulsion for the political style of Jackson's party. Throughout the early 1820's Giddings echoed Whittlesey's fear that the Jacksonians were preparing "some great effort to Revolutionise [sic] the country" by making politics a process of popular opinion. Whittlesey and Giddings shared a deferential view of government, assuming that men of probity, piety, and social standing should make wise decisions for the good of the nation. The followers of "Old Hickory," however, selfishly conspired to throw aside such restraining influences and to expose politics to the "secular, misguided passions" of the general will. Giddings quickly decided that the only way to avoid national anarchy was by supporting the ex-Federalist leaders of National Republicanism, Henry Clay, John Quincy Adams, and Daniel Webster. These men became Giddings' political heroes, for their firm patriotism and sound moral judgment reflected "right principle." [29] Sincere partisan conviction began merging with Giddings' ethical and emotional needs to broaden his spheres of activity. Fortunately, just as Giddings' taste for political life started to sharpen, Whittlesey's need for a liaison grew greater than ever.

Immediately after Jackson swept into office in 1828, National Republicans set out to select a candidate around whom the heterogeneous foes of "Old Hickory" could organize. By early 1831, Whittlesey, Giddings, and many others agreed that Henry Clay was best equipped to play this role,[30] but the great problem became the creation of a powerful organization in Ohio which could help boost Clay into the White House. Whittlesey discovered the key to solving this problem within the newly arisen Antimasonic movement, which had swept into the Reserve from New

York State during the late 1820's. Antimasonry, a melange of prejudice and egalitarianism, had its origin in the mysterious abduction of a New York Mason who had promised to expose the "lurid rites" of the Order. A widespread network of societies soon sprang up throughout the North, dedicated to the exposure and abolition of the perverted aristocracy which Masonry seemed to nurture.[31]

Since many important politicians of both major parties held high Masonic titles, the movement quickly developed into a deeply equalitarian political movement as well as a moral crusade.[32] Here Whittlesey discovered an impulse which could unite anti-Jacksonian voters. National Republican coalition with the Antimasons became the process through which the Whig Party in the Reserve had its genesis, and Whittlesey lost little time before trying cooperation. In the elections of 1830 he dropped his Masonic affiliations, courted the support of his former detractors,[33] and felt extremely anxious for Giddings' help in the maneuver. "I want to know all and something more," was his injunction.[34] Giddings' meticulous reporting conformed to this request, and with some Antimasonic help Whittlesey was easily re-elected.[35]

Notwithstanding Whittlesey's return to Congress, Antimasons and National Republicans still eyed each other suspiciously. Cooperation had proved only haphazard. One of the local irritations turned out to be Giddings himself, for he and the Antimasons had long shared an open hatred for each other. The young lawyer had been willing to advise and promote Whittlesey's fortunes, but unlike his mentor he refused to abandon his Masonic affiliation. Giddings was proud of his high standing in the Order and believed that the Masons exerted a beneficial influence on social morality. He hotly resented Antimasons for attacking a constructive institution while "villifying the characters of men who have paid for the privilege which they and their families have attained." [36]

The Antimasons reciprocated in kind, indicting him as a perfect example of subversive, impious interests,[37] while mocking him

13

as "Squire Giddings loaded down with . . . offices and honors."
They charged him with influence-seeking and with hypocrisy for
being active in the Bible Society while holding office in Ohio's
heathenish Grand Lodge.[38] Giddings' bitter rejoinders, defending the Christian character of Masonry and the need for morality
in politics, filled columns until June, paralleling Whittlesey's efforts to court the Antimasonic vote.[39] It was little wonder the election featured only spotty cooperation.

The thought of Henry Clay as President in 1832 finally made
Giddings cast aside his deep Masonic pride. So did his almost
slavish loyalty to Whittlesey's best interest: "On this subject, my
duty to the publick requires me to do all that I can," Giddings
assured him.[40] In late 1831 Giddings sent to Whittlesey his annual
list of constituents who might appreciate political literature
from their congressman and took pains to include "a good proportion of antimasons." [41] Early in 1832 Giddings announced he
would no longer attend lodge meetings,[42] and then he hastened
to Columbus to lobby for complete fusion by "having the institution [of Masonry] abolished throughout the State." [43]

Giddings' sudden espousal of Antimasonry certainly smacked
of hypocrisy, for he was Whittlesey's sycophant no matter what the
loss of consistency. Yet, for the first time in his life, Giddings had
forced himself to deal with politics as a mass movement. The
propaganda of Antimasonry spoke of attacking a bastion of privilege and influence which Giddings highly respected. He had chosen to promote actively such a program in order to combat the
Jacksonians' very similar rhetoric. Giddings may not have lost any
of his personal elitism, but he was discovering, through his involvement in Antimasonry, that public opinion had to be courted
if parties and programs were to succeed in the heady atmosphere
of the 1830's. In later years Giddings was to base his entire antislavery strategy on mass appeals to the national conscience. His
work with the Antimasons undoubtedly did much to convince
him that such techniques could be effective.

The anti-Jacksonians carried neither Ohio nor the nation in
1832, but the coalition which was formed in the Reserve signaled

the emergence of one of the strongest, most stable local Whig machines in the North.[44] Whittlesey's search for a broadly based alternative to the Democrats showed gratifying signs of success. Giddings' aid in inducing coalition had been invaluable, if hardly colorful, and Whittlesey's political debt to his protegé mounted still further as Giddings continued his work in 1834 and 1836. It soon became common knowledge that Giddings stood next in line for Whittlesey's seat in Congress. Giddings, in turn, not only developed a wish to obtain public office but became fully imbued with the programs of the Whig party he had worked so zealously to create.

His immediate attention began to focus upon personal advancement in his new party, so again he solicited Elisha Whittlesey's aid. Since his finances seemed "tolerably good" by late 1832, Giddings believed he could easily absorb the loss of income which public office would bring with it.[45] He asked Whittlesey's help in securing a judgeship. This effort proved fruitless, as did another in 1836 when Giddings failed in a bid for election as state senator.[46] Giddings' desire for a political career would remain unfulfilled until Whittlesey decided to retire from public life.

Meanwhile, Giddings discovered a new activity which warded off attacks of the "hypochondria." By 1835 he and Wade had become wealthy men, and Giddings realized that legal routine made him feel bored and nervous. Real estate investment seemed an inviting prospect, for it supplied new challenges. Speculation, Giddings explained to his wife, "keeps the mind active and drives away the hypo. Indeed, this was my principle [sic] motive for entering into this business." Clearly, his object was not primarily monetary: "I can no longer sit down in our office to the business of being a lawyer, and if I do not find something to . . . give play to the imagination I shall be as badly affected as I was last year." [47] As attacks of "the hypo" came with increasing frequency,[48] Giddings followed his law partner, law teacher, and many other friends into three years of hectic land-jobbing, promoted by the easy-credit atmosphere of Jacksonian America.

15

The associates, concentrating on real estate outside the rapidly growing city of Toledo in western Ohio, immediately began dealing in thousands of acres and tens of thousands of dollars. Even circumspect Edward Wade, Benjamin's younger brother, found himself entangled in a web of short-term loans, options, and contracts.[49] Giddings found plenty to keep him busy, and became, on paper at least, a man of independent means. As his credit rating and bank balance rose, his interest in law declined still further. In 1836 he dissolved his partnership with Ben Wade and announced his retirement.[50]

The very year that Giddings decided to end his practice the first signs of strain began appearing in the economy. Andrew Jackson, worried by the increasing rate of bank failures, adopted austerity measures, but these proved insufficient. By early 1837 the nation was in the throes of a deep depression. Paper assets gradually vanished, financial institutions closed their doors, and Joshua Giddings was only one of thousands being pressed by their creditors for impossible sums. But the sudden loss of prestige hurt Giddings far more than the threat of bankruptcy. His wealth had testified to success, respectability, and social acceptance. Now that he was stripped of his affluence, his hard work seemed as meaningless to him as his large bundle of worthless land titles—his only tangible asset.

Giddings immediately returned to the office, took a new partner, and announced that business would commence as usual.[51] But business was unusually bad. Most of Giddings' old clients had been claimed by other firms, notably by the partnership of Benjamin Wade and Rufus Ranney, which Wade had set up after Giddings' retirement. Wade himself, placing competition over friendship while also trying to liquidate his own debts, exposed Giddings to humiliating jibes as they faced each other in local courtrooms. The once-reticent Wade now had developed a sharp tongue, and once, just as Giddings was making the concluding speech for the prosecution in a libel case, "Frank" made a shambles of his presentation. Giddings was summing up with Iago's famous lines from *Othello*: "He who steals my purse steals trash. He who filches

16

from me my good name, robs me of that . . ." (here he faltered) "Which you never had!" Wade exclaimed. The courtroom exploded with raucous laughter and, as if to compound the insult, Giddings lost the case.[52] A long-standing friend had deserted him. He and Wade were from then on bitter political and personal enemies. Besides, such an experience seemed shamefully beneath the dignity of one who had once done successful battle with Ohio's best legal minds.

Humiliation at the bar and the loss of Wade's friendship, however, constituted only parts of Giddings' developing crisis. Concurrent with the panic and the painful return to the dull business of law, a deep rift between himself and his closest friend, Whittlesey, hurt Giddings deeply. The older man, it seems, had confided to several associates that, had Giddings run for Congress as Whittlesey's successor in the 1836 elections, a Jacksonian victory in the district would have been inevitable. Evidently, Giddings' inability to win a seat in the state senate did not pass unnoticed in high Whig circles. Giddings received news of these remarks and complained bitterly.[53] Although Whittlesey vigorously denied the rumors, Giddings accused his teacher of consciously doing "gross injustice to the feelings of a friend . . . ," and spared no ink while dwelling on fourteen years of loyal service which Whittlesey saw fit to repay with "remarks . . . which . . . have more weight than the best-directed effort of an avowed enemy." Whittlesey, Giddings alleged, had all but ruined his own reputation as well as their friendship.[54]

In the space of six brief months Giddings had plummeted from prosperity to near bankruptcy. His promising political prospects were in danger of extinction. His legal reputation and high social standing had vanished. Whittlesey and Wade, his two closest friends, now acted like betrayers. Long trips to the homes of distant creditors and degrading efforts to get extensions added much to his distress.[55] Many of his personal moorings had been suddenly, painfully, wrenched from him. Antislavery agitation in politics eventually was to restore his equilibrium, but, for the moment, anger, despair, and helplessness were all that Joshua Giddings was capable of feeling.

17

NOTES

1 Joshua Reed Giddings (hereinafter JRG) to Joseph Addison Giddings (hereinafter JAG), December 5, 1839, Joshua R. Giddings MSS, Ohio Historical Society, Columbus, Ohio (hereinafter OHS). All citations subsequently made to Giddings MSS refer to this collection.

2 JRG to Lura Maria Giddings (hereinafter LMG), January 8, 1840, Giddings MSS.

3 JRG genealogical fragment, George W. Julian MSS, George Washington Julian Collection, Indiana State Library, Indianapolis, Indiana (hereinafter ISL); George W. Julian, *The Life of Joshua R. Giddings* (Chicago, 1892), 11–12.

4 *Ibid.*; Whitney R. Cross, *The Burnt-Over District: The Social and Intellectual History of Enthusiastic Religion in Western New York, 1800–1850* (Ithaca, 1950), 139–40.

5 Walter Buell, *Joshua R. Giddings, A Sketch* (Cleveland, 1882), 17–18; Julian, *Giddings*, 16.

6 Julian, *Giddings*, 16, 19.

7 *Ibid.*

8 *Ibid.*, 19–20.

9 Kenneth E. Davison, "Forgotten Ohioan: Elisha Whittlesey, 1782–1863" (Ph.D. dissertation, Case Western Reserve University, 1952), *passim.*

10 Julian, *Giddings*, 21.

11 JRG to JAG, June 1, 1842, Giddings MSS.

12 JRG to Laura Waters Giddings (hereinafter LWG), December 1, 1838, Giddings MSS.

13 Julian, *Giddings*, 23–24; Elisha Whittlesey to JRG, January 9, 1821, JRG to JAG, December 11, 1838 (quotation), Giddings MSS.

14 Julian, *Giddings*, 29; JRG to Elisha Whittlesey, June 22, 1822, Elisha

Whittlesey MSS, The Western Reserve Historical Society, Cleveland, Ohio (hereinafter WRHS).

15 Hans L. Trefousse, *Benjamin Franklin Wade: Radical Republican from Ohio* (New York, 1963), 23.

16 Harlan H. Hatcher, *The Western Reserve: The Story of New Connecticut in Ohio* (Cleveland, 1966) *passim*. An illuminating treatment of the transplantation of New England institutions to the Ohio frontier can be found in Page Smith, *As a City Upon a Hill: The Town in American History* (New York, 1966), 37–53. Smith stresses the conservative nature of this process and of the people who participated.

17 Buell, *Giddings*, 28–30.

18 JRG to Elisha Whittlesey, February 7, 1821, August 27, 1830, Whittlesey MSS, WRHS.

19 JRG to Elisha Whittlesey, July 29, August 22, 1822, Whittlesey MSS, WRHS.

20 Elisha Whittlesey to JRG, January 18, February 19, September 18, 1824, December 24, 1825, Giddings MSS; JRG to Elisha Whittlesey, January 7, 1827, Whittlesey MSS, WRHS.

21 JRG memoir fragment, Julian MSS, ISL; JRG to Elisha Whittlesey, January 7, 1827, Whittlesey MSS, WRHS.

22 JRG memoir fragment, Julian MSS, ISL; JRG to Ephriam Brown, August 23, 1831, Ephriam Brown MSS, WRHS; JRG to Elisha Whittlesey, January 4, March 26, 1831, Whittlesey MSS, WRHS.

23 Julian, *Giddings,* 23.

24 Mary Bright Land, "Old Backbone: 'Bluff' Ben Wade" (Ph.D. dissertation, Case Western Reserve University, 1950, 2 vols.), I, 1–23.

25 *Ohio Luminary* (Ashtabula), February 12, 1830; Julian, *Giddings,* 402; JRG to Elisha Whittlesey, January 10, 1828, Whittlesey MSS, WRHS (quotation).

26 JRG to JAG, June 1, 1842, Giddings MSS.

27 JRG to LWG, June 28, 1836, Giddings MSS.

28 Elisha Whittlesey to JRG, May 13, 1824, Whittlesey MSS, WRHS.

29 JRG to Elisha Whittlesey, January 9, 1826, January 10, 1828, Whittlesey MSS (both letters quoted). Whittlesey viewed the "crisis" of Jackson's possible election as "awfully appalling" and hoped that high-minded politicians would rally to defeat the Democrats: "We live in a time when office and distinction dwindle to nothing when compared

with the salvation of the Republic." to JRG, Elisha Whittlesey, July 21, 1828, Giddings MSS.

30 Elisha Whittlesey to JRG, January 17, 1831, Giddings MSS; JRG to Elisha Whittlesey, January 4, 1831, Whittlesey MSS, WRHS.

31 David Brion Davis, "Some Themes of Counter-Subversion: An Analysis of Anti-Catholic, Anti-Masonic and Anti-Mormon Literature," *Mississippi Valley Historical Review*, XLII (January, 1963), 205–24.

32 Lee Benson, *The Concept of Jacksonian Democracy: New York as a Test Case* (Princeton, 1961), 21–46.

33 Davison, "Whittlesey," 88–90; Elisha Whittlesey to JRG, September 3, 1830, Giddings MSS.

34 Elisha Whittlesey to JRG, September 14, 1830, Giddings MSS.

35 JRG to Elisha Whittlesey, August 2, August 24, September 2, September 12, 1830, Whittlesey MSS, WRHS.

36 JRG to Elisha Whittlesey, February 17, 1828, Whittlesey MSS, WRHS. In this same letter Giddings went on to indict the Antimasons for their irreligion, as men who "heretofore professed much Christian Zeal [but who] are now associating upon the most intimate terms with the vilest scoffers of all religion. . . ." Convinced that the Antimasons were motivated by "superstition, malevolence, and the most impudent falsehood . . . ," Giddings' conservative temperament led him to view the movement in the same way that he saw the Jacksonians, as a frontal assault against all political morality.

37 *Ohio Luminary* (Ashtabula), February 12, 1830.

38 *Ibid.*, February 19, 1830.

39 *Ibid.*, March 30, April 7, May 22, June 5, 1830.

40 JRG to Elisha Whittlesey, August 27, 1830, Whittlesey MSS, WRHS.

41 JRG to Elisha Whittlesey, November 22, 1831, Whittlesey MSS, WRHS.

42 *Ohio Republican,* January 9, 1832.

43 JRG to Elisha Whittlesey, June 26, 1832, November 17, 1832, (quotation), Whittlesey MSS, WRHS.

44 Harold W. Davis, "The Social and Economic Basis of the Whig Party in Ohio, 1828–1840" (Ph.D. dissertation, Case Western Reserve University, 1932), 194.

45 JRG to Ephriam Brown, November 21, 1832, Brown MSS, WRHS.

46 JRG to Elisha Whittlesey, November 23, 1832, Whittlesey MSS,

WRHS; Julian, *Giddings,* 34. There is little information available concerning the circumstances of Giddings' nomination and campaign. Obviously he ran as an anti-Jacksonian. There is some indication that certain voters still suspected him of Masonic bias. This factor, as well as personality clashes between Giddings and other politicians, contributed to his defeat. See the Ashtabula *Sentinel,* August 16, 1836.

[47] JRG to LWG, March 11, 1836, Giddings MSS.

[48] Benjamin F. Wade to JRG, May 18, 1835, Giddings MSS.

[49] Benjamin F. Wade to JRG, June 12, 1836, JRG to LWG, March 11, June 28, 1836, Giddings MSS; Land, "Wade," I, 27.

[50] Julian, *Giddings,* 35.

[51] *Ibid.,* 35–36.

[52] Albert G. Riddle, *The Life of Benjamin F. Wade* (Cleveland, 1888), 127–28.

[53] JRG to Elisha Whittlesey, January 27, 1837, Whittlesey MSS, WRHS.

[54] Elisha Whittlesey to JRG, January 29, 1837, JRG to Elisha Whittlesey, March 29, 1837 (quotation), Whittlesey MSS, WRHS.

[55] JRG to LMG, April 27, 1837, Giddings MSS.

Chapter 2

CRISIS
AND
COMMITMENT

◄ ►

1837-1838

At first Giddings nearly let his woes get the better of him, for he began indulging in the worst self-pity, and his degree of despondency became unusually acute. Once, while he was out of town seeking credit, his daughter Lura Maria failed to write him as promised. "If you loved me as you ought," he complained piteously, "you would certainly think of me when I am away, far from you and among strangers, in poor health, with no one to comfort me, console me, or cheer me." Life is uncertain, he warned her; he might die before returning home and she might never see her father again. Lura, he feared, would be left alone, never to learn respect and the maning of duty. These prospects, he wrote, "give me gloomy forebodings as to your future happiness." [1] Such baleful sentiments contrasted markedly with letters written home in happier days. Then he had been careful to include descriptions of incidents which might capture the fancy of the children. [2]

Giddings felt a deep need to be coddled by the family, but

he was also sure that retreat to hearth and home could not offer him the inner peace which escaped him. Although he felt a man of his age who had "buffeted the waves of adversity as long as I have" certainly deserved the luxury of a full domestic life,[3] Giddings' makeup ruled out this solution altogether. Mental and emotional dynamism, the tension-charged activities of pushing toward difficult and clearly outlined goals, had too long been dominant in his personality.

The dangers of psychological speculation about a person long dead are obvious, but Giddings' personal crisis demands attention here, for it resulted in his commitment to antislavery politics. Many historians still persist in characterizing such reformers as "disturbed personalities," men who hated slavery because of personal insecurities. Giddings, like anyone else, had his quirks, but his eventual adoption of political antislavery appears to represent a quite realistic, rather healthy readjustment to a crisis which might have otherwise left his personality permanently scarred.[4]

Giddings' inner imperative to aim high had always provided him with a critical reference point, which certain people find essential for living peacefully with themselves and others. Although completely unhappy with himself, he found it impossible to rearrange his old psychological patterns. The personal stresses with which he had always felt comfortable could not be discarded for a life of rural simplicity, and he informed his wife quite directly of this fact: "The constant habit of intellectual excitement into which my business has led me," he explained, "has unfitted my mind for enjoyments other than those of active employment. . . ." If "left at home with my family . . . ," he assured her, "I presume melancholy and depression would constantly prey upon my mind." [5]

Giddings was emphatic about what he could not do, but he could not discover any alternative course. In May of 1837 he lapsed into a period of brooding indecision, the only one he would ever experience. In desperation, he elected to flee his problems as his father had so often done. After saddling his horse he headed East, back to Hartford and Enfield, where he visited relatives for a time.[6] But during his solitary journeys through the green hills of New York State and down the Connecticut Valley, Giddings was unable to come to terms with himself. By late June, when he had retraced his steps as far as Jefferson, he still could tell his wife nothing about what he proposed to do. Probably unable to bear the humiliation of facing his family while still so confused, Giddings bypassed his homestead and headed West. By July, he had wandered into the sparsely settled regions around Chicago.

Belief in the redemptive effect of nature upon the individual permeated much of the popular thought of nineteenth-century America. Many religious souls held to the belief that the frontier, unsullied by material corruption, provided a place where man could confront God directly and obtain new spiritual purity. Giddings' flight into the wilderness in search of new values clearly partook of an experience shared by many pious Christians, anxious for an emotional reconciliation with the Deity.[7] Giddings, desperate for inspiration from any source, found the solitude of the Illinois prairies regenerating. He discovered, in the "beautiful" grandeur of the "solitary and lonely" grasslands, the deep spiritual qualities in life which had hitherto eluded him. Never had he seen such a *"boundless* place, where in any one direction the eye could not rest on a hill or mountain[,] forest tree or shrub." He responded in a poetic, nearly animistic, fashion to his surroundings and began submerging his anxieties by seeing similarities between his difficult situation and God's larger world of nature. He felt sympathy for the occasional larks and blackbirds which rose out of the tall grass, "fluttering [as] though trying to find a limb or twig to alight upon, but finding none their weary wings . . . again guide them through the boundless grass. . . ." Doubtless Giddings imagined that the journeys of the birds closely resembled his own fretful quest for self-direction, and perhaps he took comfort in this thought. Whether he drew any deeper analogies remains unknown, but he was certain that nothing would restore his perspective more completely than to "spend two or three months rambling

24

around these western wilds, to travel, live poorly and sleep on the floor or ground as occasion should require." [8]

Clearly Giddings' anxieties were finally dissipating. He was turning away from his self-centered esteem of material success by connecting himself with nature's spiritual qualities. Many of Giddings' most pious contemporaries, spokesmen for churches in the Reserve, had long preached this romantic approach to religion, and now he started taking the message seriously. Although the exact dynamics of the process remain uncertain, it is clear that Joshua Giddings began reorienting himself through the experience of religious conversion. While in the Illinois prairies and after his return to Jefferson, Giddings turned for guidance to a piety which he had thus far de-emphasized in his desire for earthly success. Soon Giddings was to draw from this source much of his commitment to anti-slavery reform.

Giddings, as noted, had long clung to the Congregationalist faith, as did most transplanted New Englanders in the Reserve. He had been an active supporter of his church since the 1820's by serving as an elder and had promoted piety through his presidency of the local Bible Society. Like many of his fellow citizens, he had also taken part in the "great revival" which had swept into Ohio from New York in the 1820's. The theology of this religious upheaval was, to put it far too simply, the fruition of a deeply pious radicalism which had long existed within the bosom of Puritanism. By the time the revival had reached the Reserve, its apostles had completely refined its content by rejecting much of that same Calvinism which had spawned the movement. Holiness consisted of an emotional recognition of one's own base impulses, followed by a "change of heart" within the penitent sinner. God no longer predestined man on account of his original sin but instead helped him to save himself and then commissioned him to apply his new piety in his daily life. The redeemed sinner should act as an example of Christ's benevolence, helping others to purge themselves of wrong impulses.

25

Holiness now consisted of concern for the spiritual well-being of others, not election by an arbitrary deity.[9]

During the late 1820's Giddings had confessed faith in the "new religion," and by 1831 he had begun grumbling about the opposition to revivalism among old-line Congregationalists whose "lives and conduct would do little credit to the morals of [even] professed unbelievers." Once, while out of town on business, he heard a revivalist minister give a sermon and felt quite homesick.[10]

But not until 1837, as Giddings reassembled his values, did he begin to grow ever more interested in the religious imperative to work for the moral improvement of those around him. Naturally he was more willing to find fault with society as a consequence of his own misfortunes. Yet his romanticism was supported and given concrete direction by the implications of his religious views. Almost automatically he assumed that his fellow men needed benevolent assistance, and he moved quickly toward active reforming. Instead of passing along offhand warnings to his children, as he once did, to exercise caution while swimming and to dress warmly in winter,[11] he dwelled upon the spiritual peace to be derived from acting upon one's Christian duty to humanity. His daughter Lura received the admonition that "you can only make yourself happy in proportion as you confer happiness on others. . . ." To the same degree that she neglected the spiritual well-being of her fellows would her own "want of enjoyment" be increased. Providing for people's spiritual health would bring Lura contentment and a feeling of accomplishment, Giddings insisted, "from the simple fact of having done as you know you ought to have done." [12] Giddings may have actually been trying to explain himself in this letter instead of giving advice to his daughter. Nevertheless, he had completely discarded his socially conscious materialism. Now he was fashioning a new set of reforming principles which were to undergird his dedication to antislavery.

Soon he began showing a greater concern for the active improvement of those who had strayed from the paths of Christian virtue. After visiting the inmates of the Columbus jail in 1837, he noted with enthusiasm that the prison minister had stimulated a revival among them. Inspired by the reverend's successes, Giddings exhorted one of his less fortunate clients, now serving a sentence, to abandon crime and adopt the principles of Christian rectitude. After finishing his impromptu sermon, Giddings judged his listener "hopefully pious." [13] By mid-1838, Giddings began trying to uplift society in general and his neighbors in particular by supporting the Ashtabula County Temperance Society. He dedicated himself to encouraging all measures designed "to promote abstinence from the use of alcoholic drinks . . . ," and in 1843 he became president of this organization.[14]

The point at which Giddings abandoned his colonizationist sentiments and expanded his reform interests to include a militant sectional stance on slavery cannot be exactly ascertained.[15] Nevertheless it would have been surprising had he not done so, for his views on religion contained potential antislavery conclusions. Furthermore, during the years between 1832 and 1836 Giddings' immediate environment, the Western Reserve, had become rampantly anti-Southern in its opinions.

During the early 1830's the religion of the "great revival" gave much impetus to the growth of abolitionism in the North and especially in the Western Reserve. Almost naturally a portion of those believing in the emotional conversion of sinners and efforts to expunge evil in society turned their attention to the South's "peculiar institution." Through evangelistic methods the revivalist-turned-antislavery-reformer believed that he could prick the conscience of the slaveowner and convert the people of the nation to sponsor a speedy extinction of human bondage. The public could be shown that slavery was a stain upon society and a sin in the eyes of God. The slave himself, a creature of God, was forced into circumstances which violated every principle of Christian benevolence. His soul was op-

27

pressed, not improved; his morals were debased, not elevated; and his conscience, rather than being enlightened, was extinguished.

The cogency of such reasoning impressed many Reserve inhabitants who adhered to revivalism. As early as 1832 the residents of Jefferson had accepted abolitionist projects, imported from the east coast, as a permanent feature of their neighborhood. In that year pious New Englanders, eager to promote holiness and reform in the West, had recruited persuasive Theodore Dwight Weld, a dynamic abolitionist, to select a site for a progressive frontier seminary. But once in the Reserve, Weld did far more than survey potential college locations. Instead he converted to the cause of emancipation Elizur Wright, Jr., Charles Storrs, and Beriah Green, all educators at Hudson, Ohio's Western Reserve College. This trio set out to commit their school and the entire Reserve to abolitionism, touching off violent protests from opponents. By 1833, Wright and Green had resigned from the college, but not before vociferously publicizing their cause and founding the first of the Reserve's many antislavery societies.[16]

Meanwhile, Weld's choice for a college, Lane Seminary in Cincinnati, had not turned out well. In 1834 over fifty disgruntled students seceded over administration refusals to admit Negroes and endorse immediate abolition. The debate which accompanied the split captured national attention as the rebels moved to the Reserve and founded Oberlin College, only fifty miles from Giddings' home. Oberlin students, with Theodore Weld as their chief spokesman, quickly turned their attention to winning adherents to the antislavery crusade throughout the countryside. The following year Weld accepted a position as Western agent for the New England-based American Anti-Slavery Society, the center of abolitionist planning for the entire nation. Weld collected numerous recruits, and they fanned out through the Reserve, initiating a careful canvass of every hamlet. They did not omit Jefferson. Many of their meetings were disrupted by jeers and cat-calls, but in spite of the difficulties they won many converts and evoked much sympathy as they exhorted audiences to work for slavery's overthrow.[17]

Abolitionist arguments made great sense to Giddings' neighbors, farmers and artisans who subscribed to old New England provincial attitudes as well as to the theology of the "great revival." Distrustful of political innovation, they had already rejected Jacksonian democracy and Masonry as antirepublican plots against the original designs of the founding fathers. Instead, they had followed old Federalist leaders into the Whig party, where they believed stern moral leadership still prevailed. The inroads made by the "slave power," as described by the abolitionists, seemed like the most perverse conspiracy of all to such conservative minds. In the opinion of many rural Ohioans the political influence of the Southern states was at odds with the nation's self-professed ideal of freedom, espoused during the days of the American Revolution. The need for reform received widespread support in the Reserve for political as well as religious reasons.[18] A combination of transplanted Yankee suspicion, the effect of the "great revival," and arduous abolitionist effort had caused Joshua Giddings' home territory to be saturated with anti-Southern feeling. It is hardly surprising, given Giddings' new opinions, that he eventually made antislavery reform his permanent vocation.

To be sure, there were many advocates of revivalism and republican purity in the Reserve and elsewhere who eschewed the slavery question. Others were openly proslavery in their opinions.[19] Prior to 1837, before Giddings developed his new viewpoints, he had maintained an utterly neutral position, showing no interest whatsoever in the antislavery crusade. Nevertheless, after this date he was to devote the rest of his life to a sectional program based on implementing Christian benevolence while banishing from politics the perversions wrought by the "slave power conspiracy."

Giddings' refusal before 1837 to adopt a sectional stance remained unchanged despite a great deal of pressure, for he had once listened to the arguments of Theodore Weld himself. This

29

self-effacing but magnetic apostle of emancipation had arrived in Jefferson in October, 1835. Weld was a controversial figure. He had often been reviled and mistreated because of his views, but despite the risks Giddings was impressed, at least initially. During his stay Weld had slept and eaten with the Giddings family, while for twelve days he had preached of the moral evils of slavery and the Christian imperative to work for its abolition.[20]

Tradition has it that Weld turned Giddings into a convert who, with Benjamin Wade, enthusiastically drew up a charter founding the Ashtabula County Anti-Slavery Society. Giddings from that day forward supposedly became a permanent advocate of "gradual emancipation immediately begun." [21] but this assertion is not borne out by the evidence. Following Weld's visit to the Reserve, Giddings did nothing in the way of acting on his new-found convictions, if he had acquired any. He made no lengthy statement of his antislavery views until 1838, when he was asked to do so by that very same Ashtabula County Anti-Slavery Society which he was supposed to have founded but in which he actually played no part at all.[22]

Giddings had not been among the Society's first members who pledged to work for "the speedy and utter extinction of slavery," and the reason for his absence was simple.[23] At the time of the Anti-Slavery Society's founding he still held his position in the local Colonization Society, an anathema to all good abolitionists. At one meeting he had seconded a resolution declaring "unabated confidence" in the Society's program of freeing and removing Negroes from the United States, and his affiliation continued for perhaps a year after Weld's departure.[24]

His endorsements are not surprising, for Whittlesey, on whom he relied for a political future, was always an enthusiastic promoter of colonization. Whittlesey later served as vice president on the National Council of the Colonization Society.[25] Common sense, if nothing else, had dictated that Giddings actively support his patron's solution to the slavery question rather than respond to the exhortations of Theodore Weld. Before 1837, none of his letters indicated any deep zeal to attack slavery, and not until January of that year did he correspond briefly with Elizur Wright, Jr., one of the original Western Reserve College rebels, asking a rather inconsequential question about the status of slavery in Wisconsin.[26] But by mid-1838, after Giddings had overcome his personal discontents, he committed himself publicly to a complete program of antislavery doctrine,[27] and once he had stated his convictions he never went back on them. Few reformers were to boast a longer career of upholding consistent principles.

Giddings' choice of antislavery politics constituted a logical re-integration of goals and aspirations, fitting quite well into his personal makeup. He had always functioned best under tension. Now that he had constructed new values, his decision to serve society in the electric atmosphere of antislavery reform was a wise and healthy one. Besides, Giddings' revivalistic religious feelings also coincided with his conservative notions of politics drawn from the old Federalist tradition. He believed, as he would later explain to a friend, that : "I would deny the existence of an over-rulling [sic] intelligent power if I thought that duty and policy were in constant conflict with each other. . . ." One must do his duty and "leave the consequences to God. . . ." His political antislavery, he acknowledged, stemmed from his conviction that "the wisdom of providence is . . . manifestly to be seen in any subject" that came to the attention of Congress. This idea was one upon which he loved to meditate.[28]

His religious convictions, his romanticism, and the needs of his own personality, not the persuasiveness of Theodore Weld, made Giddings decide to assume the burdens of active political reform, for in this manner he could serve his country, his party, and his God, while avoiding the "hypochondria." It was a decision which meant taking on new tensions while finding release from old ones. No exhaustive change of personality was involved, only a significant redirection of his focus of activity. He did not emerge from his crisis as a disturbed individual clinging to antislavery as a device for channeling neurotic anxiety. To be sure, Joshua Giddings in 1838 was an unusual person, but nonetheless he was

very much in control of himself. He had decided, while successfully resolving a personal crisis, to defend unpopular convictions in order to give his life a deeper meaning than most were
willing to seek.

Giddings did not wait long before exposing his views to the
public. Mid-1838 brought rumors of Elisha Whittlesey's desire to
retire. He asked for confirmation, and Whittlesey, in a curt note
which indicated how sour their friendship had become, replied:
"It is my determination not to be a candidate this fall." Whittlesey had decided to resign his seat, before his last session expired,
because of pressing family commitments,[29] and Giddings quickly
declared his intention to run for both the unexpired term and
the seat in the Twenty-sixth Congress which would open in
December, 1839. Ultimately, Whittlesey did help. The influential
Ashtabula *Sentinel*, long Whittlesey's spokesman and for the
next twenty years Giddings' chief political organ, called on the
local Whig convention to nominate Giddings as Whittlesey's logical successor. The delegates complied, the district Whig machine
worked to perfection, and Giddings defeated his Democratic opponent by a three-to-one vote.[30]

The Sixteenth District of Ohio, which Giddings now represented, was comprised of Ashtabula, Geauga, and Trumbull Counties and constituted more than just an unshakable bastion of Whiggery. Most of its constituents were also fully imbued with the
sectional convictions so common to the rural Reserve,[31] and early in the campaign Giddings saw to it that his potential antislavery supporters knew where he stood. During the canvass he
replied publicly to a query from the Ashtabula County Anti-
Slavery Society by explaining his views on slavery's political aspects: both slavery and the slave trade in the District of Columbia
and in territorial waters were illegal and disgraceful. Congress
had the moral duty and legal power to abolish these injustices,
but the interstate slave trade was not subject to congressional
controls. Moreover, he maintained that the Fugitive Slave Law
of 1793, although unfortunate, was constitutional. On the ques-

tion of the "gag rule," which automatically excluded the petitions of antislavery Northerners from the House of Representatives, Giddings affirmed his opposition. All citizens, black and white, had both the "moral and legal right" to petition Congress on any subject. To prohibit this right was a gross violation of the Constitution. Slaves, on the other hand, while holding an undisputed moral right to petition the government, were regrettably lacking in the legal status to do so.[32]

Antislavery men announced they were "pleased with the independent stand Mr. Giddings has taken. . . ." They felt he had well satisfied the doubts of some potential voters,[33] for Giddings' endorsement of political antislavery represented a break with Whittlesey's successful technique of straddling the issues.[34] He campaigned on this platform, drawing most of his strength from Whittlesey's weakest regions, while gaining only a small majority in his predecessor's citadel, Trumbull County, where antislavery spirit had always lagged behind.[35] Giddings' convictions, while rearranging the district voting patterns, had now pushed him to the point of public commitment.

In late November, 1838, he set off for Washington. Uri Seeley, an obscure but dedicated antislavery constituent, advised him just before he departed to show no hesitation in speaking out for freedom: "when policy coincides with great principles then it becomes every individual—& more especially a person that occupies the station you occupy—to lift Samson like." [36] Counsel of this kind, plus experiences in Washington as a new representative, would soon intensify Joshua Giddings' dedication.

NOTES

1 JRG to LMG, January 29, 1837, Giddings MSS.

2 JRG to JAG, May 21, 1835, Giddings MSS.

3 JRG to LWG, April 22, 1837, Giddings MSS.

4 Reliance on tension and the pursuit of long-range goals, the hall-marks of Giddings' personality, fit surprisingly well into a framework suggested by Martin Duberman in his article "The Abolitionists and Psychology," *Journal of Negro History*, XLVII (July, 1962), 183–91. It is on this framework that I am relying. Duberman, using the tenets of ego psychology, offers the notion first postulated by Gordon Allport that a mature, healthy personality rationally picks difficult goals which can be achieved only by maintaining a high level of tension. In Allport's psychological lexicon such words as "conscience," "will power" and "character" have valid meanings of their own. Commitment to a cause can indicate maturity and stability rather than a guise which hides an urge to relieve neurotic anxiety. Perhaps some foes of slavery were deranged, but so were many other people in the nineteenth century. Giddings' long-term personal and family relationships, however, suggest that he was not one of these. For an attempt to apply the older stereotype to Giddings and his crisis see Robert P. Ludlum, "Joshua R. Giddings, Radical," *Mississippi Valley Historical Review*, XXIII (June, 1936), 31–53.

5 JRG to LWG, April 22, 1837, Giddings MSS.

6 Julian, *Giddings*, 35.

7 For excellent treatment of this theme of nature in nineteenth-century thought see Henry Nash Smith, *Virgin Land* (Cambridge, 1950), Chaps. 7–8, and Alan E. Heimert, *Religion and the American Mind from the Great Awakening to the Revolution* (Cambridge, 1966), 103–7. See especially Perry Miller, *The Life of the Mind in America from the Revolution to the Civil War* (New York, 1965), 27–36.

[8] JRG to LWG, July 20, 1837, Giddings MSS.

[9] Heimert, *Religion and the American Mind, passim.;* Gilbert Hobbes Barnes, *The Antislavery Impulse, 1830–1844* (New York, 1933), 3–37.

[10] JRG to Ephriam Brown, July 13, 1831, Brown MSS, WRHS (quotation); JRG to LWG, June 20, 1836, Giddings MSS.

[11] JRG to JAG, April 24, 1835, Giddings MSS.

[12] JRG to LMG, January 29, 1837, Giddings MSS.

[13] JRG to LWG, January 26, 1837, Giddings MSS.

[14] Ashtabula *Sentinel,* June 9, 1838, April 9, 1843.

[15] Giddings spent nearly all of 1838 in Jefferson. Few family letters exist for this year.

[16] Barnes, *Antislavery Impulse,* 38–40.

[17] *Ibid.,* 74–78, 87–90.

[18] The factual material for this paragraph, but not the interpretation, is drawn from Edward C. Reilley, "The Rise of Antislavery Sentiment in the Western Reserve" (Ph.D. dissertation, Case Western Reserve University, 1940) *passim.* Reilley gives this problem a heavily economic interpretation, which overlooks religion and other cultural influences that contributed greatly to the sectional opinions of Reserve citizens.

[19] William C. McLoughlin, in the Introduction to Barnes, *Antislavery Impulse,* xxviii.

[20] Barnes, *Antislavery Impulse,* 82; Theodore Weld to Lewis Tappan, December 14, 1841, in Gilbert Hobbes Barnes and Dwight Lowell Dumond (eds.), *Letters of Theodore Dwight Weld, Angelina Grimké Weld, and Sarah Grimké, 1822–1844,* 2 vols. (New York, 1934), II, 879–80 (hereafter cited as *Weld-Grimké Letters*).

[21] Barnes, *Antislavery Impulse,* 82; Benjamin Platt Thomas, *Theodore Weld, Crusader for Freedom* (New Brunswick, 1950), 102.

[22] Ashtabula *Sentinel,* June 21, 1834.

[23] *Ibid.*

[24] *Ibid.,* July 12, 1834, June 16, 1836.

[25] Davison, "Whittlesey," 134–172.

[26] Elizur Wright to JRG, January 22, 1837, Joshua R. Giddings-George W. Julian MSS., Library of Congress (hereinafter LC).

[27] Ashtabula *Sentinel,* September 29, 1838.

JOSHUA R. GIDDINGS

28 JRG to James A. Briggs, April 29, 1843, James A. Briggs MSS, WRHS.

29 JRG to Elisha Whittlesey, June 23, 1838, Whittlesey MSS, WRHS; Elisha Whittlesey to JRG, June 28, 1838, Giddings MSS.

30 The endorsement is found in the Ashtabula *Sentinel,* July 28, 1838. Election results are reported in *ibid.,* October 20, 1838. For evidence of Whittlesey's aid in Giddings' election, see JRG to Milton Sutliffe, September 10, 1838, Joshua R. Giddings-Milton Sutliffe MSS, Norton Collection, WRHS. These letters, still in private hands, have been made available through the joint auspices of the Norton family of Cleveland and The Western Reserve Historical Society.

31 Willard D. Loomis, "The Antislavery Movement in Ashtabula County, Ohio, 1834–1854" (M.A. thesis, Case Western Reserve University, 1934), 1–36; Davison, "Whittlesey," 79.

32 Ashtabula *Sentinel,* September 29, 1838.

33 *Ibid.,* October 6, 1838.

34 Davison, "Whittlesey," 133–34.

35 Ashtabula *Sentinel,* October 20, 1836.

36 Uri Seeley to JRG, November 28, 1838, Giddings MSS.

Chapter 3

A
NEOPHYTE IN
WASHINGTON

⊰ ⊱

1838-1841

Washington in 1838 looked little different to Giddings than Jefferson had in the 1820's. In many respects the capital city had the appearance of an overgrown frontier town. Thoroughfares were constantly clogged with mud or choked with dust, and small, drab-looking brick dwellings lined each avenue. The major administrative buildings cast their jagged, unfinished profiles against the sky, giving the city a rude, disorganized look.[1] Giddings found a room with comfortable furnishings in a boarding house only a mile from the Capitol. Although he made no quick friendships among his colleagues at the new residence, his messmates, he was relieved to discover, were all "professors of religion, two Presbyterian and one Methodist." There was little of the "general corruption of morals . . ." he had expected to encounter, and, except for missing his family, he felt quite at ease.[2]

Considering his political opinions, however, Joshua Giddings was definitely more than just another ordinary new congressman. Alongside his developing antislavery views, already far beyond the bounds of propriety, lay an unorthodox but none-theless profound loyalty to the Whig party, which he had helped to build. The unity of Whiggery was supported by a fragile web of allegiance and expediency, many threads of which crossed and re-crossed the Mason-Dixon line. Unforgiving sectionalism, as all Whigs knew, could easily disrupt the party, and Giddings did not consciously wish to destroy it. He was as eager to defeat the Democrats and enact the Whig economic program as he was to do justice to his antislavery beliefs.[3] The two loyalties were en-tirely contradictory. But Giddings, from the start, attempted to knit them together into a morally and politically consistent sys-tem in which he could consider Whiggery and antislavery as syn-onymous ideas, even though they were not.

No two great personalities of the nineteenth century present-ed more jarring contrasts while more clearly highlighting the contradictions which Giddings found within Whiggery than convivial Henry Clay and dour John Quincy Adams: slavehold-er and Yankee, political buccaneer and high-principled patriot, high-living Southerner and staid New Englander. Yet among all the people Giddings assessed during his first days in Washing-ton, he admired these men most. He met both at successive New Years' social functions, and soon saw each in action in Congress.

Henry Clay embodied the economic principles of Whiggery to which Giddings was deeply dedicated. Clay's programs for inter-nal improvements, homestead laws, and a national bank prom-ised much for Giddings' district and made great sense to a former land speculator who had lost his fortune in the panic of 1837. But above all, Henry Clay espoused economic nationalism. He aimed at making the United States transcend its regional variations through common industrial and agricultural devel-opment, and Giddings, despite his growing hatred of slavery in the South, believed fully in the wisdom of these principles. His first conversation with Clay, which took place at a lavish Whig soirée, was casual, unrestrained, and in the spirit of party brotherhood. Giddings found in the urbane Clay "much hidden feeling beneath a cool, dispassionate exterior" and left him with an even "higher admiration" than he had previously entertained.[4] Clay's profile, as Giddings, a believer in phrenology, noted, "is the best in our house." [5] Soon after his talk with Clay, Giddings sat in the Senate gallery, heard the Kentuckian deliver a rhetorical masterpiece on the tariff, and was completely enthralled.[6]

While Clay spoke for an expanding nation, John Quincy Adams, who also claimed Whig allegiance, upheld the values of a more provincial political style, characteristic of an earlier generation of Yankees. Imbedded in his viewpoint was a profound concern for preserving the ideals of the Republic as defined in 1787, through an emulation of the highly moral statesmanship ascribed to New England's Revolutionary generation. By acting on such convictions, John Quincy Adams had transformed himself into a sectional agitator, at odds with much of Henry Clay's national vision. He had returned to the House of Representatives after his defeat by Andrew Jackson, and by 1836 he had assumed a new role as he turned his legal expertise and sharp tongue against the "gag rule." This rule, the product of Southern fears for the health of slavery and Northern desires to avoid the sectional conflict, had been instituted when abolitionists began flooding Congress with antislavery memorials. The "gag" dictated that all petitions to Congress protesting any aspect of slavery be automatically tabled without being printed, discussed, or acted upon in any manner.[7] Adams, though certainly not an abolitionist, believed this rule a dangerous deviation from the aims of original republicanism. He was now waging a ceaseless attack against the slaveholders and their Northern "doughfaced" allies, the defenders of a clear abridgment of constitutionally guaranteed civil liberties. Adams' motives were conservative and legalistic, but in the process he had become the most efficient liaison between the government and Northern antislavery opinion.[8]

Giddings, who had also declared himself opposed to the gag rule for some of the same reasons, could hardly find words which did justice to his conversation with the stern old Puritan. His admiration for Adams, which never diminished, was unbounded, resulting in a lifelong friendship.[9] Giddings discovered in Adams the ideal politician, a living incarnation of the high-minded independence which all public men, especially Whigs, ought to embody. Adams impressed Giddings as a "specimen of genuine greatness, consecrated with . . . republican simplicity" developed in the era of the American Revolution. He was certain that Adams' presidency and now his battles against the exclusion of antislavery petitions would "hereafter fill the brightest pages of American history." [10] Besides meeting for the first time one who was to be his closest friend, Joshua Giddings had discovered a powerful reinforcement of his own antislavery convictions. John Quincy Adams confirmed that the party contained men whose sound judgment led them to battle the dangerous political innovations wrought by the "Southern influence." After his first meeting with Adams, the new Ohio congressman doubtless felt more certain than ever that moral duty required him to speak out against slavery.

But loyal Whiggery demanded that no Northern member hold undue hatred toward slaveholders. Initially Giddings felt none,[11] but he began to modify his opinion after mid-December, when the gag rule again passed. Efforts led by Adams to defeat it were beaten down with relative ease,[12] and, as debate wore on, Giddings began to notice "a vast difference in the character of the members of the north and the south," especially on the subject of slavery. Southern men displayed "self-important airs" and "overbearing manners," while representatives from the North acted "diffident, taciturn, and *forbearing*." Giddings concluded that "southern Bullies" had forced everyone else into silence, and no one was even willing to protest the slave markets which did business across the street from the House of Representatives. "This kind of fear I have never experienced, nor shall I submit to it now," he swore in his diary. Soon he began to consider the idea of presenting resolutions instructing Congress to investigate and report on how many slaves in the District of Columbia had committed suicide within the previous five years, rather than submit to being sold and sent away from their families.[13]

Though anxious to speak on the "gag" and other questions, Giddings felt hesitant because "the etiquette of Congress requires young members to be modest," and he was reluctant to enflame debate in the House.[14] But concern over violating congressional rules of propriety did not last long. On January 30, 1839, while wandering the streets of Washington, Giddings caught his first glimpse of the slave trade. It was an experience which he found profoundly shocking, like nothing he had ever seen in Jefferson.

The slave gang was composed of about sixty-five men, women, and children all chained together. Only the weakest women and children too young to walk were allowed to sit in the large wagon which accompanied the procession. Beside the group rode a slavedriver, cracking a whip over laggards. Giddings' reaction to this "barbarous spectacle" in the streets of the Capitol was one of hot indignation.[15] That evening he called on Adams' closest associate, William Slade of Vermont, and asked for advice on how best to take up the issue of slavery in the District of Columbia. Slade, after overcoming initial reservations, found that he and Giddings agreed on most points, and the two men became friends at once. Both had come to be antislavery Whigs by mixing religious, Antimasonic, and Federalist convictions. After several years of working virtually alone with Adams, Slade doubtless felt happy to discover a new ally in Giddings.[16]

After conversing with Slade, Giddings sent a letter to Gamaliel Bailey, one of Ohio's outstanding abolitionist leaders, begging for support. Bailey's reform career was to be among the longest and most productive in ante-bellum America, and in 1839 he spoke for nearly all of the Midwest's abolitionists through his vigorously edited newspaper, the *Philanthropist,* located in Cincinnati. Before taking the perilous step of opposing slavery, Giddings understandably wanted encouragement. Bailey's reply came by return mail, and it was all that Giddings could have wished for: "Abolitionists will help you. . . . What we all wish is *action now.* Do something, only make a *beginning.*" Meanwhile,

Giddings prepared his wife, telling her: "Do not be frightened if you should hear of some attacks on this subject of the slave trade before Congress ends, Notwithstanding the 'gag.' " [17] In Congress, four days later, he watched the House debate and refer a petition from the white citizens of the District of Columbia which prayed for the continued exclusion of all antislavery petitions. Giddings countered by submitting one from his constituents which called on Congress to abolish slavery in the District of Columbia. After heated words with Hugh Garland of Louisiana and Edward Stanly from North Carolina, Giddings saw his petition tabled by the gag rule.[18]

The cumulative impact of Southern behavior, the gag rule, and, above all, the slave trade infused in him a new sense of urgency: he "no longer felt . . . the Representative of *Freemen* . . . while compelled to remain silent and witness my country's disgrace." From then on he did not care if speaking out did nothing to "soothe and reconcile" contending parties.[19] On February 13, 1839, Giddings captured the Speaker's attention and rose from his seat.

The subject under discussion was an amendment to the District of Columbia appropriations bill, which set aside $30,000 for a bridge over the east branch of the Potomac River. The issue had not the remotest connection with slavery, but Giddings seized upon it, for it would allow him to speak of the terrible activities he had seen in the District without being cut off by the gag rule. He moved to strike out the amendment and went on to explain his reasons.

It would be wasteful, Giddings maintained, to make such an appropriation, for soon the government would be moved to a free state because of growing Northern hostility to slavery and the slave trade. His constituents viewed with "disgust and abhorrence" the spectacle of Congress being surrounded by practices usually condoned only among "barbarous and uncivilized nations." No liberty-loving Northerner would remain content to "continue the seat of Government in the midst of a magnificent slave mart . . ." where high-sounding congressional debates mingled with "the voice of the auctioneer proclaiming the sale of human, intelligent beings."

The House exploded in frenzied cries of "Order! Order!" Giddings, however, explained that he was only trying to detail his opposition to the appropriation. James K. Polk, the Southern Democratic Speaker, upheld him, and Giddings next directed objections to the gag rule. His Northern constituents would be taxed to pay for the bridge. At the same time, Congress tabled their petitions protesting slavery in the District and kept their representative "bound hand and foot by a sort of legislative straight-jacket" to keep him from voicing their sentiments for freedom. Congress told Northern men, "We will not hear your objections to the slave trade; but we will tax you to build a slave market." Giddings would never vote for any appropriation for the District until all Northern antislavery petitions were received and acted upon.[20]

Thomas Glasscock of Georgia jumped to his feet and interrupted, crying loudly that the Speaker stop Giddings from "pouring out his foul aspersions and gross calumnies upon the citizens of this District." [21] He called Giddings a "damned liar" and accused him of slandering the characters of slaveholders. The House degenerated into chaos as loud voices filled the hall, "a perfect scene of disorder and uproar . . . ," Giddings later described it. With Adams and Slade dissenting sturdily, Polk finally called him to order for irrelevancy.[22]

Giddings sat down amidst glowers and insults. Adams, his full face wreathed by a glowing smile, walked over to Giddings' seat, laughed heartily, and congratulated him.[23] An influential Whig paper in Cleveland immediately advised Giddings' constituents to order him home at the earliest opportunity, while that august Whig voice of the nation, the *National Intelligencer,* declared that his speech misrepresented the facts.[24]

Amid this barrage of criticism from his own party Giddings felt no less a loyal Whig, for he found it easy to reconcile his conflicting Whig and antislavery ideologies. Although his conclu-

43

sions revealed few traces of astuteness and often made him an inept "practical" politician, they did furnish him with several much more essential convictions and aims. Giddings considered himself one who acted in the best interests of his party by becoming the most effective antislavery agitator in Congress during the 1840's.

Though Glasscock and the other Southern Whigs were hardly less devoted to the gag rule and slavery than the Democrats, Giddings maintained from the first that the Democrats, both Northerners and Southerners, were responsible for every proslavery measure. Whigs, on the other hand, even slaveowning ones, were potentially redeemable. As early as 1838, Giddings had convinced himself that every political influence behind the reenactment of the gag rule had Democratic origins.[25] On the gag rule vote, and in a later fray, when Adams tried to get a hearing for a petition praying the recognition of Haiti, Giddings noted that nearly every Northern Democrat voted with the "Southern interest," while a far greater number of Northern Whigs took a sectional position.[26]

Giddings seized upon this block of Northern Whig votes and concluded that agitation served the best interests of the party, while Whiggery, in turn, contained the potential to become antislavery's best agency. While overlooking the fact that many Northern Whigs supported repeal of the gag rule simply to diminish the Democratic administration in the eyes of antislavery constituents,[27] Giddings believed that Whig congressmen had a clear appreciation of their moral duty as politicians and could become dedicated antislavery men. Such votes indicated the latent and potentially powerful antislavery basis of the party. Northern Whigs, unlike the Northern Democrats, were not bound hand and foot to Southern opinion and could act upon their principles. In cases where Whigs lacked conviction, Giddings himself would try to instill some by impressing his colleagues with the sins of slavery.

Even as early as 1838, when the gag rule came up for debate, Giddings instructed his district's editors to take an uncompromising stand on repeal: "I want our friends to put it on a *broad* & *right* basis. Let the question before the people be the same as it is here. . . ." If Whigs all over the North face the issue squarely, "the locos cannot sustain themselves before the public." [28] With the goal of Northern supremacy achieved, the Whig economic program and Giddings' antislavery views could become realities. As for the Southern branch of this party, it would either have to see the logic of antislavery action, or at least accept it as the only strategy for victory. Otherwise, such men simply were not Whigs. [29] For nearly twenty years Giddings sent advice like the above to editors and made innumerable speeches while trying to convince politicians of the evils of slavery. Through his faith in the conversion experience and his assumption that morality and politics were inseparable, Giddings ultimately discovered harmony between antislavery and Whiggery. More deeply, he also reconciled his reform activity with his participation in the political process.

Giddings drew from his unique views extra measures of fulfillment often denied to other advocates of reform. He connected his crusade not with political life as it was but as he fully expected it soon *would be.* Convinced that congressional regeneration was always possible, his dissatisfaction with conditions as he found them only renewed his zeal to maintain his principles. The pitfall of expediency was later to entrap many antislavery partisans less imbued with Giddings' optimism and more reconciled to day-to-day bargaining. But in spite of numerous setbacks and stunning examples of his colleagues' lack of sensitivity, Giddings served longer and more consistently in Congress than any other ante-bellum representative. Although always exposed to the "art of compromise," his technical position as politician seldom distracted him from his true vocation as critic and reformer. Joshua Giddings insured his effectiveness as an antislavery spokesman by partaking as little as possible of a conventional political mentality.

Although Giddings vigorously denied it, his conclusions led

him to strict sectionalism, for the idea of either converting Southern politicians or simply ignoring their wishes would naturally result in the destruction of national parties. But Giddings knew nothing of this inevitability in 1839, for he felt his doctrines were the essence of political conservatism and should be easily comprehended by the South. They were, as he once declared, "not new, as they are as old as the Constitution, nor are they *antislavery*, for they have been, for half a century, agreed to by the southerner." [30] Giddings based his views simply on a translation of Southern states-rights arguments, and, given this idiom, Southerners should be able to see the justice of his proposals. After all, as he often assured the public, he had no plans to end slavery in the South. He was not an abolitionist.

Abolitionists of every shade of opinion always appreciated this fact, although it completely eluded the slaveholder. One abolitionist, dubious about Giddings' position, told him that his doctrines were "entirely negative. Not a single one of them is opposed to the continuance of slavery. . . . You propose [only] to confine slavery in all its bearings south of Mason's and Dixon's line, and when you have gotten there, to 'rest from your labors.' " [31] This critic was completely accurate in his judgments. To be sure, Giddings hoped privately to end slavery in America, but he never campaigned directly for that goal.[32] Instead he insisted that the Constitution intended slavery to have no influence in the national government. The founding fathers, as he asserted time and again in speeches, essays, and letters, had wanted the political role of the "peculiar institution" to end at the borders of those slave states in existence in 1789. Back in 1787 New England delegates to the Philadelphia Convention had wished to abolish slavery, for it was out of harmony with the egalitarian meaning of the Declaration of Independence. But Southern representatives, for selfish economic reasons, had balked at entering any union in which the central government might have the power of emancipation. To be doubly safe from any such threat Southern men had insisted, just as they still insisted, that the federal government be powerless to deal with the institution.

The Southerners' wish, Giddings stated, had been granted in the Tenth Amendment. All power to abolish or promote slavery had been left in the hands of the several states. New York had ended slavery within its borders, while Virginia had elected to preserve it. The federal government could neither create slavery in Ohio nor cripple the system in South Carolina. Yet in a national government based on the "self-evident" truths of the Declaration of Independence Giddings felt there could not be, nor was there, any *recognition* of humans as property. The federal government had no obligation to protect slaveowners' "chattel." [33]

But Southern politicians, Giddings maintained, had quickly insisted on measures which contradicted the states-rights aims of the founding fathers. Over the years the federal government had been progressively perverted by proslavery innovations which forced it to violate its own charter of freedom. Such Southern programs constituted illegal and immoral commitments, for they slowly made the support of slavery a national policy. In 1795 the federal government assumed the burden of protecting slavery and the slave trade in the District of Columbia, and by 1820 Southern demands had resulted in the creation of a slave state, Missouri, carved out of federal lands. Soon after, federal troops had been increased in the South and extra government monies had been expended to guard against slave revolts.

Within territorial waters along the Southern coasts, Giddings asserted, the United States Navy lent unconstitutional protection to the coastwise slave trade, while since 1835 the federal troops had collaborated with slavery by returning fugitive bondsmen during the Florida War. Not content with these illegalities, Southern votes had instituted the gag rule in 1836 to shut off all protest from the North, thus ravishing still other sections of the Constitution which guaranteed citizens' rights of free speech and petition to the government. In Giddings' view,

47

slaveholders had succeeded in nationalizing the "peculiar institution" despite the Constitution.[34]

As a result, the moral stain of slavery rested as much upon every Northern citizen as upon every slaveholder. Given Giddings' belief in the unity of politics and morality and his long-cherished Federalist bias, the need to return to the "true doctrines" of 1787 presented him with a compelling personal imperative. He always claimed that his was the conservative lineage of Alexander Hamilton and George Washington. He never fully appreciated that his activities constituted a most radical sort of behavior. Until 1861, his entire program consisted simply of trying to convince others to "denationalize" slavery totally by a reverse application of all the arguments which most Southerners made to defend that institution. "The North cannot disturb slavery in the South," they would declare. Giddings agreed heartily and then exhorted his colleagues to follow such logic to its obvious conclusion and vote to abolish slavery in the District of Columbia and the slave trade on the coasts.

Giddings' constitutional arguments, of course, were vulnerable in their inconsistencies. He could never come to grips with the abolitionists' observation that the founding fathers, by the three-fifths compromise, had defined a slave as three-fifths of a man, and his explanation of the section providing for the federally administered Fugitive Slave Law of 1793 was implausible. Giddings maintained that Northerners were not legally bound to enforce that law even though the law said otherwise.[35] Such incongruities, however, did not matter to Giddings, for his situation contained dilemmas not answerable by the use of cold reason anyway. Had he admitted to himself the Constitution's proslavery nature his career as an elected reformer would have ended forthwith. He could not then have sworn as a federal official to uphold the government. Some abolitionists with aims more sweeping than Giddings' did acknowledge the Constitution's true nature and advocated disunion as the only possible recourse. But Giddings was irrevocably wedded to the idea that politics and antislavery action were inseparable. In order to implement this belief by confronting moral questions in Congress, he instinctively overlooked the basic predicaments others saw in the Constitution. The preciseness of his doctrines, however, meant little inasmuch as they provided a serviceable basis from which he could act. From 1838 to 1861 none was to be more vigorous in antislavery circles than Joshua Giddings, and all the while he deemed himself a constructive influence on his party associates. Most of his colleagues, however, often feared and seldom understood this vocal representative who behaved so little like a legislator.

But how well he was liked by his associates was the least of Giddings' preoccupations during his first session. He believed his "retiring and simple habits" suited him poorly for the "gay and social circle" around him. At parties and soirées he imagined himself "allmost [sic] a stranger" as he pushed through the clusters of guests "at expense to my own comfort, as well as the ease of many small and delicate ladies." [36] Instead, he devoted his time to working on the Committee on Claims and thinking about his family.

The Claims Committee assignment allowed Giddings to use his legal knowledge. It was the only congressional committee which acted as a court of law, for its job was investigation of the enormous number of monetary claims by private citizens upon the federal government. Giddings found most of his fellow members derelict in their responsibilities,[37] and he spent fatiguing hours managing his committee's work. Anxious to meet his duties, he usually arose by five o'clock. After a brisk mile of walking around the Capitol grounds and a breakfast of steak, sausage, cornbread, and coffee, he often began work by 6:30, reading applications and searching for precedents.[38] He took great pride in the two hundred and twenty claims bills which he personally expedited in his first session;[39] on the strength of such achievements he soon became the committee's chairman. With a schedule like this one he could find little time for the "hypo-chondria." [40]

Nevertheless, Giddings sorely missed his family. He never made enough money to take his wife and children to Washington, and especially during his first terms he constantly longed to return to Jefferson and "enjoy the family circle, once more to meet around the family altar & unite in Thanksgiving to our common parent." [41] What pleased him most was intimate family news—the more the better. "You make me think myself allmost [sic] at home," he told his wife Laura. "As for instance when you told me of the . . . children, and all but Grotius gone to meeting, that he was sitting upon the carpet looking at pictures and talking to you occasionally and telling you to 'give his love to Pa.' " [42]

When the mailbox was empty, Giddings became depressed, and sometimes angry. Often, he became short-tempered about Laura's procrastination in replying to his letters. Sometimes he rebuked his children for the same offense: "The truth is, you are not aware of the anxiety I have for you and your brothers. I have no doubt that as far as I am concerned you are of much more importance than you are aware of." [43] The older children received endless, often stern advice about manners, morals, and religion, as well as small mementos. Giddings always hoped that he could somehow bring up his children by mail.

Despite his protectiveness, Giddings was an excellent father who tried to make his children develop a sense of independence, responsibility, and free choice. Joseph once received a stern lecture for wasting his time with novels when Giddings felt he should be reading his law books.[44] Earlier, however, Giddings had advised his wife that their son was progressing nicely, should not be coddled, and should be allowed "to be placed . . . upon his own resources." [45] Lura Maria, a bright girl, was granted her request to leave home and finish her education at Hartford Women's Seminary in Connecticut. Giddings continually wrote to her about how a proper young lady should think and act, corrected her spelling faults, and worried much about her.

But he also told her he would always have "confidence in the principles in which you have thus far been bred. . . ."[46] He praised the poetry and essays which Lura sent him, while making careful, friendly criticisms.[47]

Giddings' children all grew to be healthy, well-balanced adults because of, and not despite, the influence of their father. Grotius and Joseph found success in law and journalism, while Lura Maria became a radical abolitionist and vigorous crusader for female equality. Comfort chose to remain a farmer. Another daughter, Laura Ann, born in 1839, married George W. Julian, Giddings' close friend and biographer, an outspoken antislavery partisan and a very successful politician. All were devoted to their parents, who had provided each with a happy childhood.[48] This fact, if nothing else, bears witness to the healthiness of Joshua Giddings' personality.

The notoriety of his first attack on the slave trade and the gag rule made a few close friendships for Giddings, despite the general hostility to his display of "fanaticism." He drew nearer to like-minded colleagues, and when the Twenty-sixth Congress opened in December, 1839, he moved into new quarters at Mrs. Sprigg's boarding house, along with two men whose views on sectional issues were very close to Giddings' own—William Slade and a new antislavery recruit, Seth M. Gates, from Genesee County in the heart of New York's "burnt-over district." Now Giddings found people with whom he could feel at home, and he enjoyed both the "good room and good company." He also spent long evenings in pleasant conversation at John Quincy Adams' house.[49]

Despite the growing closeness of the group, there was little unanimity within the antislavery movement in late 1840. Democrats and Whigs were evenly divided in the House, and Northern Whigs worried over the prospect of abolitionist opposition to the election of William Henry Harrison as president. Antislavery agitation often became submerged in other partisan issues. Slade, Gates, and Giddings dutifully cast their ballots for

51

a succession of Southern Whig caucus nominees and helped elect Robert M. T. Hunter, a Virginia slaveholder, as Speaker.[50]

While Giddings rejoiced at the victory,[51] he noticed criticism from a new quarter, stinging denunciations from Joshua Leavitt, editor of the Boston abolitionist journal, the *Emancipator*. Leavitt, a Congregationalist minister, had forsaken his parish for a reform career during the early 1830's. He had been pivotal in organizing the American Anti-Slavery Society's petition campaigns, and he possessed broad practical talents and a tough-minded idealism, which were to insure him an antislavery career equal in length and importance to Giddings' own. Leavitt expressed utter disgust at the antislavery Whigs' apostasy in voting for a Speaker "who, twelve months ago, trampled upon liberty and the Constitution" by endorsing the gag rule. "Let us rally under our own banner," Leavitt appealed, "and . . . we [will] put men in Congress who do not care a straw for other questions in comparison with that of slavery. . . ." [52]

Leavitt's call to action constituted a momentous shift by many abolitionists away from their old program of propaganda to a new plan of direct political involvement. Alienated from a faction led by William Lloyd Garrison which espoused anti-clerical and antigovernment ideas, veterans like Leavitt, Elizur Wright, Jr., Henry B. Stanton, and Gerrit Smith had dropped out of the American Anti-Slavery Society. Their "new organization," the Liberty party, proposed to abolish slavery by slowly capturing the government, while rejecting Garrison's insistence that abolitionists divorce themselves from all institutions connected with the maintenance of slavery. Hoping to preserve their principles while plunging into politics, these men nominated the ex-slaveholder-turned-abolitionist James G. Birney to oppose Willian Henry Harrison and Martin Van Buren in the 1840 presidential election.

The party was destined never to elect a single candidate to office. Many of its members were one day to find their abolitionist commitment untenable in the face of political compromise. Unlike Giddings, their aim was ending slavery, not just denationalizing it—a program far more vulnerable than his to political vitiation. Ultimately, the Garrisonians alone continued to espouse the unsullied ideal of Negro emancipation. In the meantime Liberty men like Joshua Leavitt were to exercise a crucial influence on the antislavery behavior of Whigs like Joshua Giddings.

Giddings noted Leavitt's criticism of his Speakership vote and quickly began muttering about "wild ultraism" which would "kill any other cause upon earth" with its doctrinaire views. He feared that the "more thorough-going abolitionists" would denounce Harrison's Whig candidacy "as a *proslavery* nomination." [53] During this session Slade, Giddings, and the rest spent most of their time fretting over the Liberty party and trying to embarrass the Democrats. Antislavery agitation was purposely muffled, except for a speech by Slade, who argued with strained logic that all abolitionists should vote for Harrison rather than Birney. Giddings judged it a "good antidote to our ultra abolitionists who refuse to vote for the Hero of North Bend." [54] Slade, who could disregard his principles for the good of the party, advised an agreeing Giddings to put a damper on agitation in order to draw public attention to issues other than slavery.[55]

Antislavery votes, Giddings decided, must not be drawn from the party he wished to renovate, especially since the Whig presidential nominee hailed from Ohio and would remember those who helped deliver his home state. Characteristically, he sent a campaign banner to little Grotius and instructed him to tell everyone "that you are for Harrison and reform, and opposed to *all 'Northern* men with Southern principles.' " [56] His main preoccupation, especially after Harrison's stand on sectional issues received a qualified private endorsement from Gamaliel Bailey,[57] became a sweeping Whig victory which would curtail the Liberty party's growth and bury the Democrats. Giddings never bothered to notice that his desire to remake Whiggery contained a contradiction. Future reform depended on how many votes the party could get as presently constituted. For the moment Giddings allowed his antislavery convictions to be overridden by his desire for victory.

The gag rule again passed after two months of stalemate, "cool weather and warm debate." [58] Giddings limited his participation to voting against every proposed formula.[59] Only once thereafter did he agitate the slavery question, aside from presenting petitions, which were quietly gagged. On this single occasion he argued that memorials praying the abolition of slavery and the slave trade in the District of Columbia lay outside the limits of the gag rule and should be received and complied with. Robert Craig of Virginia "imperiously demanded" that the Speaker stop Giddings from wasting the House's time. Speaker Hunter agreed, and Giddings for the rest of the session said nothing about slavery.[60]

Instead, there was much to be done to organize the party for the elections, and Giddings did his part enthusiastically. He introduced several resolutions calling for financial retrenchment, and he scored the Democrats in a formal speech for expenses which were "extravagant and in contrast with the economical professions of the administration." [61] At the same time, he scribbled furiously, sending letter after letter and finally form letters to Whigs in his district. Each one exhorted its receiver to organize for Harrison and victory. "You *must* arouse Ohio," Giddings repeated. "Make some demonstrations for the public . . . meetings and the like. . . . Heal all the other difficulties . . . and unite the whole force if you can, but be doing it as fast as possible." [62]

Harrison and his running mate, John Tyler, a "states-rights Whig" from Virginia, swept Ohio and the nation in one of America's most raucous campaigns. Ashtabula County delivered the heaviest Whig majority of any in the state, and Giddings easily won re-election.[63] His speech against the slave trade had received very friendly notices from the local Whig press, and the district convention deemed him "worthy of the confidence and support of a free people." [64] On the surface, Giddings' desire for a united and aroused Ohio seemed fully satisfied. Appearances, however, were deceiving, for the 1840 elections saw rearrangements of loyalties within the local electorate.

The first schism opened when office-hungry Benjamin Wade attempted to win the congressional nomination. Giddings had heard rumors of Wade's activities early in 1840, had taken successful steps to abort them,[65] and by February had assured Joseph that after the nominating convention Wade would still be "engaged in the *law business.*" Memories of Wade's courtroom insults had not faded, and this second affront was enough to extinguish any last affection for "Frank." Giddings began using Wade's ambition as an object lesson for the children; *"avoid his vices,"* he warned Joseph, "and instead pursue *your real worth and moral virtue."* [66]

Yet this feud held minor implications compared to the appearance of the Liberty party in Ohio. In April, 1840, a national convention of the "new organization" met in Albany, New York, and nominated James G. Birney for president. By September, an Ohio convention chaired by Gamaliel Bailey and a converted machine Democrat, ex-Senator Thomas Morris, had drawn up a complete slate of independent candidates. Back in Ashtabula County a convention of political abolitionists denounced Harrison and Van Buren, and nominated a candidate for Congress to oppose Giddings.[67]

The new party received only three per cent of Ohio's votes in the separate congressional election, but its greatest appeal centered in Ashtabula County. The ninety-seven Liberty party votes there represented the largest single cluster polled by the party in Ohio.[68] The unusually wide-spread popularity of antislavery within the Sixteenth District made it a possible site for a Liberty party success. Giddings took immediate steps to forestall this possibility. Long editorials appeared in Giddings' sounding board, the Ashtabula *Sentinel*, picturing Harrison as favorable to signing bills abolishing slavery in the District of Columbia and Van Buren, completely subservient to the South, as vetoing such legislation out of hand. The Whig party, said the *Sentinel*, represented the only practical hope for successful antislavery action, while Liberty men hindered things. Their presence insured the triumph of proslavery Democrats, for a vote for Birney had the effect of being a vote for Van Buren.[69]

This argument and Giddings' own stand on sectional issues had a powerful effect on the voters of the Sixteenth District.[70] Giddings' antislavery attitude, certainly radical by national standards, appeared moderate and responsible to most people in the Reserve when compared to Liberty party principles. Giddings thus enjoyed the luxury of speaking as emphatically about slavery as he wished, for the Whigs, both nationally and locally, much preferred his re-election to a Liberty party victory. Left-wing opposition enabled Giddings to take a position which neutralized the appeal of this more extreme group. He used such tactics to defeat third-party candidates in three straight elections while exhorting Whigs all over the North to follow his example. In short, the Liberty party's presence in the Sixteenth District helped to insure Giddings' continued success as a maverick Whig, but only as long as he spoke out often against slavery. Agitation seemed even more imperative to Giddings as he left for Washington in December, 1840.

NOTES

[1] Allan Nevins, *Ordeal of The Union, Fruits of Manifest Destiny, 1847–1852* (New York, I, 1947), 39–42.

[2] JRG Diary, January 3, 1839, JRG to LWG, December 1, December 16, 1838 (quotations), Giddings MSS.

[3] In his pre-election antislavery exposition Giddings made it clear that in choosing between the Whig slaveholder Henry Clay and the Northern Democrat Martin Van Buren he would support the former. (Ashtabula *Sentinel*, September 29, 1838.) Giddings also was deeply impressed with John Bell of Tennessee upon first meeting him in Washington and hoped that this slaveholder would one day become president. See JRG Diary, December 15, 1838, Giddings MSS.

[4] JRG Diary, December 30, 1838, Giddings MSS.

[5] JRG to LMG, January 1, 1839, Giddings MSS.

[6] JRG Diary, January 2, 1839, Giddings MSS.

[7] Russel Blaine Nye, *Fettered Freedom: Civil Liberties and the Slavery Controversy, 1830–1860* (Ann Arbor, 1949), 32–41.

[8] Samuel Flagg Bemis, *John Quincy Adams and the Union* (New York, 1956), 326–61.

[9] Adams, an aloof personality, offered Giddings his deepest friendship and once wrote Giddings a poem describing his feelings. In part:
> Intent, with anxious aim to learn,
> Each-other's character we scan,
> And soon the differences discern,
> Between the fair and faithless man
> And here with scrutinizing eye
> A kindred soul with mine to see,
> A longing bosom to descry,
> I sought, and found, at last in thee.

Original in JRG Autograph Book, Giddings MSS.

10 JRG Diary, January 1, 1839, Giddings MSS.

11 *Ibid.*, December 15, 1838, Giddings MSS.

12 U. S. *Congressional Globe,* 25th Cong., 3d Sess., VII, 21–23, 25–27, 31–32.

13 JRG Diary, December 14, 1838, Giddings MSS.

14 JRG to Ephriam Brown, November 21, 1838, Brown MSS, WRHS.

15 JRG Diary, January 30, 1839, Giddings MSS.

16 *Ibid.*; Louis Filler, *The Crusade Against Slavery, 1830–1860* (New York, 1960) , 147; JRG to LMG, February 1, 1839, Giddings MSS.

17 Gamaliel Bailey to JRG, February 7, 1839, Giddings-Julian MSS, LC; JRG to LWG, February 1, 1839, Giddings MSS.

18 Joshua R. Giddings, *A History of the Rebellion, Its Authors and Causes* (Cleveland, 1864) , 130; JRG Diary, February 4, 1839, Giddings MSS.

19 JRG to "Sir," February 26, 1839, Joshua R. Giddings MSS, Miscellaneous Collections, The New-York Historical Society, New York City. (This collection is hereinafter cited as Giddings Miscellaneous MSS, NYHS.)

20 JRG Scrapbook, 1839, undated, untitled clipping, Giddings MSS; U.S. *Congressional Globe,* 25th Cong., 3d Sess., VII, 180; Giddings, *History,* 130–31.

21 U.S. *Congressional Globe,* 25th Cong., 3d Sess., VII, 181; Giddings, *History,* 131.

22 JRG Diary, December 12 [13], 1838, Giddings MSS (quotation) ; Giddings, *History,* 130–31.

23 JRG Diary, December 12 [13], 1838, Giddings MSS.

24 Cleveland *Herald,* February 20, 1839; *National Intelligencer,* quoted in the Painesville *Telegraph,* March 14, 1839.

25 JRG to John Crowell, December 13, 1838, Giddings MSS; JRG to Elisha Whittlesey, December 26, 1838, Whittlesey MSS, WRHS.

26 U.S. *Congressional Globe,* 25th Cong., 3d Sess., VII, 23–27, 44–45, 59.

27 Barnes, *Antislavery Impulse,* 119; Davison, "Whittlesey," 144.

28 JRG to John Crowell, December 13, 1838, Giddings MSS.

29 "Pacificus" [pseud. JRG], *Western Reserve Chronicle,* January 3, 1843.

[30] *Ibid.*, November 30, 1842.

[31] R. W. Taylor to JRG, in the Warren *Liberty Herald*, July 24, 31, 1844.

[32] Here an abolitionist is defined as anyone who campaigned openly for the immediate, uncompensated end to slavery in the South. This criterion is used by James M. McPherson in *The Struggle for Equality: Abolitionists and the Negro in the Civil War and Reconstruction* (Princeton, 1964), 3. All of Giddings' previous biographies have misdefined Giddings' position, calling him an abolitionist. See the treatments of Giddings by Robert P. Ludlum, "Joshua R. Giddings, Antislavery Radical (1795–1844)" (Ph.D. dissertation, Cornell University, 1935) and Richard W. Solberg, "Joshua R. Giddings: Politician and Idealist" (Ph.D. dissertation, University of Chicago, 1952).

[33] "Pacificus" [pseud. JRG], *Western Reserve Chronicle*, November 8, 1842.

[34] *Ibid.*, November 29, December 13, 1842.

[35] *Ibid.*, November 15, December 20, 1842; Staughton Lynd, "The Abolitionist Critique of the United States Constitution," in Martin Duberman (ed.), *The Antislavery Vanguard: New Essays on the Abolitionists* (Princeton, 1965), 209–39.

[36] JRG Diary, January 3, 1839 (quotation), JRG to LMG, January 1, 1840 (quotation), Giddings MSS.

[37] JRG to Elisha Whittlesey, February 3, 1839, Whittlesey MSS, WRHS.

[38] JRG to LMG, December 7, 1838, Giddings MSS.

[39] JRG to Elisha Whittlesey, January 27, 1839, Whittlesey MSS, WRHS.

[40] JRG to LWG, December 9, 1838, Giddings MSS.

[41] JRG to LMG, February 17, 1839, Giddings MSS.

[42] JRG to LWG, January 27, 1839 (quotation), JRG to LMG, January 15, 1842, Giddings-Julian MSS, LC.

[43] JRG to LMG, January 8, 1840, Giddings MSS.

[44] JRG to JAG and Comfort Peace Giddings (hereinafter CPG), April 26, 1840, Giddings MSS.

[45] JRG to LWG, January 5, 1838 [1839], Giddings MSS.

[46] JRG to LMG, March 18, 1840, Giddings MSS.

47 JRG to LMG, April 2, 1840, Giddings MSS.

48 Julian, *Giddings*, 21–22.

49 JRG to LWG, December 1, 1839 (quotation), JRG to LMG, December 1, 1839, Giddings MSS.

50 U. S. *Congressional Globe*, 26th Cong., 1st Sess., VIII, 51–55.

51 JRG to Elisha Whittlesey, December 17, 1839, Whittlesey MSS, WRHS.

52 Boston *Emancipator*, December 26, 1839 (quotation). For treatments of parts of Leavitt's career to date, see Barnes, *Antislavery Impulse*, 20, 33–35, 107, 133, 164, 176, 178–79; and Filler, *Crusade Against Slavery*, 24, 63, 172, 174.

53 JRG to Edward Fitch, December 21, 1839, Edward Fitch MSS, OHS (quotation); JRG to [Anon.], December 28, 1839, Giddings MSS (quotation).

54 JRG to John Crowell, March 21, 1840, William Henry Harrison MSS. For Slade's speech, see U.S. *Congressional Globe*, 26th Cong., 1st Sess., VIII, Appendix, 401–3.

55 William Slade to JRG, July 25, 1839, Giddings MSS.

56 JRG to Grotius Reed Giddings (hereinafter GRG), June 17, 1840, Giddings MSS.

57 Gamaliel Bailey to JRG, January 1, 1840, Giddings MSS.

58 JRG to LWG, January 19, 1840, Giddings MSS.

59 U.S. *Congressional Globe*, 26th Cong., 1st Sess., VIII, 89–90, 93–94, 121, 150–51.

60 *Ibid.*, 295.

61 *Ibid.*, 79, 148–49, 150–51, 320 (quotation); JRG to LWG, April 12, 1840, Giddings MSS.

62 JRG to ——, December 28, 1839, original of a form letter, Giddings MSS (quotation); JRG to Elisha Whittlesey, January 19, February 10, May 18, 1840, Whittlesey MSS, WRHS.

63 Ashtabula *Sentinel*, October 17, November 7, 1840.

64 *Western Reserve Chronicle*, April 2, 1839; Painesville *Telegraph*, March 14, 1839; Ashtabula *Sentinel*, September 26, 1840 (quotation).

65 Wade received only two votes in the district convention, Ashtabula *Sentinel*, September 26, 1840.

[66] JRG to JAG, February 8 (quotation), February 13, 1840, Giddings MSS.

[67] Theodore Clarke Smith, *Liberty and Free Soil Parties in the Northwest* (New York, 1897), 39, 41–42; *Emancipator*, September 17, 1840.

[68] Cincinnati *Philanthropist*, December 9, 1840; Ashtabula *Sentinel*, November 7, 1840.

[69] Ashtabula *Sentinel*, August 22, 1840.

[70] *Ibid.*, October 17, 1840.

Chapter 4

CONSPIRACIES
AGAINST
SILENCE

◄ ►

1841-1843

As soon as Giddings had settled himself at Mrs. Sprigg's, he discovered he had developed an unwanted reputation. Seekers of government monies now regarded him as the most influential member of the Claims Committee, and the deluge of entreaties quickly became wearisome. "I am thronged with claimants allmost [sic] constantly . . . ," he complained. "All sorts of folks are pressing me and I keep working away." Sometimes he stayed up until 4:00 A.M., trying to reduce the backlog of cases. Dragging himself into his House seat by nine-thirty after such evenings became painfully frequent routine.[1] But preparation to agitate the slavery question did not lag because Giddings lacked spare time.

Adams, Seth Gates, William Slade, Giddings, and two less important congressmen, Nathaniel Borden and John Mattocks, consulted together early in the session. After a few nights' discussion they agreed on Giddings' idea of bringing slavery issues "collaterally into debate, where other matters constituted the main subject of discussion." Thus there would be less chance of being cut off by the gag rule.[2] Giddings' assurance that he expected a "quiet session" was undoubtedly offered with deliberate irony to the old colonizationist, Elisha Whittlesey.[3]

After the House settled down to business, Adams moved to repeal the gag rule, but his proposal was defeated by a close margin. Soon after, on January 21, 1841, the Clerk announced that it was Massachusetts' day to present memorials. The former president rose again and offered a petition which kept slavery pre-eminent in the minds of congressmen for two weeks. Adams' constituents prayed for the Congress to prohibit any more slave states from entering the Union, and by parliamentary trickery he forced the House into admitting that such a request fell beyond the gag rule's limits. Southern congressmen, tangled in a web of rules Adams wove around them, stood one after another to denounce the Northern abolitionists and their congressional allies. The old Puritan handed back as much abuse as he got.[4]

Finally, on February 8, the Southerners switched the subject. By pre-arrangement they successfully moved to resolve the House into the Committee of the Whole to discuss appropriations for the Seminole War in Florida,[5] and an opportunity to attack slavery "collaterally" presented itself. Well prepared for the occasion, Giddings immediately objected to the bill and announced his intention to speak. While the Southerners had succeeded in silencing Adams, they found to their dismay that they had unleashed Joshua Giddings.

Giddings' speech, a masterpiece of planning and parliamentary tactics, lasted for three hours. A perfect example of Giddings' style as an agitator, his aim was to demonstrate that the Florida War, in its inception, goals, and methods, involved the federal government in capturing and re-enslaving runaway Georgia Negroes. The United States government, Giddings charged, made war upon the Seminoles only to hunt down escaped slaves who had found refuge with the Indians. This unconstitutional, immoral obligation had been originally foisted upon the government by Georgia slaveholders anxious to receive compensation for their losses of human property.

As an amateur historian, Giddings ably proved himself. He filled his speech with quotations and references drawn from War Department dispatches, Claims Committee reports, and clauses from Indian treaties. Each citation buttressed Giddings' contention that the army was being "prostituted in Florida to the base purpose of leading an organized company of Negro catchers. . . ." The patriotic cry of the once-proud militia, "liberty or death," had been forgotten, Giddings charged. " 'Slaves' has become the watchword to inspire them to effort."

Giddings' exposé sprang from his hope that his states-rights antislavery arguments could reach the Southern mind. He did not aim at abolition, he asserted. He wished only to show how the conduct of the Florida War violated the Southerners' own correct constitutional doctrine that the federal government should have nothing to do with slavery. Giddings appealed to the "gentlemen of the South who hold to a strict, rigid construction . . ." to point out the specific clause in the Constitution which authorized the federal government to use the army to recapture fugitives. All should agree that no such clause existed. Did not Northerner and Southerner, even Giddings himself, vote for the first section of the gag rule which declared that the federal government "has no power whatever over the institution of slavery in the several States of this Union"? One hundred ninety-eight representatives had supported this statement. Why should Southern men not follow their own logic and realize that federal activities like the Florida War were unconstitutional and must be ended at once?

Finally, Giddings switched the direction of his exhortation toward the Northern conscience. Army operations in Florida were expensive, and most of the cost came from "the hard earnings of free whites." As a result, the citizens of the North shared active complicity; their money contributions made them "purchasers of human beings." The sin and guilt of slavery spread further over the soul of every Northern citizen the more each was forced to subsidize the recapture of humans who exercised their right to freedom guaranteed "by the laws of Nature and Nature's God. . . ." Economic waste compounded the injustices, and Giddings, his voice projecting toward the Whig side of the aisle, rhetorically asked the House to choose between the benefits to the nation which would accrue if $40,000,000 were spent to catch Florida Negroes and those which allocating a like amount for internal improvements would bring about. Not only was the free Northerner robbed of his innocence but his material property also suffered.[6]

Giddings conducted himself with "perfect calmness and self-possession." Not once did he indulge in personal attacks as members gathered around, although few encouraged him as Adams did. Most had intimidating looks in their eyes. Cries to silence him rang out, and "the House was nearly all the time agitated like the waves of the sea";[7] Giddings later described it as a "peaceful riot."[8] Every demand that he be gagged was countered by Giddings' appeals to his research; and, as Joshua Leavitt, now the Washington reporter for the *Emancipator,* noted respectfully, "The Gentleman from Ohio had examined his ground too carefully to make a mistake. . . ."[9] The Speaker could find no reason for quieting this new threat to the conspiracy of silence against discussing slavery.

Giddings judged that his speech had "raised quite a dust. . . ."[10] For an agitator, he often showed a surprising penchant for understatement. The next day six of the South's most uninhibited rhetoricians rose one after another to attack Giddings' conduct and character in an effort to repress the representative from Ohio. But in their anger they failed to notice that they, too, were discussing the slavery question on the floor of the House; such oversights were never pointed out by the anti-slavery Whigs.

Giddings sat placidly, hearing Mark Cooper of Georgia begin the onslaught by accusing him of barefaced hypocrisy, and he made no reply when Black threatened him with "the infliction of *lynch* law . . . , an elevation of which he [Giddings] little dreams." Charles Downing, a Whig from Florida, called on the party not to touch Giddings, "even with a pair of tongs." When fellow Whig Waddy Thompson from South Carolina pursued the attack further, Giddings assured him he could not be baited. But after Julius Alford, a Georgia Whig, exclaimed he would sooner spit on Giddings than listen further to his "abolitionist" insults, Giddings shot back: "If I could wash your blood from my soul as easily as I can wipe . . . spittle from my face, you would not live another day." [11] Alford, shouting threats, jumped up and started toward his opponent, but Giddings, at six feet two inches and two hundred twenty-five pounds, sat quietly as other congressmen grabbed Alford and steered him back to his seat.[12] The combative congressman always remained outwardly unflappable when threatened.

The Southerners, all Democrats, and the great majority of Whigs judged Giddings' speech distasteful and dangerous. Although the district press applauded his effort,[13] president-elect Harrison, newly arrived in Washington, added his voice to those in the House as he promised privately to purge the party of subversive influences like Giddings. His inaugural address, delivered three weeks later, denounced those whose acts were "harbingers of disunion, violence and civil war." [14]

But Joshua Leavitt and Gamaliel Bailey, recognized directors of the Liberty party, exhausted their vocabularies for enough complimentary adjectives to print in their newspapers, the *Emancipator* and the *Philanthropist,* respectively.[15] Partisanship meant little to these abolitionists. Good works, no matter who did them, simply merited support, while timidity meant stinging criticism. The tactical flexibility of Leavitt and Bailey, not the number of votes their party could muster, constituted their major impact on American politics. In this case, they prodded Giddings' desire to speak openly and often on antislavery topics, for if he could satisfy such "unbending" Liberty men his chances of uniting the political antislavery movement under the Whig banner would be all the greater. "It has never been my habit to oppose our antislavery friends when I thought them wrong," Giddings once revealed to an Ohio third-party leader. "I have rather tried to

persuade them to what I believe correct policy." [16] Throughout
the early and mid-1840's Liberty party spokesmen did a most
effective job of arousing Joshua Giddings.

In May, 1841, during the interim between the end of the Twenty-sixth Congress and the opening of the Twenty-seventh, Giddings returned home to be with his family while Joshua Leavitt
hurled new barbs at the antislavery Whigs. The upcoming session
was a special one, called for by Harrison only to enact the Whig
economic program. Leavitt did not expect "great things" to hap-
pen but told Giddings privately that agitation "should be tried"
anyway.[17] Meanwhile, the *Emancipator* carried incessant criticism
of Giddings and the others for continuing to support their slave-
ridden party. Although Leavitt's caustic jibes drew open protest
from William Slade,[18] they did bring quick results.

The Twenty-seventh Congress reported a Whig majority of forty, and the outcome of electing a Speaker was never in doubt. But
when the caucus selected slaveholder John White of Kentucky to
run, Slade, Adams, Gates, and Giddings bolted the nomination
and voted for Northern Whig candidates. The cadre of antislavery
Whigs had begun to snap the ties of party regularity.[19] Despite
this disquieting display, the new Speaker placed Adams at the
head of the Committee on Foreign Affairs and appointed Giddings as chairman of the Claims Committee.[20] Giddings appreciated White's largesse, for in spite of the Speakership bolt White
"walked up to the subject like a man. . . ." Other Southerners were
not so forgiving and "swore terribly about it." Henry A. Wise of
Virginia demanded to know whether Giddings would report favorably on bills compensating owners of lost slaves, and Giddings shot
back that he would never think of such a thing.[21]

During this brief session the Whigs were almost exclusively preoccupied with economic legislation. The antislavery circle joined
with its Whig brethren to repeal the subtreasury system, pass a
bankruptcy bill, and create a second Bank of the United States.[22]
Party rancor caused by the vetoes of the Virginia slaveholder John
Tyler, who became president when Harrison suddenly died, added

67

to Whig distractions. The gag rule campaign, which Adams began on a promising note by moving successfully to have the rule dropped, finally broke down. Giddings initially glowed over Adams' victory,[23] but after long, hysterical speeches by Wise and Kenneth Rayner of North Carolina the House readopted the "gag" for the duration of the session. As a concession to the North, it was decided to appoint a select committee to consider revising the rules and to submit a report when the second session convened.[24] Giddings, allowing his devotion to Henry Clay to override his antislavery principles, announced he supported this plan in order to "get at [the] business" of the Whig economic program, for enough time had already been wasted.[25] Only Adams of all the antislavery Whigs voted against this formula.[26]

Although Giddings rationalized his inconsistency by hoping that the protracted debate had helped "the cause" by pushing Wise and some of his zealous associates out of the party,[27] Joshua Leavitt was incensed at the antislavery Whigs for capitulating to the gag rule, even temporarily. He scorched Giddings and the others with a merciless editorial in the *Emancipator,* calling them apostates who had sacrificed principle to pure party expediency.[28] Giddings and William Slade immediately protested. The compromise for which they had voted was not a permanent enactment of the gag rule since it dictated withholding petitions for the present session only. "Why . . . should [you] deem it necessary," Giddings asked Leavitt, "to diminish the influence of the few individuals who are now placed between you and the common enemy . . . ?" In a private communiqué he pleaded that Leavitt clear the air of misunderstandings by admitting his error.[29] Leavitt, though characterized by Seth Gates as "a most inveterate and upandicular man," assumed a quite pragmatic posture. Despite the substantial correctness of his charges, he printed a public retraction and called on all men regardless of party to organize against the gag rule when Congress met again in December, 1841.[30] Giddings' appeals for unity and Leavitt's tactical retreat signaled the beginning of a temporary but enormously significant coordination between the antislavery Whigs and the political abolitionists.

68

Between September and December, 1841, the emphasis quickly did become organization. Leavitt, now eager for harmony instead of contention, asked Giddings to reserve him a room at Mrs. Sprigg's boarding house. He also sent along a friendly reminder that "the dictates of sound wisdom" made not the Whig economic program but "opposition to slavery . . . the *leading object* of public policy." [31] Gamaliel Bailey's *Philanthropist* published a long notice signed by Leavitt and other abolitionists appealing to "all who hate slavery" to send in their petitions.[32]

Soon after Giddings, Gates, Slade, and Leavitt settled themselves at Mrs. Sprigg's boarding house, Adams moved that the House repeal the gag rule, and his attempt failed by a mere three votes.[33] The sign augured well for the developing group of insurgents, but they needed help in researching antislavery issues, for the congressmen were constantly plagued with committee duties, and Leavitt, as Washington reporter for the *Emancipator,* had his readers to attend to. Giddings and Leavitt decided that Theodore Weld, now in semi-retirement, should come to Washington to assist in the work. Writing earnestly and persuasively, Leavitt assured Weld that the insurgents were "thoroughly aroused and are determined to carry the war in upon the enemy, to shift the plan of the campaign and attack slavery at every point." They planned to "open the whole field for discussion in a shape in which the gag . . . cannot touch them," by discussing the Florida War, the various slave trades, diplomatic recognition of Haiti, the constitutional rights of Negroes, and many other issues. Weld could not resist. Giddings found him a niche at the Library of Congress and, after collecting contributions from the other members of the cadre to pay for Weld's rent, reserved another room at Mrs. Sprigg's.[34]

John Quincy Adams did not feel at all sure about the programs of the little association. Their ideas appeared too radical to suit him. He was a civil libertarian, purely and simply, and his gag rule assaults were governed solely by this concern. Back in 1839 he had declared that Congress possessed no legal power to abolish slavery in the District of Columbia but that nonetheless Congress must accept and report on petitions praying for this measure.[35] Such a stance left him at partial odds with Giddings and the others, so he tried to solve this problem by limiting their aims.

Adams met with the insurgency members to convince them that restoring the right of petition should be their single objective. He offered a six-point program designed to coordinate an intensive campaign against the gag rule alone, but Slade, Giddings, Gates, and the rest acted noncommittal. Nothing came of Adams' proposal.[36] While acting with Giddings and his friends, he never joined their group; the insurgency was far too serious about implementing its broad program. Nevertheless, during this crucial year Leavitt and Weld worked closely with Giddings and Adams, and their collaboration was most effective. Giddings' prediction was nearly accurate when he promised that this "select committee," as he liked to call it, would "fill a larger space [in history] than that of any other select committee of this or any former Congress." [37]

The most fruitful issues for agitation were to be found in the *Creole* case. The *Creole* was an American ship which worked the coastwise slave trade. In 1841 slaves on board had risen in mutiny, killed a seaman, and forced the captain to take the vessel to Nassau, where all except the murderer were declared free under British law. The American owners denied British jurisdiction over their slave property and passionately demanded that the Negroes be returned and tried as murderers. John C. Calhoun, the deep South's most articulate defender, introduced resolutions to this effect in the Senate, and Secretary of State Daniel Webster sent strong letters to Whitehall voicing the same requests.[38]

The "select committee" asked Weld to draw up resolutions on this subject in line with the idea of the municipal nature of slavery, a doctrine which closely resembled Giddings' own views.[39] According to the municipal theory, if slavery's laws had no effect beyond the borders of the Southern states, then once the *Creole* entered national waters her slaves immediately reverted to their God-given state of freedom and were legally and morally right in using violence to throw off their oppressors. Weld composed nine resolutions;[40] Giddings stuffed them in his briefcase and waited patiently for the Southerners to bring up the issue in the House.

Leavitt and Gamaliel Bailey prepared the public by featuring long editorials in their newspapers which asserted Weld's arguments while castigating Calhoun and Webster for their actions.[41] The conspiracy against silence was fully mobilized.

While Giddings awaited an opportunity to introduce the *Creole* resolutions, the storm over the gag rule continued to rage. The antislavery Whigs, constantly on their feet, presented hundreds of petitions, each carefully phrased to fall beyond the literal application of the rule. Every one thus became open to debate.[42] Adams convulsed the House by presenting a request from certain Southern citizens demanding his own removal from the chairmanship of the Foreign Relations Committee. "Old Man Eloquent" obtained the right to defend himself and spent the next four days launching one draconian assault after another at the gag rule and its supporters.[43] "We are determined to give the slaveholders a hard pull," Giddings bubbled. "I enjoyed the sport yesterday first-rate. . . ." [44] One of Adams' petitions echoed Weld's *Creole* doctrine, and Southern members exploded, demanding that it be tabled, which it was. "Well, Sir," declared Adams, "I will submit if I must, but," he added ominously, "you may hear more of this subject before the session is over." [45] Giddings held on to the resolutions, still hoping that the Southerners would broach the question first.

Congress was stunned by this explosion of agitation, and Whigs began to worry about open splits within the party. As if the widening division between the followers of John Tyler and Henry Clay were not enough, party leaders now discovered overt sectionalism in the organization—Joshua Leavitt conferring with Giddings and William Slade just outside the hall itself! Southern Whigs decided to make a terrifying example of John Quincy Adams by censuring him whenever they could. The Democrats, of course, were anxious to abet any plan to dispense with him, and Adams himself obliged by giving his opponents an early opportunity.

On January 24 he presented a petition from forty-six citizens of Haverhill, Massachusetts, praying for a peaceful dissolution of the Union, and asked Congress to state why this request should *not* be granted. Henry A. Wise cried out through the shouts of indignation that filled the chamber and offered a motion of censure. This motion was soon expanded to include charges of a high breach of privilege and contempt of Congress. Adams again claimed the right of self-defense and obtained it. For the next eleven days, his "trial" consisted of one broad-ranging attack after another by the former President upon the "slave power" and its pernicious effects on the American political process.

Never had the Congress experienced such antislavery agitation, as the insurgents worked late into the night helping Adams to prepare his "defense." [46] "He has entered the lists of slavery and cuts right and left," Giddings exclaimed in admiration. "He makes bloody work." Giddings watched the slaveholders "literally shake and tremble through every nerve and joint" as Adams followed up one philippic with yet another.[47] Finally, the House began to realize just how "bloody" Adams' activities had become. On February 7 the motion of censure was tabled by a purely sectional vote, and Giddings wrote in jubilation to his family: "Well, we have triumphed, the *north* for once has triumphed . . . the charm of the slave power *is now broken*." [48] Representatives of the free states, he convinced himself, finally realized it was "time that the rights and interests of the north were maintained." He was sure they had "mustered sufficient courage. . ." to stand by Adams and had begun to "come up to the work . . ." of antislavery. The slaveholders displayed "downcast countenances," but some Southern Whigs, Giddings thought, were changing their minds. Adams' victory promised the "opening of a new era in our political history . . . a moral revolution. . . ." Giddings never more graphically revealed his belief in the power of the conversion experience in politics. It appeared as if the Whig party had finally begun to realize that the dictates of conscience must be served.[49]

Moral revolutions do not always generate their own power, however, and Giddings began acting on his promise to "spring" additional agitation on the Southerners "when they think not of it." [50] On February 28 he offered an exact replica of Adams' now-famous Haverhill petition. Hot words were exchanged, but the slaveholders, "burned by their own iron before...," as Theodore Weld explained to his anxious wife, stifled any impulses to censure Giddings.[51] Eleven days later, the representative from Ohio struck again by beating down a claim for slaves lost to the British during the War of 1812. Once more much Southern bluster was heard, but that was all.[52] The "moral revolution" appeared imminent, but Southern congressmen still refused to mention the *Creole* affair. After fourteen weeks of impatient waiting, convinced of the improved tone of the House, Giddings finally decided to present Weld's resolutions anyway. He did so on March 21.

Southern fear, instead of inducing conversions or acquiescence, had led to a strong desire for revenge, and Giddings had no appreciation of this fact. He also lacked Adams' stature and resourcefulness. Southern members, as well as many Northerners, had vowed for some time to put down the nettlesome insurgents for good by censuring Giddings, and resolutions affirming the right of slaves to rebel and kill within territorial waters provided ample excuse.[53]

A motion to table the *Creole* resolutions immediately failed, 52–125, with the entire insurgency, most of the Southerners, and all Democrats voting "nay" in order to keep the issue alive. Isaac Holmes of South Carolina muttered about fools rushing in "where angels fear to tread." Meanwhile John Minor Botts of Virginia offered a motion of censure on the grounds that Giddings had betrayed his public trust by trying to create "excitement, dissatisfaction and division..." among the people. After a bit of parliamentary maneuvering, John Weller, an Ohio Democrat, called for the previous question. This motion, if passed, would cut off all debate and require an immediate vote on Botts' censure resolution. By this neat juggling of the rules, Giddings would be deprived of any chance to defend himself. There would be no repeat of Adams' lengthy performance. After another short exchange, Weller's call to invoke the previous question passed, 118–64; the rules now dictated that Botts' bill of particulars be voted on immediately. The House then adjourned to forestall such an abrupt-looking conclusion.

The next day, Giddings tried to defend himself but was ruled out of order, and the resolutions of censure came to their inevitable vote. They passed, 125–69, with the entire Democratic party and almost all Southern Whigs casting their votes for the measure.[54] Giddings immediately resigned his seat, bade farewell to the insurgency and a tearful Adams, disregarded a threat to hang him for his actions, and left for home to get re-elected. He assured the family that he had not disgraced either himself or his constituents.[55] Congress had now leveled a direct challenge to the antislavery Whigs. The outcome of Giddings' re-election attempt would determine which conspirators would succeed: those for or those against open discussion of the slavery question. Giddings' vindication, as Seth Gates put it, was "of the very highest importance to the cause of freedom." [56]

No one was more aware of the high stakes riding on the outcome of Giddings' re-election attempt than the Whigs in Washington. Efforts by the insurgency to exonerate Giddings on the floor of the House were beaten down by Whig votes,[57] and a move by Seth Gates to develop concerted party support fell through because of the unwillingness of the Ohio delegation to involve itself. "You must trust to God and your own efforts. . . . The Lord send you deliverance for your Whig colleagues won't," Gates told Giddings disgustedly. Leavitt felt "deep anxiety" for Giddings' chances[58] as he noticed the Cleveland *Herald,* the largest Whig paper in the Reserve, criticizing Giddings as indiscreet and a "firebrand," while calling for Elisha Whittlesey to come out of retirement. The powerful *Ohio State Journal* accused Giddings of an "offense against prudence and patriotism." The *National Intelligencer* declared the *Creole* resolutions "repugnant to the spirit of the Constitution . . . ," and Giddings "inconsiderate" and "wrong" in offering them.[59] Gates' warnings appeared to be all too accurate.

The Democrats, of course, stopped at nothing in trying to smear the Whigs with "abolitionism." The Cleveland *Plain Dealer,* a lone, loud Democratic voice on the Reserve, could not "find words odious enough . . ." to do justice to Giddings' conduct, while the *Ohio Statesman,* Ohio's leading Democratic organ, carried on in a similar vein. One Democratic paper attacked the *Creole* resolutions as thoroughly absurd. It would make equal sense for Giddings to work for "the total anihiliation [sic] of all the musquitoes [sic] both in Florida and in the U. States . . . and for the removal of the Allegheny Mountains beyond the Mississippi—they being at present a public nuisance." [60]

William Slade reflected on all this invective, saw the situation more clearly than had Gates, and made an astute observation about the impact of the censure: "This outrage will . . . wake up a spirit in the country. . . . The slaveholders are taking the business . . . out of our hands. We have nothing to do but stand still and see the salvation." [61] Slade's prediction was right on the mark. The full, diverse spectrum of antislavery and abolitionist sentiment united in the Reserve to support Giddings' resolutions and re-election. The Liberty party presses ran editorials similar to those printed in their great abolitionist detractor, the *Liberator,* which suddenly showed no embarrassment about supporting a candidate for political office. Despite his "no-government" opinions, William Lloyd Garrison demonstrated that he was flexible enough to act like an average antislavery voter.[62] Every Whig paper in the Sixteenth District completely ignored the views of the national party and demanded that Giddings be returned.[63]

The most restrained sentiments came from the Geauga *Freeman,* whose defense of Giddings rested on a literal interpretation of constitutional principles. The groundswell to re-elect him was "not an endorsement of his antislavery views, but rather a defense of the right of free speech." Others acknowledged the issue of civil liberties but added, as did the *Western Reserve Chronicle,* that Giddings' resolutions themselves met with "the hearty approval of at least nineteen-twentieths of his constituents." [64] Nonpartisan conventions all over the Reserve resolved that Giddings should present the *Creole* doctrines as soon as the voters had sped him back to Washington,[65] and Giddings reported with pride and accuracy to Adams: "There is a spirit of independence going forth among the people that shows our population to have been descended from the Pilgrim Fathers." [66] Reserve voters, with their conservative habits, simply could not abide arbitrary curtailment of Giddings' rights as their representative. The result of the election was a foregone conclusion. May 3 found Giddings in his carriage, bumping along side roads, avoiding admirers, detractors, and curiosity seekers as he made his way back to the Capitol.[67] He carried a 7,469 to 393 majority over his Democratic opponent and a firm commitment from his electorate that he should again present the *Creole* resolutions.[68] Joshua Giddings had become an antislavery hero.

The news of his arrival sped through the Capitol, "as quick as it would if a whole menagerie of monkeys and jackasses had come upon the good people unexpectedly." Amidst a large number of downcast faces and uneasy looks, Giddings lumbered into the House and claimed his seat. Adams, beaming, walked over, pumped Giddings' hand and asked if Giddings "had heard anything from the late Congressional election in Ohio[?]" Giddings chuckled and inquired of the old man's health. "Much better since you are here," he was assured.[69] Giddings' reappearance meant the conspiracy against silence had been broken. Agitation could proceed apace. Even Henry A. Wise knew this and told Giddings his re-election was "the greatest triumph ever achieved by a member of the House." [70] Besides, Giddings' constituents had demanded that the *Creole* resolutions be aired again.

Some antislavery Whigs felt uneasy about such a course of action. Seth Gates believed "the cause" would be weakened by "playing the same game over again" and fretted lest Giddings betray "a desire to aggravate, provoke and bully the house." Even Adams could not "ward off a doubt of the expediency of agitating it at all. . . ." But Giddings was not to be put down. One item on the House agenda was a bill to reduce the army because the Florida War had ended. Many members opposed this measure because Anglo-American relations had become badly strained, partly on account of England's refusal to return the *Creole* Negroes. William Slade thought the subject fit Giddings' purposes nicely.[71]

While Giddings waited for the bill to come up for debate, he acted noncommittal about speaking and enjoyed "much sport by exciting the anxiety of some northern dough-faces . . ." by keeping his intentions carefully shrouded with cryptic remarks. Meanwhile he warned his family to "look out for *thunder* and *lightening* [sic] about next week or the week after." [72] On the evening of June 3, with the House nearly vacant, Giddings rose to speak. Fifteen minutes later nearly every absent member had bolted down his dinner and rushed to his seat.[73] Whatever the congressmen's opinions of Giddings, none wished to miss out on the "thunder and lightening."

First he offered a few brief remarks on the Florida War, during which he was "interrupted, called to order, cheered, threatened, encouraged, assailed etc. . . ." But then he announced there should be no ill will between the United States and England over the *Creole* issue, since the Negroes had only exercised their obvious legal and moral right to freedom. A hush fell upon the House. "All were now silent and solemn," Giddings recalled. "They had not believed I would dare to tread upon that ground." [74] The nine brief resolutions for which Giddings had so recently been censured were now being presented again, but this time in the form of a full-dress speech.[75]

As Giddings expatiated upon the *Creole* case, the House remained relatively calm. A few "second rate slaveholders" like Edward Black tried to interrupt him, but the Speaker summarily squashed their objections.[76] Most listened attentively as Giddings came as close to an unprovoked personal attack as he ever would while castigating Daniel Webster for trying to force England to return the Negroes. But Giddings never once slurred Webster's personality, only his actions.

The point, however, was not precisely what Giddings said, for he was showing the conspiracy of silence to be broken forever. Through the process of his censure, re-election, and reassertion of the *Creole* resolutions, Giddings had successfully defied his party and nearly all of Congress. The continued independence of the antislavery Whigs was now insured. Congress would henceforth be unable to escape sectional issues by forcing the agitators out of the sanctuary which he had fashioned. As Giddings himself put it, once the *Creole* doctrines were restated, the gag rule "morally ceased to operate," even though it remained on the books until late 1844.[77]

NOTES

[1] JRG to LWG, December 9, 1840, January 2, 1841 (quotation), JRG to LMG, January 20, 1840, Giddings MSS.

[2] Giddings, *History,* 148.

[3] JRG to Elisha Whittlesey, December 10, 1840, Whittlesey MSS, WRHS.

[4] Julian, *Giddings,* 92; U.S. *Congressional Globe,* 26th Cong., 2d Sess., IX, 116–17.

[5] One of the most succinct, complete treatments of the gag rule struggles is James M. McPherson, "The Fight Against the Gag Rule: Joshua Leavitt and the Antislavery Insurgency in the Whig Party, 1839–1842," *Journal of Negro History,* XLVIII (July 1963), 177–95.

[6] U.S. *Congressional Globe,* 26th Cong., 2d Sess., IX, Appendix, 346–52.

[7] Joshua Leavitt to Readers, *Emancipator,* February 18, 1841.

[8] JRG to LMG, February 14, 1841, Giddings MSS.

[9] Joshua Leavitt to Readers, *Emancipator,* February 18, 1841.

[10] JRG to LWG, February 14, 1841, Giddings MSS.

[11] U.S. *Congressional Globe,* 26th Cong., 2d Sess., IX, 158–59, 165–67, 170–72.

[12] *Ibid.,* 159; Julian, *Giddings,* 98.

[13] Favorable reviews of the speech appeared in the Painesville *Telegraph,* March 17, 1841, the *Western Reserve Chronicle,* March 9, 1841, and the Ashtabula *Sentinel,* March 20, 1841. See also Edward Wade to JRG, April 3, 1841, Giddings MSS.

[14] Giddings, *History,* 151–52.

[15] *Philanthropist,* March 3, 1841; *Emancipator,* February 18, 1841.

[16] JRG to Salmon P. Chase, January 4, 1842, Salmon P. Chase MSS,

Historical Society of Pennsylvania, Philadelphia, Pa. (hereinafter HSP).

17 Joshua Leavitt to JRG, March 31, 1841, Giddings MSS.

18 William Slade to Editor, *Emancipator,* May 6, 1841.

19 U.S. *Congressional Globe,* 27th Cong., 1st Sess., X, 2; Seth M. Gates to James G. Birney, June 7, 1841, in Dwight Lowell Dumond (ed.), *Letters of James Gillespie Birney, 1831–1857,* 2 vols. (New York, 1938), II, 629–31. For descriptions of the antislavery Whig strategies on the Speakership issue see Seth M. Gates to Gerrit Smith, June 7, 1841, Gerrit Smith-Miller MSS, Syracuse University Library, Syracuse, N.Y. (hereinafter SUL).

20 U.S. *Congressional Globe,* 27th Cong., 1st Sess., X, 36.

21 JRG to LWG, June 9, 1841, JRG to JAG, June 24, 1841, Giddings MSS (both letters quoted).

22 U.S. *Congressional Globe,* 27th Cong., 1st Sess., X, 274, 313, 350, 372.

23 *Ibid.,* 26–28. Giddings noted excitedly that Southern men were "perfectly *horrified, stultified, electrified, stupified* and *edified* . . ." by this vote. See JRG to JAG, June 10, 1841, Giddings MSS.

24 U.S. *Congressional Globe,* 27th Cong., 1st Sess., X, 51–52, 53–56, 57–63.

25 *Ibid.,* 55–56.

26 *Ibid.,* 63.

27 JRG to JAG, June 17, 1841, Giddings MSS.

28 *Emancipator,* June 24, 1841.

29 *Ibid.,* July 15, 1841 (quotation); JRG to Joshua Leavitt, July 19, 1841, Giddings MSS.

30 Seth M. Gates to JRG, December 6, 1843, Giddings MSS (quotation); *Emancipator,* July 22, 1841.

31 Joshua Leavitt to JRG, October 29, 1841, Giddings MSS.

32 *Philanthropist,* November 3, 1841.

33 U.S. *Congressional Globe,* 27th Cong., 2d Sess., XI, 1–3, 8–9.

34 For Weld's synopsis of Leavitt's letter and the above quotations see Weld to Lewis Tappan, December 14, 1841, in Barnes and Dumond (eds.), *Weld–Grimké Letters,* II, 879–82. In a subsequent letter to his wife Weld characterized the various members of the insurgency. Giddings, he found, was "fearless, self-possessed and not to be put down by threats or bluster." Gates struck Weld as "timid" about speaking, but still "a

man of mind and moral courage." All the insurgents, Weld reported, "treat brother Leavitt and myself exactly as though we were not fan[a]tics, and we talk over with them at the table and elsewhere abolition just as we should at home." Theodore Weld to Angelina Grimké Weld, January 1, 1842, in *ibid.,* 882–84.

35 JRG Diary, January 19 [22], 1839, Giddings MSS. Gilbert Hobbes Barnes paints an erroneous picture of total unanimity within the insurgency and with respect to Adams on matters relating to slavery. See Barnes, *Antislavery Impulse,* 181–90. Barnes' thesis that "abolitionism' came permanently to Washington via Weld, Leavitt, and the insurgents is most questionable and is supported chiefly by his treatment of the insurgency.

36 Charles Francis Adams (ed.), *A Memoir of John Quincy Adams, Comprising Portions of His Diary from 1795 to 1848,* 12 vols. (Boston, 1874–77), XI, 62–63, 68; see also the draft of this plan in Adams' handwriting in Adams Family MSS, 1842, reel 32 (microfilm), Massachusetts Historical Society, Boston, Mass. (hereinafter MHS).

37 JRG to LWG, January 18, 1842, Giddings MSS.

38 U.S. *Congressional Globe,* 27th Cong., 2d Sess., XI, 110; *Emancipator,* January 21, 1842; Ashtabula *Sentinel,* March 26, 1841.

39 Theodore Weld to Angelina Grimké Weld, January 9, 1842, in Barnes and Dumond (eds.), *Weld-Grimké Letters,* II, 886.

40 Bemis, *John Quincy Adams,* 425; Sherman W. Savage, "The Origins of the Giddings Resolutions," *Ohio Archaeological and Historical Quarterly,* XLVIII (October, 1938), 20–39.

41 *Emancipator,* January 21, 1842; *Philanthropist,* January 12, 1842.

42 McPherson, "Leavitt," 189.

43 U.S. *Congressional Globe,* 27th Cong., 2d Sess., XI, 157–59, 160–64, 167–68.

44 JRG to LWG, January 23, 1842, Giddings MSS.

45 U.S. *Congressional Globe,* 27th Cong., 2d Sess., XI, 143.

46 Bemis, *John Quincy Adams,* 427–38; Nye, *Fettered Freedom,* 41–42.

47 JRG to Salmon P. Chase, February 5, 1842, Chase MSS, HSP (quotation); JRG to LWG, February 6, 1842, Giddings MSS (quotation).

48 JRG to Daughter, February 8, 1842, Joshua R. Giddings-Julian MSS, LC.

49 JRG to Salmon P. Chase, February 5, 1842, Chase MSS, HSP; JRG to LWG, February 6, 1842, Giddings MSS (both letters quoted).

50 JRG to "Sis," February 16, 1842, Giddings-Julian MSS, LC.

51 U.S. *Congressional Globe*, 27th Cong., 2d Sess. XI, 268; JRG to Daughter, March 2, 1842, Giddings-Julian MSS, LC; Theodore Weld to Angelina Grimké Weld, February 27, 1842, in Barnes and Dumond (eds.), *Weld-Grimké Letters*, II, 937–38.

52 U.S. *Congressional Globe*, 27th Cong., 2d Sess., XI, 308.

53 McPherson, "Leavitt," 192.

54 U.S. *Congressional Globe*, 27th Cong., 2d Sess., XI, 342–46.

55 Giddings, *History*, 188–89; JRG to LMG, March 22, 1842, Giddings MSS.

56 Seth M. Gates to James G. Birney, March 24, 1842, in Dumond (ed.), *Letters of James Gillespie Birney*, II, 685–86.

57 U.S. *Congressional Globe*, 27th Cong., 2d Sess., XI, 354, 356.

58 Seth M. Gates to JRG, March 25, 1842, Giddings MSS (quotation); Seth M. Gates to James G. Birney, April 4, 1842, in Dumond (ed.), *Letters of James Gillespie Birney*, II, 688 (quotation).

59 Cleveland *Herald*, March 28, 1842; *Ohio State Journal*, March 30, 1842; *National Intelligencer*, March 28, 1842.

60 Cleveland *Plain Dealer*, March 30, 1842; *Ohio Statesman*, March 30, 1842; *Sunday Mercury*, reprinted in the Cleveland *Plain Dealer*, March 30, 1842 (quotation). See also the Washington *Globe*, reprinted in the *Ohio Statesman*, March 30, 1842.

61 William Slade to JRG, March 26, 1842, Giddings MSS.

62 *Philanthropist*, April 6, 1842; *Emancipator*, March 31, 1842. William Lloyd Garrison, showing a far more intense interest in politics than his recent biographers have acknowledged [see John L. Thomas, *The Liberator, William Lloyd Garrison: A Biography* (Boston, 1963)], declared that Giddings "will be returned by an overwhelming (it ought to be unanimous) vote, to the confusion and disgrace of his profligate censors. . . ." Boston *Liberator*, April 1, 1842.

63 Ashtabula *Sentinel*, April 16, 1842; Painesville *Telegraph*, April 6, 1842; *Western Reserve Chronicle*, April 5, 1842.

64 Geauga *Freeman*, quoted in the *Ohio State Journal*, April 20, 1842; *Western Reserve Chronicle*, April 5, 1842.

65 Complete coverage of these conventions can be found in the *Phil-*

anthropist, the *Emancipator,* and the Ashtabula *Sentinel* for the month of April, 1842.

[66] JRG to John Quincy Adams, April 7, 1842, Adams Family MSS, MHS (quotations from the Adams Papers are from the microfilm edition, by permission of the Massachusetts Historical Society) ; see also JRG to Seth M. Gates, April 1, April 9, April 18, 1842, Gerrit Smith-Miller MSS, SUL.

[67] JRG to LWG, May 3, 1842, Giddings MSS.

[68] *Emancipator,* June 9, 1842; Ashtabula *Sentinel,* May 7, 1842.

[69] JRG to LWG, May 5, 1842, Julian MSS, ISL.

[70] JRG to JAG, May 19, 1842, Giddings MSS.

[71] Seth M. Gates to Gerrit Smith, April 8, 1842, Gerrit Smith-Miller MSS, SUL; Adams, *Memoir of Adams,* XI, 153.

[72] JRG to JAG, May 19, 1842, Giddings MSS.

[73] JRG to LWG, June 5, 1842, Giddings MSS. When Giddings rose to speak, a congressman demanded to know whether the House could expect an antislavery speech. "Yes, with God's blessing I will not omit that part," Giddings shot back. The hall then began to fill up.

[74] *Ibid.,* (quotation) ; Joshua R. Giddings, *Speeches in Congress* (Boston, 1852) , 21; U.S. *Congressional Globe,* 27th Cong., 2d Sess., XI, 575–76.

[75] Giddings, *Speeches,* 21–31.

[76] JRG to Daughter, June 10, 1842, Giddings-Julian MSS, LC.

[77] Giddings, *History,* 197.

Chapter 5

CLAY, TEXAS,
AND THE
LIBERTY PARTY

⋅◖ ◗⋅

1843-1845

Giddings passed his summer in Jefferson in a leisurely fashion. The normal round of congressional elections was postponed until 1843 because of redistricting squabbles in the state legislature. Only the contests for state and local offices went off as scheduled.[1] Giddings did his share of campaigning but spent most of his time with the family. The elections proved disastrous for Ohio's Whig party, as the Democrats scored enough victories to capture both houses of the legislature as well as the governorship. The reason was simply that the Liberty party, now based on a solid organization and run by capable hands, had drawn off many antislavery Whig voters. The party's polling power, while still small, had tripled since 1840, most of its gains being made in the Reserve.[2]

Giddings' placid summer thus merged into a hectic winter, for he felt that he had to counter this growing threat. Shortly thereafter, there appeared in the *Western Reserve Chronicle* a lengthy series of essays under Giddings' pseudonym, "Pacificus."

He wrote these articles for the benefit of two audiences: Whigs whose antislavery convictions needed prodding and Liberty men who had to be persuaded to cast their ballots once more for Whig candidates. Giddings mustered every argument, no matter how contrived, and put them to these purposes. "Pacificus" assured the public that all good Whigs stood for the Constitution and would, once enlightened, enforce the "denationalization of slavery" with a vengeance. In addition to the normal items required in this program, "Pacificus" told his readers that the Whigs sponsored the total exemption of the North from complicity in the return of fugitive slaves and countenanced the arming of Negro escapees so that they could resist violently all Southern slave catchers venturing into states where free law prevailed.[3] "Pacificus" was trying to picture the Whigs as committed to practically everything short of subsidizing the Underground Railroad as an internal improvement.

Giddings, however, did not drop his case at this point. Instead, he went far beyond the standard assertions that Liberty party votes only helped to defeat antislavery Whigs,[4] and what followed would have pleased the "progressive" historian of the 1920's. "Pacificus" attempted to unite the Whig economic program with antislavery doctrine by defining both as parts of larger "Northern rights" which true friends of "the cause" should support. He argued that protective tariffs, national roads, and homestead bills were as much antislavery measures as the abolition of servitude in the District of Columbia. Giddings also began emphasizing these notions in his letters and speeches.

Despite what some older historians would have thought of this reasoning, Giddings' arguments constantly revealed their moral substrata. He aimed at dispersing to the broadest possible audience every appeal he could discover. Economic arguments constituted a single language which Giddings hoped would be comprehended by two quite different groups, Whigs and Liberty men. As he once revealed to his wife, "There is no argument so strong as that adressed [sic] to a man's pocket." [5]

Giddings' tendency to expose his moral preoccupations revealed itself embarrassingly in his reasoning that internal improvements constituted an antislavery measure. The building of highways, canals, and harbors would not only bring wealth, but would also disseminate culture and knowledge throughout the North, for the sophisticated East would be bound more closely to the roughhewn West. But Southerners always realized that any such material or intellectual advances were "dangerous to the interests of slavery, which must ever depend on ignorance and stupidity, and is jealous of the progress of knowledge which teaches men to know the rights that God has given him." Therefore the South, as well as the Democrats, always opposed internal improvements. Giddings offered much the same reasons for the supposedly unanimous Southern hatred of high tariffs.[6] These Southern incursions, "Pacificus" assured his readers, were "as clearly violations of the rights of the free States as . . . appropriations for the express purpose of capturing fugitive slaves." [7] In summation, "Pacificus" thus appealed to the followers of Henry Clay and James G. Birney at the same time: *"Why do you divide your political influence . . . while you agree in principle and are laboring for the same objects?"* [8]

Giddings' political logic was, of course, faulty. The more he preached to the Liberty men as a Whig the more he antagonized his own party. The longer he remained a Whig the greater became Liberty party opposition. But his views of human nature and human institutions would never permit him to see the obvious contradictions of his position.

As reformers went, Giddings retained a far greater faith than many in those devices which hold societies together, especially the political process and churches. Certainly his belief in the oneness of morality and politics often made him deeply hostile to men of public affairs whose compromises and connivings insured the stability of national parties. In this sense, Giddings reflected an anti-institutional bias. Nevertheless, he did not believe, as did some antislavery spokesmen, that institutions should be torn down because they utterly corrupted those who participated in them. Giddings stopped short of this position by relying on his faith in the conversion experience. He maintained that people were simply ignorant of their sins and that by providing men with enlightening moral arguments it was possible to improve institutions without overthrowing them. Furthermore, he insisted that even the most imperfect human agencies could be useful to the great task of regenerating each individual. Giddings assumed that people stimulated to act on moral truth would naturally improve their churches, parties, or places of business by working from within such associations.

Partly for this reason Giddings preferred the larger Whig organization to the morally more consistent Liberty party, which represented a fragmentation of American politics. Whigs, no matter how hostile, tolerated men like Giddings and so he was "able to talk to them, to argue with them, to place inducements before them." Suppose he were to join the third party, he once asked a Liberty man, what advantage would be gained? "Could I speak and act more freely? . . . Could I be more independent in the declaration and promulgation of the principles of human rights?" The principal problem facing reformers was "*ignorance* in regards to the encroachments of the Slave power"— the difficulty lay in "getting the truth before the public mind. . . ," and Giddings felt certain that the Whig party commanded a larger audience than did any third organization.[9] For the same reasons, he long opposed the "come-outer" movements within various nationally established denominations. Instead, he viewed this question as one of local polity and called on all ministers to expose the un-Christian nature of slavery or be dismissed by their individual congregations.[10] This general evangelistic outlook, as well as the practical problems posed by the Liberty party, made Giddings act as a cyclone of agitation in 1843 and during the first session of the Twenty-Eighth Congress in 1844.

The insurgents greeted him warmly when he arrived at Mrs. Sprigg's. The boarding house was filled to capacity with congressmen curious to meet the likes of Theodore Weld and Joshua Leavitt, and the two abolitionists were forced to share the same room.[11] Despite the cramped quarters, the insurgents quickly began searching the "ancient records" for fruitful topics to agitate.[12] But Giddings' reception in the House was not nearly so friendly. John Snyder, a Pennsylvania Democrat who sat next to him, had hired a carpenter to build a partition between the two desks. On it he posted a sign explaining his invention as "a Partition between Abolitionism and Democracy." Giddings retaliated by tacking up a label of his own, a couplet by Alexander Pope:

Great wit to madness nearly is allied,
And *thin partitions* do their bounds divide! [13]

A Vermont wag, calling himself a "Sprig from the Green Mountains," doubtless drew a chuckle from Giddings by suggesting Snyder procure three more boards, fashion a pen for himself, and finish the work "so gloriously *begun*." [14]

Despite this display of ill will, and over Southern objections, Giddings reassumed the chairmanship of the Claims Committee,[15] and the post proved crucial to antislavery agitation. As chairman, Giddings kept track of all claims for lost slaves, and he constantly wheedled his co-workers to report such bills favorably, so that he could protest them in the House with lengthy speeches.[16] One Southern congressman, exasperated that one of his constituents' claims had been so treated, scored Giddings for "having so much sympathy for a nigger while refusing to do justice to a white man," [17] but such complaints never put Giddings off. On three occasions during this session and once during the session which followed, slave claims became his vehicle for filling the hall with hours of oratory.[18] Each speech reiterated the familiar themes of states-rights antislavery and appeals to return the nation to the original intentions of the founding fathers.

If the repetition bored many listeners, Giddings nevertheless kept most of them awake with pungent barbs and digs. As he probed for the congressional conscience he once questioned the criteria Congress used to arrive at the dollars-and-cents value of a man: "Which is deemed more valuable, black, white, or a mixture of both . . . ?" Perhaps the House should fix the sum by considering the lost slave's political affiliation, Giddings suggested, with cost assigned on the basis of whether he was a Whig, a Democrat, or, most crucially, "whether he goes the Liberty party." True to his intentions as a Whig agitator, Giddings asserted that each slave claim had roots in some act of Democratic servility, dating back to the days of Jackson himself. At one point he declared if he could cartoon Democratic behavior in Congress he would sketch a Northern Democrat "holding a gag in the mouth of his constituent with one hand, while the other is employed to examine his pockets to pay for the expenses of the slave agency." Whigs received the invariable exhortation to end all federal support of slavery at once.[19]

After every sally of this sort Giddings saw each objectionable bill voted down by a large majority. The triumph always appeared "perfect," especially after Southern men told him they would "rather vote with Father Adams to lay it on the table than to permit the discussion to go on." He concluded on every occasion that conversion was imminent, that the "revolution in the public mind is going forward more rapidly than I ever expected." [20] Even though all his speeches met with massive counterblasts and, on one occasion, threats by a knife-wielding representative from Louisiana, such hostility never lessened Gidding's firm conviction that ignorance was being dispelled and that Christian ethics and politics were about to unite.[21]

Giddings, however, often concerned himself with other goals than enlightening Congress and converting the public. When the Twenty-eighth Congress opened in December, 1843, Giddings, fresh from another re-election, turned instead to piecemeal humanitarianism. Early that month he received a desperate appeal from a Negro who had been jailed by Washington authorities for being unable to prove his freedom. The Negro maintained he had manumitted himself many years earlier. Giddings immedi-

ately introduced resolutions requesting that Congress set up
an investigating committee to report whether free Negroes were
being unjustly arrested and sold into slavery because of the
District's laws. He also asked the committee to make recommen-
dations for changing the laws if found to operate unfairly. After
a lengthy debate in which he put down a Southern protester
by doubting "the ability of the gentleman to *prove* his [own]
freedom . . . ," his suggestions were referred to the Judiciary
Committee by a surprising 75–40 vote. Although nothing came
of this effort, Giddings henceforth developed a deep concern
for improving the lot of the Negro in the District of Columbia.[22]

The major concerns of this session of the Twenty-eighth
Congress lay elsewhere, however. The gag rule, presidential politics, and the issue of Texas' annexation occupied the nation's
attention. Although each was of crucial concern to Giddings,
there was no longer a unified insurgency on which he could
rely. Gates and Slade had retired in 1843, and Joshua Leavitt
acted not "as friendly and social as formerly," because of Giddings' strident and successful opposition to the Liberty party.
Theodore Weld had returned to the seclusion of private life,
and Adams' infirmities made him more feeble every month.
Giddings felt quite alone.[23] Unsuccessfully, he implored Weld
to come back to Washington: "My good friend I never wanted to
see you more in my life. I never wanted to use you as much as
at present. . . . I was never qualified nor prepared for the station
in which by a train of circumstances I have found myself." [24]

Nevertheless, Giddings' innate optimism soon overcame his depression. He turned his attention to his new Whig messmates, Luther Severance and John Morse of Maine, John Dickey and Robert McIlwaine of Pennsylvania, and Daniel R. Tilden of Ohio,
urging them "to look into antislavery matters." Before long he
reported that he had created a "phalanx" which would "drive
slavery into the Atlantic or Gulf of Mexico." Perhaps even slavery
in the District could be abolished. Giddings had fashioned a new
group of insurgents to replace Slade and Gates, and they were soon

working out their plans.[25] His only worry was that the old champion of civil liberties, John Quincy Adams, would oppose his efforts to abolish the coastwise and District slave trades. Again, the former President remained outside the insurgency. This difference of opinion, however, did nothing to lessen Adams' and Giddings' profound mutual regard, and they continued, as always, to spend long evenings conversing in "Father Adams' " drawing room.[26]

But Adams' leadership in the fight against the gag rule went unchallenged. He obtained appointment as chairman of a special committee to revise the House rules, and early in the session the committee filed a report which omitted the gag.[27] Five weeks of furious argument followed, during which Giddings and his new friends thrust in remarks at the most irrelevant moments. Once, when debate turned from the gag rule to naval appropriations, Giddings rose, objected, and delivered a twenty-minute speech protesting the use of the navy for the "base purpose of catching fugitive slaves" during patrols along Southern coasts. In reply, Alexander Duncan, an Ohio Democrat, lectured Giddings scornfully on the "eternal truth" of Negro inferiority.[28] On another occasion, Giddings objected to an appropriations bill for Indian treaties because it contained a clause subsidizing the recapture of escaped bondsmen.[29]

Concurrently, Adams succeeded in getting a petition praying the abolition of the three-fifths compromise, by which the Constitution permitted Southern states to count their slave populations on a three-fifths ratio for purposes of representation, referred to a committee and reported.[30] This maneuver prompted Aaron V. Brown of Tennessee to vilify Adams as an agent of Haitian insurrectionists "who shed the blood of a sleeping infant and stuck a pole through its warm and quivering body, and under that standard marched with torch in one hand and sword in the other." [31] Giddings' motion to refer a petition calling for the end of federal support of the slave trade failed by merely one vote. Another petition which he offered for referral prayed for the secession of New York State and its annexation to free Canadian soil, and it took

91

three votes to table this strange request because of the absence of a quorum. Southern men, furious with Giddings, assailed him scurrilously.[32]

Giddings listened and rejoiced inwardly that "the panic of the Southern members [was] becoming more and more apparent ... ," and he was sure that they could no longer control the Northern Democrats. While the South retreated, anti-"gag" feeling was advancing. Southern Whigs acted as it they were "becoming acquainted with the views of the Whig Abolitionists and [were] reconciled to them. . . ." Giddings, sensing a "moral revolution," felt certain of repeal: "We are preparing to follow up like Blucher [sic] at Waterloo." And a "Waterloo affair" it almost was. After Giddings brought the attack to a climax with a one-hour oration in which he hoped to "speak to the whole nation and to posterity . . . ." the House finally readopted the "gag" by a scant one vote.[33] By late February, 1844, the days of the rule were clearly numbered.

Despite the bright prospects of ending fetters to free speech, every antislavery man began worrying over the issue of Texas' annexation. Shortly after the Twenty-eighth Congress convened, President Tyler made clear his intention to push for the admission of this slave republic, which had earlier revolted from Mexican control and was now petitioning for membership in the Union. Tyler, unlike his predecessors, felt little concern over the possibility of war with Mexico as a result of granting statehood to Texas. The untimely death of Secretary of State Abel Upshur in February, 1844, resulted in the elevation of slavery's ardent defender, John C. Calhoun, to this pivotal office. Negotiations went forward, and by April a treaty of annexation had been signed and sent by Tyler to the Senate for ratification.

At first Giddings had not viewed the threat as serious and saw annexation simply as a "glorious thing" with which to "open the eyes" of the North to the arrogance of the "slave power." But in April, after resolutions against admitting Texas had been soundly defeated in the House and the Senate had received the treaty,[34] his complacency suddenly vanished. Now he feared that "every possi-

92

ble effort" was being made to transfer the people of the free states "into the domain of the slaveholding fugitive criminals of Texas . . . in direct and open violation of the Constitution." [35] His sleep was disturbed by thoughts of "giving a preponderance to the South . . ." in national politics, and he felt pressed with a "weight that breaks down . . . hopes and spirits." [36]

Though despondent, Giddings threw himself into a fit of activity. He posted one letter after another to Ohio editors, calling for all Whigs to resist annexation. "Nothing," he warned, "will save us . . . but bold and determined ground." With the presidential elections a mere eight months away, the Democrats appeared to be threatened by internal tensions on the Texas issue. A strong Whig stand against admission would rouse the North, reconcile the Liberty party, and blow the Democrats "sky high." [37]

While the Senate was debating the treaty and Giddings was fretting, the leading Whig nominee, Kentucky's Henry Clay, was trying to plot out the surest path to the presidency. On April 27, 1844, he published his famous "Raleigh Letter," airing his views on Texas. Annexation without Mexico's assent was tantamount to war. To consider it "at the present time," he qualified, would be inexpedient and dishonorable. So saying, Clay hoped to eliminate sectional questions from the election.[38]

Giddings' strategy, however, hardly squared with Clay's hopes, for the Ohioan read the Raleigh Letter, judged it a "statesman-like paper," and announced with relief that Clay's "flat-footed" opposition to annexation amounted to an endorsement of the "Pacificus" essays. The Whigs would win by an overwhelming margin if they met antislavery issues as boldly as Clay had done.[39]

Giddings' spirit soared even higher when in June the Senate rejected the treaty. Soon after, the Democrats passed over Martin Van Buren and nominated Tennessee's James K. Polk on an expansionist platform which promised both Texas and all of Oregon. After a private meeting with Clay himself, Giddings felt even surer that the wily party leader would make the denationalization of slavery and the proscription of Texas the focal points of the campaign.[40]

93

Just to make certain all Whigs understood, he delivered a lengthy speech on May 21 which castigated Tyler for his "treason" in negotiating with Texas, and he emphasized the immoral and unconstitutional implications of admitting another slave state. Giddings also dwelt at length on the notion that any increase in Southern political strength would bind Northern business interests to the slave economy's need for international free trade, and hence to poverty. A firm Whig commitment to antislavery principles would, on the other hand, leave the Democratic party in fragments after the votes had been tallied.[41] If Clay had hoped to mute sectional issues with the Raleigh Letter, Giddings was not very obliging. As the campaign went on, his activities became exceedingly embarrassing to "Harry of the West" and his Southern supporters.

Self-deception prompted by his faith in the capacity of men to see moral truths was one of Giddings' principal weaknesses. Never did this flaw show more clearly than in his reaction to Henry Clay's bid for the presidency. Prior to the Raleigh Letter his estimate of Clay had dropped off sharply, and with good reason. As early as 1839 the Kentuckian had denounced antislavery petitioners on the floor of the Senate, and the new representative's disappointment at that time had been keen indeed. Clay's second attack on abolitionists, an 1842 speech delivered in Indiana, had been deemed by Benjamin Wade an "unpardonable sin against the North." [42] Giddings had once toyed with the idea of switching his support to fellow Ohioan John McLean, the ambitious Whiggish Supreme Court justice, and had agreed with Seth Gates' contention that the only way to make an effective stump speech was to "rub along without saying much about Clay." [43]

But considering Giddings' deep state of depression over Texas' annexation, it was natural that he interpret the Raleigh Letter as a godsend. Besides, Clay had always taken pains to keep on friendly terms with him.[44] The Kentuckian's outward displays of sincerity, plus Giddings' abiding faith in man's ability to redeem himself, enabled the Ohio congressman to campaign for Clay and antislavery measures at the same time. Furthermore, the need to advance antislavery principles within Whiggery was even more acute, for Liberty party growth now threatened not only Clay's prospects for the presidency but also Giddings' own congressional career.

Political life in the Reserve had become increasingly chaotic every year since 1842. In 1843 the Democratic state legislature had rearranged the congressional districts, carefully assigning Giddings new boundaries which could only hurt him. His new district, the Twentieth, included Cuyahoga and Lake Counties, and both contained powerful centers of orthodox Whig opinion. Trumbull County, which had turned staunchly antislavery during the censure fracas, was excluded.[45] Giddings now faced a large block of hostile voters, especially in Cleveland, whose newspaper the *Herald* had castigated the *Creole* resolutions while calling for Giddings' defeat in 1842.

Benjamin Wade saw in this new arrangement an opportunity to advance his political fortunes. He lined up conservative leaders in Cleveland and dispatched an emissary to visit Giddings' loyal friend Henry Fassett, editor of the Ashtabula *Sentinel*. The messenger threatened, in Wade's name, to open a competing newspaper unless the *Sentinel* ceased operating as Giddings' mouthpiece. Fassett ordered Wade's spokesman out of his office. Not long after, a new weekly, the Conneaut *Reporter,* sponsored by Cleveland money, suggested that Giddings be replaced in the 1844 elections.[46]

Of greater consequence than Ben Wade's maneuvers was the activity of the Liberty party, which had greatly increased its strength within the district. After converting tough-minded local Whig wheelhorses like Edward Wade, Benjamin's more principled antislavery brother, and former state senators James H. Paine and Leicester King, the party had augmented its vote ten times over since 1840. The Liberty men had even established a newspaper of their own in Giddings' district. In its second issue the Warren *Liberty Herald*'s capable editor, L. L. Rice, declared Giddings tainted by the proslavery Whig party and his own restricted doctrines,

95

while endorsing Edward Wade for Congress.[47] Of the Wade brothers it was Edward, not Ben, who promised Giddings a hectic summer of campaigning.

The strong opposition to annexing Texas within the district and Whig fear of the Liberty party united majority opinion behind Giddings' renomination.[48] But the Liberty party itself remained hostile. Along with reminders that Henry Clay was a slaveholder and duellist, Gamaliel Bailey's *Philanthropist,* as well as the *Liberty Herald,* issued one call after another for antislavery men to support James G. Birney for president and Edward Wade for representative. The time had arrived, declared editor Rice, "when Mr. G. deserves to be dealt with . . . without mincing words . . . ," [49] and Liberty party opinion agreed. Giddings was crucified as an opportunist for his support of slaveholding candidates for Speaker of the House, and the "Pacificus" arguments were rejected as antiabolitionist nonsense. His "many and strenuous" efforts to seduce Liberty men from their "allegiance to freedom" had utterly failed. "We shall . . . give a largely increased Liberty vote, the labors of J. R. Giddings and Co. notwithstanding." [50]

This unpleasant situation, compounded by the overwhelming issue of Texas, turned Giddings' campaign into the most frantic he had yet experienced. No longer did he try to reason with the Liberty men. Instead he began attacking them furiously as foes of Northern rights, plotters who were contriving to place James K. Polk in the presidency and Texas in the Union by drawing votes from Henry Clay. While parrying still other criticisms from the Democrats, Giddings' claims that Clay's convictions would save the nation became ever more extreme as the need increased to overwhelm Liberty party arguments. To buttress his contentions, he joined Cassius M. Clay, the Whiggish Kentucky antislavery man whose espousal of abolitionism stemmed strictly from racist and economic doctrines. Clay's major concern was improving the lot of the nonslaveholding Southern white by eradicating the competition of slave labor. By September the two men had canvassed every major town in the Reserve, and Giddings had gotten along quite well with his campaign partner, despite the marked ideological differences between them.[51]

But Henry Clay began undoing whatever progress Giddings was making against the third party. As the campaign progressed, the Kentuckian, fearing the loss of Southern support, began to feel misgivings about his original stand on Texas. Soon, copies of the Raleigh Letter appeared with key phrases deleted; then in August and September Clay issued his two famous "Alabama Letters," which nearly qualified out of existence his opposition to annexation. Subsequently, yet another dispatch signed by Clay disavowed all efforts on his behalf by his relative Cassius.[52]

Giddings sent off shocked requests for clarification to "Ashland," Clay's home in Lexington, Kentucky, while trying to explain away the second Alabama letter as a "locofoco trick."[53] Clay's replies smacked of evasion, but Giddings put on a bold face and continued to speak of Henry Clay and "northern rights" in the same breath. Finally, the worried presidential hopeful politely told Giddings to tone down his antislavery statements. All of Giddings' efforts to drown out the Liberty party's appeal, Clay assured him, were "vain and fruitless."[54] Liberty men, ecstatic at the summary fashion in which Clay had crippled Giddings' campaign, stepped up their attacks.[55] Seth Gates, disgusted, advised Giddings to give up Clay as a lost cause: "He is as rotten as a stagnant fishpond, on the subject of slavery and always has been. . . ." Gates, after reading the "Alabama Letters," had immediately joined the Liberty party.[56]

When the results of the October elections were announced, Giddings had defeated Edward Wade and the Democratic opponent by a better than two-to-one combined margin. His antislavery Whig appeals had done their work well, but only in the Twentieth District. The Democrats again controlled both houses of the state legislature, while more Democratic representatives than usual were assured seats in Congress.[57] Prospects looked unpromising for a Clay victory in Ohio with the presidential election but three weeks away.

97

As it turned out, Clay did carry Ohio on the strength of a Whig fraud perpetrated upon the Liberty party. Just as Birney headed west on his campaign tour, carefully timed news releases began appearing, complete with a notarized letter purportedly from Birney to a Michigan Democrat. The letter, an utter forgery, showed Birney admitting his candidacy was designed solely to aid James K. Polk. In late October Whig papers all over the North ran banner headlines: "MR. BIRNEY'S REAL POSITION: THE DECEPTION EXPOSED!" [58] Although Birney immediately pronounced the letter fraudulent, the Whigs, including Giddings, exploited it effectively and unscrupulously. Understandably, the third party charged Giddings with complicity in originating the false letter episode, and he vehemently denied it.[59] No evidence exists to prove the Liberty men accurate on this count, no matter how justified some of their other indictments of his behavior might have been.

Under these circumstances, the revenge of Birney's supporters must have been especially pleasurable. The key to the presidential election proved to be New York, and the Liberty party's ability to woo away Whigs like Seth Gates swung the state and the nation to Polk. "The die is cast. The story is told," mourned Giddings. The annexation of Texas now appeared inevitable, with "only one hope . . . left to our Whigs," from now on "to meet promptly all attempts to encroach on the rights of the free states. . . ." [60] When Congress opened in December, 1844, he was in his seat, fully prepared to do just that.

NOTES

1 Edgar Allen Holt, *Party Politics in Ohio, 1840–1850* (Columbus, 1930), 191–94.

2 Smith, *Liberty and Free Soil Parties,* 65.

3 "Pacificus" [pseud. JRG], *Western Reserve Chronicle,* November 8, November 15, November 22, December 13, 1842.

4 *Ibid.,* November 3, December 13, 1842.

5 JRG to LMG, February 17, 1839, Giddings MSS.

6 "Pacificus" [pseud. JRG], *Western Reserve Chronicle,* December 6, 1842.

7 *Ibid.*

8 *Ibid.,* December 27, 1842.

9 JRG to Salmon P. Chase, February 19, 1843 (quotation), October 12, 1843, Chase MSS, HSP.

10 JRG to Editor, Ashtabula *Sentinel,* June 19, 1845. The opinion of some historians, most notably Stanley Elkins, that the antislavery movement was heavily anti-institutional falls down with respect to Giddings and to Liberty party leaders as well. Men such as Joshua Leavitt and James G. Birney were engaged in the most difficult sort of institution-building, that of creating a political party. See Stanley M. Elkins, *Slavery: A Problem in American Institutional and Intellectual Life* (Chicago, 1959), 140–93.

11 JRG to LWG, January 1, 1843, Giddings MSS.

12 Joshua Leavitt to James G. Birney, February 10, 1843, in Dumond (ed.), *Letters of James Gillespie Birney,* II, 716.

13 *Philanthropist,* January 11, 1843.

14 "A Sprig from the Green Mountains" to JRG, December 28, 1842, Giddings MSS.

15 JRG to Son, December 21, 1842, JRG to JAG, January 12, 1843, Giddings MSS; Giddings, *History,* 197–99.

JRG to LMG, April 19, 1844, Giddings MSS.

17 U.S. *Congressional Globe,* 27th Cong., 3d Sess., XII, 241.

18 *Ibid.,* 241–42, Appendix, 80–82, 194–98; 28th Cong., 1st Sess., XIII, Appendix, 500–4.

19 *Ibid.,* 27th Cong., 3d Sess., XII, Appendix, 194–98.

20 JRG to JAG, January 26, 1843 (quotation), JRG to LWG, February 12, 1843 (quotation), JRG to CPG, January 21, 1843, Giddings MSS; JRG to LMG, April 19, 1844, Giddings MSS.

21 JRG to Daughter, February 13, 1843, Giddings-Julian MSS, LC; JRG to LWG, February 19, 1843, Giddings MSS.

22 JRG to JAG, January 7, 1844, Giddings MSS; *Emancipator,* January 11, 1844; U.S. *Congressional Globe,* 28th Cong., 1st Sess., XIII, 78–80 (quotation), 85–89, 627.

23 Giddings, *History,* 216; JRG to LWG, December 10, 1843 (quotation), Giddings MSS.

24 JRG to Theodore Weld, February 21, 1843, Theodore Dwight Weld MSS, LC; JRG to Theodore Weld, January 28, 1844, in Barnes and Dumond (eds.), *Weld-Grimké Letters,* II, 1021 (quotation).

25 JRG to David Lee Child, December 9, 1843, David Lee and Lydia Maria Child MSS, Boston Public Library (hereinafter BPL), (quotation); JRG to Seth M. Gates, December 15, 1843, Gerrit Smith-Miller MSS, SUL; JRG to JAG, December 24, 1843, Giddings MSS (quotation).

26 JRG to JAG, December 25, 1843, JRG to GRG, January 1, 1844, Giddings MSS.

27 Julian, *Giddings,* 148–49.

28 U.S. *Congressional Globe,* 28th Cong., 1st Sess., XIII, 112.

29 *Ibid.,* 224; JRG to Messrs. Gales and Seaton, February 22, 1844, Giddings Miscellaneous MSS, NYHS.

30 JRG to CPG, January 7, 1844, Giddings MSS.

31 U.S. *Congressional Globe,* 28th Cong., 1st Sess., XIII, 132.

32 *Ibid.,* 177–79, 353.

33 JRG to James A. Briggs, January 1, 1844, Briggs MSS, WRHS (quotation); JRG to JAG, January 7, 1844 (quotation), JRG to LWG,

February 4, 1844 (quotation), Giddings MSS; U. S. *Congressional Globe*, 28th Cong., 1st Sess., XIII, 343 and Appendix, 652–56.

[34] JRG to Seth M. Gates, December 15, 1843, Gerrit Smith-Miller MSS, SUL; U.S. *Congressional Globe*, 28th Cong., 1st Sess., XIII, 401.

[35] JRG to James A. Briggs, March 20, 1844, Briggs MSS, WRHS.

[36] JRG to LMG, April 19, 1844 (quotation), JRG to JAG, April 13, 1844 (quotation), JRG to LWG, May 19, 1844, Giddings MSS.

[37] JRG to Oran Follett, April 14, 1844 (quotation), in Belle Hamlin (ed.), "Selections from the Follett Papers," *Quarterly Publications of the Historical and Philosophical Society of Ohio*, X (January, March, 1915), 15; JRG to James A. Briggs, April 2, April 19, 1844, Briggs MSS, WRHS; JRG to Son, March 24, 1844, Giddings MSS.

[38] Glyndon G. Van Deusen, *The Life of Henry Clay* (Boston, 1937), 373.

[39] JRG to LMG, April 28, 1844 (quotation), JRG to JAG, April 28, 1844 (quotation), Giddings MSS; JRG to James A. Briggs, April 19, April 29, 1844, Briggs MSS, WRHS.

[40] JRG to JAG, June 12, 1844, Giddings MSS; JRG to Oran Follett, May 12, 1844, in Hamlin, "Follett Papers," 15–16; JRG to James A. Briggs, May 20, 1844, Briggs MSS, WRHS.

[41] U.S. *Congressional Globe*, 28th Cong., 1st Sess., XIII, Appendix, 704–8.

[42] JRG Diary, February 7–9, 1839, Giddings MSS; *National Intelligencer*, October 29, November 12, 1842; Benjamin F. Wade to JRG, January 2, 1843, Giddings MSS.

[43] Elisha Whittlesey to John C. McLean, October 6, 1843, John McLean MSS, LC; Seth M. Gates to JRG, July 31, 1843, Giddings MSS (quotation); JRG to Seth M. Gates, August 30, 1843, Gerrit Smith-Miller MSS, SUL; JRG to James A. Briggs, July 19, 1843, Briggs MSS, WRHS.

[44] Julian, *Giddings*, 159–60.

[45] Cleveland *Herald*, March 15, 1843; *Western Reserve Chronicle*, April 11, 1843.

[46] Henry Fasset to JRG, January 26, 1844, Giddings MSS; Conneaut *Reporter*, April 11, 1844.

[47] Smith, *Liberty and Free Soil Parties*, 59; Warren *Liberty Herald,* September 28, 1843.

[48] Conservative Whigs in the new district rallied around Giddings' renomination because of fear of the Liberty party and opposition to Texas' annexation. The Cleveland *Herald,* which had always opposed Giddings bitterly, endorsed his renomination on July 17, 1844.

[49] Warren *Liberty Herald,* September 18, 1844.

[50] *Ibid.,* May 29, July 24, 1844 (quotation) ; *Philanthropist,* October 9, 1844.

[51] David L. Smiley, *The Lion of Whitehall: The Life of Cassius M. Clay* (Madison, 1962) , 71–74; *Emancipator,* September 11, 1844.

[52] Van Deusen, *Clay,* 380–84; Warren *Liberty Herald,* October 2, 1844.

[53] JRG to Henry Clay, July 6, 1844, Giddings MSS; Mercer (Pa.) *Luminary,* quoted in the Warren *Liberty Herald,* October 2, 1844 (quotation) .

[54] Henry Clay to JRG, July 19, September 11, September 21, 1844 (quotation) , Giddings-Julian MSS, LC.

[55] Warren *Liberty Herald,* October 16, 1844; *Philanthropist,* October 9, 1844.

[56] Seth M. Gates to JRG, October 2, 1844, Giddings MSS.

[57] Smith, *Liberty and Free Soil Parties,* 80–81.

[58] *Ohio State Journal,* October 26, 1844.

[59] Smith, *Liberty and Free Soil Parties,* 78–80; Betty Lorraine Fladeland, *James G. Birney, Slaveholder to Abolitionist* (Ann Arbor, 1955) , 216–18. For Giddings' denial see JRG to the editor of the *Ohio American,* reprinted in the Warren *Liberty Herald,* May 14, 1845.

[60] JRG to Oran Follett, November 14, 1844, in Hamlin, "Follett Papers," 19–20.

102

Chapter 6

THE ONSET
OF SECTIONAL
POLITICS

◄ ❧ ►

1845-1846

On December 3, 1844, Giddings should have felt joyful, for during this second day of business in the House of Representatives John Quincy Adams moved that the "gag" be stricken from the rules. His resolution passed, 108–80. Giddings' six-year effort to restore the right of petition was finally successful. Still, he could not rid himself of a gloomy outlook. Rescinding the gag rule meant little so long as the Speaker persisted in loading the strategic committees with proslavery majorities, thus preventing favorable reports on requests to abolish servitude and the sale of human beings in the District of Columbia.[1]

What most depressed Giddings, however, was the possibility of a new slave state entering the Union, for the Democrats declared Polk's election a mandate for expansion and wasted no time. The House had just begun to consider joint resolutions for the annexation of Texas. Giddings' pessimism deepened as Southerners and Northern "doughfaced" Democrats acted vigorously to facilitate immediate admission. Only by "hoping against hope" could he entertain any possibility of keeping Texas out of the Union.[2]

But as debate in both Houses continued into January, 1845, Giddings' spirits began to revive. Most Northern Whigs spoke out manfully against admission and were joined by many of their Southern associates, who feared that annexation meant war with Mexico and the conquest of vast territories unsuited to slavery. Most heartening to Giddings, however, were the signs of strain appearing within the Democratic party. A number of Northern "locofocos," disregarding party policy, had also decided to raise their voices in protest against admitting another slave state. The most prominent figure in this splinter group was John Parker Hale, an earnest, persuasive representative from New Hampshire. Hale, who had also voted consistently against the gag rule, was presently causing havoc in New Hampshire politics by issuing a personal manifesto against annexation. A man of unshakable convictions, Hale had already impressed Giddings as "a man the slaveholders can't use," and the Ohioan's assessment was to prove correct over the next fifteen years.[3]

Another Democrat willing to break from orthodoxy was Jacob Brinckerhoff of Ohio, who spoke for German minorities in the southern part of the state. Much of his dissent stemmed from less principled considerations than did Hale's or Giddings'. His electorate, ardent supporters of Martin Van Buren, felt disgruntled at Polk's nomination, especially after Polk overlooked certain patronage requests which Van Buren had pledged to satisfy. Brinckerhoff's hostility to Polk's program smacked of simple political revenge.[4]

Overlooking their differing motives, Giddings discovered in Hale and Brinckerhoff a "boldness and independence" which confirmed his belief in the politician's capacity to act morally. If he could only stir this latent quality among other Northern Democrats, "fearful inroads" could be made on the "slaveholding influence." Southern "locos" might find themselves unable to "whip their northern men . . ." into line. Were he successful, the joint

104

resolutions could be defeated. With these tactical goals guiding his thinking, Giddings began fashioning a speech on the Texas question.[5]

While he composed his remarks, he fretted over rumors of pre-concerted efforts to keep him from the floor and grew increasingly disgusted with the staleness of the debate. He felt sure that no speech yet delivered had put forth the broad range of arguments essential to awakening the consciences of Northern politicians.[6] On January 21 he obtained the Speaker's recognition and, with the hope of splitting the Democratic party along sectional lines, began to evangelize.

Giddings spent the first half of his time discussing the economic and political implications of annexing Texas. Union with Texas would visit poverty upon the North, for her $50,000,000 debt would be assumed by the government and the free trade agreements between Texas and England would have to be maintained as legal compacts with a sovereign nation. Beyond such temporary dislocations, he contended, the addition of more slaveholding congressmen would permanently destroy the whole process of representative government. Giddings reckoned by the three-fifths compromise that the Southern states already sent thirty-nine extra legislators to the House: "In this way our intelligent people of the North are degraded to the political level of Southern slaves." Could any Northern representative vote to increase this injustice and "then say he has maintained northern rights . . . ," in an effort to justify himself to his constituents?

Giddings next switched his subject to a direct attack on the "peculiar institution." He picked as the vehicle for his remarks Secretary of State Calhoun's recent statement to the English government that slavery was an economic and moral good, guaranteed by the Constitution. Annexing Texas was crucial to the financial and social security of the South, Calhoun had argued, for otherwise slavery might be abolished there. Giddings charged Calhoun with placing pecuniary profit over the natural rights of man, when all liberty-loving Americans should instead "rejoice" at the prospect of ridding Texas of slavery. He then hit at much broader points.

105

If Texas were annexed, the burden of the ensuing war would fall on Northerners, while the Southern states would keep their troops at home to guard against slave insurrections. Moreover, slaves would rebel and defect to the enemy. Northern soldiers would be called upon to leave Mexico, move into the South, and perform the disgusting act of re-enslaving Negroes trying to escape a cruel and Godless system.

Calhoun had justified slavery as a positive benefit for the nation. "There is no humanity or morality in it," Giddings countered, for the system robbed each slave of his liberty, "the highest injury you can inflict upon him, except to deprive him of his life." The wholesome qualities of the system, Giddings charged, were reflected in "the infinite shades of complexion that mark the slave population around us." It was not unusual for the "Christian" slaveholder to vend his own illegitimate offspring to "those who deal in human flesh." Giddings challenged his colleagues to step outside, view the slave trade, "and then say whether you are convinced of the benign influence and moral purity of slavery." Furthermore, the slave lost not only his liberty and his family but even his life to the "peculiar institution." Through a system of crude calculation based on the highly suspect 1840 census, Giddings computed that 36,000 slaves a year, one hundred a day, died under the lash or from overwork. "This tide of human gore is constantly flowing, and we are called upon to lend our official influence to extend it." The whole scheme should have been anathema to God-fearing Americans, who knew that "there is a Power above that will visit national sins and crimes with national judgments. . . ." [7]

It was by far his most abrasive performance. Threats of slave insurrections and charges of miscegenation and genocide were hardly appropriate subjects for a practicing legislator trying to argue his point of view. Giddings, however, was not an ordinary politician. He designed his rhetoric to change a nation's feelings rather than to plant seeds of doubt in congressmen's logical minds. Convinced of the moral power of his words, he could nearly forget he was in Congress and could instead feel that he spoke directly to the American conscience, residing somewhere in the Capitol. Under such conditions no amenities were worth preserving, for truths must be told, sins revealed, and divine retribution promised. Over a decade later, Charles Sumner's "Crime Against Kansas" speech followed roughly the same outline.

Despite the fact that Giddings spoke "more scathingly" than ever before, most congressmen "sat silently and attentively . . ." as he shocked his audience time and again. The only rejoinders came from Andrew Johnson, a roughhewn Tennessee Democrat, who called Giddings a victim of "monomania," and from colorless, conservative Robert C. Winthrop, one of Massachusetts' leading Whigs, who apologized to Southern men for Giddings' "extremism" while he also spoke against annexation.[8] Winthrop's criticism marked the opening of a profound dislike between himself and Giddings, which was soon to have wide political implications. For the moment, however, Giddings believed his speech had struck a telling blow. In the evening, after he had concluded his remarks, he confided to a friend: "Texas will *not* be annexed this session." [9]

On January 25 Giddings' prediction proved pathetically optimistic, for the joint resolutions easily passed the House and went to the Senate. For a moment he was even willing to admit that "We were greatly deceived in our estimate of moral principle. . . ." There was no chance of the Senate's rejecting the measure. Giddings found solace only in his deep conviction that all members of the House were responsible "to God and their consciences" when they answered to the roll call. At least he had tried his best to prevent this "great crisis" which had now consigned "generations [of slaves] to chains and bondage and a premature death." [10] The Senate approved a slightly modified version of the resolutions; on February 28, the House concurred. Texas became a part of the United States, despite Giddings' belated effort to suspend the three-fifths compromise in the new territory.[11]

While awaiting the Senate's verdict on Texas, Giddings sloughed off his depression and busied himself with other matters

107

related to slavery. He could never afford to waste time brooding over major reversals like the passage of the annexation resolutions. Had he begun to doubt the ultimate value of his exhortations, his entire motivation as reformer would have been destroyed. Bitter disillusionment or political compromise would then have been his only choices. Instead, he assumed that the pernicious effects of the "slave powers'" victories would show the people the dangers of further apathy and that duty impelled him to hasten the day of awakening. His resiliency, earnestness, and ever-present romantic optimism always led him, undismayed and independent, back into the wars against the "slave power."

This time he chose another slave claim connected with the Florida War as his point of attack. The proposal set aside $149,000 as compensation to owners of female runaways for lost offspring who would otherwise have been born in slavery, a patently ridiculous proposal at best,[12] and Giddings protested the bill as such in an hour-long speech, satirizing it as a "moral curiosity." [13] Although Giddings drew many chuckles from his listeners with his heavy witticisms, Edward Black of Georgia sat in his seat fuming and red-faced. Finally, Black's choler overwhelmed him and he began screaming insults at Giddings, while delivering one of the most vicious and unprovoked personal attacks ever heard on the floor of the House. He mixed obscenities with groundless charges as he accused Giddings of being a slave stealer and a horse thief. "Go home," Black cried, "and ascertain if you have any character there; for before God and country you have none here." Black guaranteed that there was not a single Southern congressman who would not like to waylay Giddings on the street and "knock him down in his tracks."

Giddings jumped out of his chair, planted himself in the middle of the aisle, and interrupted with strong words of his own: "Do you think the people I represent would send a coward here? . . . I have never seen an infernal coward that did not talk loud. . . ." Black, yelling curses, grabbed his cane and headed for Giddings with full intention of beating him senseless. Giddings stood his ground, but made no move to defend himself, and Black, quickly intercepted by several agile colleagues, was wrestled back into his seat. He could do nothing but sit and listen sullenly as Giddings glared at him, promising to "speak out and expose" every machination of the "slave power" no matter how often attacked.[14] Giddings won by this display of nerve more than just the respect of his fellow congressmen—including some Southerners. His courage and flash of temper while facing Black's uplifted cane also guaranteed his physical safety in the House for the rest of his career, just as the censure and re-election had secured his complete freedom of speech. He would often be verbally assailed, but never again would anyone dare attempt to make good a threat against him.

Giddings' freedom from the possibility of bodily harm was never more valuable to him than during the first session of the Twenty-ninth Congress. From December 1, 1845, the opening day of this fateful assembly, debate on the issues before Congress filled the atmosphere with electricity. The nation faced the grim prospect of two wars, one with England over Oregon and one with Mexico over Texas. Beneath both sets of diplomatic tensions lay virulent sectional feelings which Giddings both shared and fostered. He developed a sour stomach as he surveyed the prospects, noted the large Democratic majorities in both Houses, and paid a visit to James K. Polk in order to introduce a constituent. He found the president "surrounded by a coterie of locos engaged in low party exultation and boasting of his message. . . ." Giddings walked out in disgust, predicting that the "slave influence" would soon reign supreme in Washington unless someone took bold action.[15] His frame of mind was not improved by the easy passage of an enabling act making Texas a full partner in the Union. The threat of war with Mexico was now even more acute, and something had to be done to stop the Democratic juggernaut.[16]

At this point Thurlow Weed, the shadowy, astute manipulator of Whig politics in New York State, wrote Giddings, putting forward a timely suggestion. He observed that the Democrats' weak spot was the Oregon issue. Polk had campaigned on the promise to end unilaterally the Anglo-American occupation of Oregon, even if such action meant hostilities with England. If Giddings could "out trump" the president by advocating war while observing that English armies would invade the South and abolish slavery, the Democrats would be blown "sky high." Southerners would discover that Polk's policies led straight to black rebellion, while Northerners would find the president deserting them on annexing Oregon, where slavery was not likely to expand.[17]

Weed's idea struck Giddings as sound. After all, John P. Hale and Jacob Brinckerhoff had demonstrated that antislavery sentiment existed among the Northern Democrats. Besides, this strategy fitted nicely into Giddings' own plans for rearranging the Whig party, activities which had greatly increased their scope since Texas had been annexed.

The previous summer, after the joint resolutions had passed, Giddings had returned to his usual efforts to encompass the Liberty party within Whiggery.[18] This time, however, gratifying events had called for changes in his planning; new elements within the Whig party had begun acting as Giddings felt all good politicians should. In Massachusetts a diverse group of young men, "Conscience" Whigs as they came to be called, had taken a strong sectional position by issuing a manifesto against the admission of Texas. The leaders of the "Conscience" Whigs, soon to be Giddings' closest allies, were one day to number among the North's foremost sectional figures. Handsome Charles Sumner, the "Conscience" Whigs' acknowledged theoretician, was highly educated, a brilliant speaker who embodied Olympian moral convictions. He partook as little of the "practical politician" as did Giddings, but he lacked Giddings' aggressive willingness to confront the South incessantly on immediate issues like slavery in the District of Columbia. By contrast, Charles Francis Adams, the son of the former President, represented a circumspect element within the "Conscience" Whigs, while a third leader, plebian Henry Wilson, blended a sincere hatred of the "slave power" with an intelligent sense of political reality utterly lacking in Giddings and Sumner. Closest of this group to Giddings' own temperament was John

110

Gorham Palfrey, a Harvard intellectual who specialized in writing essays and history. His religious convictions had helped him to overcome his quiet nature and he attacked slavery with a vigor of which Giddings thoroughly approved. Sumner viewed the Negro as a distasteful abstraction, while Palfrey, who had personally emancipated slaves left to him in a relative's will, had a working knowledge of slavery which few Northern politicians, even Giddings, could ever match.[19]

United in their opposition to Texas annexation, this heterogeneous association of men had begun attacking as "tools of the slave power" Massachusetts' established, antisectional Whig leaders. Daniel Webster, Edward Everett, Abbot Lawrence, and a man whom Giddings had already come to distrust, Robert C. Winthrop, represented the Massachusetts orthodoxy, the "Cotton" Whigs. The two factions had soon begun contesting for control of the state organization, and Winthrop and his conservative associates had taken vigorous measures to squash the mavericks. In July, 1845, after Charles Sumner had delivered an eloquent, ornate antiwar speech on the Texas question to the state convention, Winthrop had risen and offered a toast, affirming his support for American foreign policy even if it led to hostilities with Mexico and the conquest of new territory. Winthrop's rejoinder had been a stinging rebuke to the "Conscience" Whigs, and open warfare had soon broken out.[20]

Giddings had quickly fastened his attention upon these events, and as early as February, 1845, he had tried to coordinate his efforts in Ohio to capture the Liberty party with the movements of the "Conscience" Whigs. He had even proposed that a national convention be called *"without party distinction,"* based on a series of gatherings held in various states. Through such a meeting he had hoped to unite "many of the locos and most of the Liberty men with the Whigs," while driving "rabid doughfaces" out of every party organization. By December he had convinced himself that the only way to victory over the slave power lay in completely dispensing with the "old school politicians of our party [who] are endeavoring to silence the agitation of the

111

slavery question." Renovating the Whig party now meant mustering out the likes of Winthrop in favor of John G. Palfrey and the younger Adams. Giddings thus had broad objectives in mind when, on January 5, 1846, he got his chance to try out Thurlow Weed's theory of "out trumping" James K. Polk. He aimed to assist "Conscience" Whigs in Massachusetts by indicting the conservatives and hoped to unite Jacob Brinckerhoff and John P. Hale with Charles Sumner and Henry Wilson in a reconstructed Whig party. After such a transformation, he reasoned, the Liberty men should be glad to drop their separate organization.[21]

He began his speech by terrorizing the Southern Democrats while warning Northern members of that party that they were about to be abandoned on the Oregon question if they did not push together for war. Polk would default on his promises, Giddings predicted, because of the disastrous effects hostilities with England would have upon slavery. English armies bent on emancipation would invade the South and the slaveholders knew it. "They see in the prospect the black regiments of the British West Indian Islands. . . . Servile insurrections torment their imaginations; rapine, blood and murder dance before their affrighted eyes." Giddings called on all Northern Whigs to unite with Northern Democrats in a vote for a war which "must prove the death of slavery," while bringing into the Union vast expanses of free territory: Newfoundland, Nova Scotia, even all of Canada.

Turning his attention to the Massachusetts conservatives, Giddings vowed that no true Whig should feel any qualms about becoming a "warhawk." Robert C. Winthrop had spoken in favor of conciliation with England, making him a fit target, and Giddings assailed him as a Southern pawn. It was a well-known fact, he said, "that the gentleman was the first . . . from New England who publicly avowed his submission to the new slaveholding Confederation with Texas," but now Winthrop wished to compromise on Oregon. Winthrop was anxious to oppose the acquisition of free territory for crass economic reasons, Giddings charged. War with England would jeopardize his selfish Boston commercial interests and the well-being of the slavery system to which he and the other "Cotton" Whigs had capitulated, and Giddings declared in conclusion that such servile hypocrisy had no place in the Whig party.[22]

The lurid scenes which Giddings painted had the effect for which he had hoped. John C. Calhoun and other Southerners began retracting their support for annexing all of Oregon, while editorial vilification of Giddings as an "insurrectionist" became so extreme that he even protested on the floor of the House.[23] He would seldom be more pleased with one of his efforts, reporting with pride that it had "undoubtedly stirred up more feeling than any other speech in the House since I have read the newspapers."[24]

As the Southerners continued to "rave and roar," Giddings became ever more certain that he was watching the disintegration of the Democratic party and the coalescence of all antislavery politicians. The Southern Democrats were "backing water" on the Oregon question, and "Polk wants to do so but cant [sic] tell how. . . ." Northern "locos" thanked him "wonderfully" for his speech and "cursed" the Southerners for abandoning their support of 54'40°. His assault on Winthrop received warm praise from Charles Francis Adams' editorials in his newspaper, the Boston *Courier*.[25] In the meantime, other developments encouraged Giddings. Antislavery Democrats were merging with Liberty men in New Hampshire to boost John P. Hale to the Senate, and Whig promises to repeal the discriminatory "Black Laws" in Ohio and New York drew high praise in Liberty party papers, normally very suspicious of antislavery measures proposed by either major party. "My sentiments are now making more progress than at any other time," Giddings wrote. "The fire is spreading. . . . From the east and the west and the north the signs of the times are most cheering," he boasted joyfully as he stepped up the attack on the "Cotton" Whigs with the aid of friendly Ohio editors.[26] Nevertheless, the "gathering storm" of war with Mexico cast shadows across Giddings' glowing optimism, for he

113

was enough of a realist to see that hostilities were inevitable. On May 11 and 12, Polk's request for a declaration of war passed both branches of Congress.[27]

In the House, only fourteen men defied the decision of the Whig caucus and voted against the war. One was Joshua Giddings.[28] Without a moment's hesitation he began to organize this small association to oppose all operations of the American army. A speaking schedule was arranged with Giddings to lead off, followed by Joseph M. Root, Columbus Delano, Daniel Rose Tilden, Robert C. Schenck, and Joseph Vance, all Ohio Whigs. While Root and Delano's later careers were to show that they valued their antislavery principles over party loyalty, Schenck, Tilden, and Vance simply opposed the war for fear of its sectional implications. By stopping hostilities quickly, they hoped to avoid future recriminations about whether or not conquered areas should be open to slavery. But Giddings, who never appreciated such subtleties of motivation, was determined only to set an example for his fellow dissenters to emulate. On May 12 Giddings "stole a march," and "with the nimbleness of a pickerel" obtained the floor to declare his total opposition to the war while taking "vengeance on the whole slaveholding crew." [29]

The theme of Giddings' speech was a simple one: the war constituted an act of unmitigated American aggression, initiated by General Zachary Taylor's violations of Mexican sovereignty. Polk's assertion that "war exists by act of Mexico" was a blatant falsehood designed to mask what had really occurred. Through the "arbitrary will of an irresponsible majority . . ." dominated by a "weak but ambitious executive . . . ," Southern politicians had decided to "purchase perpetual slavery . . ." through aggressive war. The only mission of Taylor's army was to extend "an institution on which the curse of the Almighty visibly rests." The clear moral duty of every patriotic American was to oppose all expenditures for the war and to insist on the immediate withdrawal of all American troops. "I will lend the war no aid," Giddings announced, "no support whatever. I will not bathe my hands in the blood of the people of Mexico . . . [in order] to waste her countryside and subject her to slavery." Columbus Delano and Joseph M. Root followed up quickly with echoes of Giddings' remarks, and his two-year effort to defeat the war had begun.[30]

Although his attempts to cajole Whiggery into blocking all military appropriations were to prove fruitless, Giddings never gave up the task. The opposition party adopted the time-honored tactic of supporting the war effort generally, while trying to make political capital by criticizing specific points of administration policy. Giddings soon noticed this approach and it disgusted him. By mid-June he began fearing the party lacked the "moral firmness to withstand the shock. . . ." Many Whigs, whose spokesmen he identified as Robert C. Winthrop and Daniel Webster, had "but one step to go before joining the Locofoco ranks," and the party, he believed, was heading for "inevitable *ruin*." As usual, he felt certain that only the therapy of some massive moral shock could save his associates from bowing to the wishes of the South.[31]

The urgency of the situation became clearer to Giddings in late June, after a long conversation with John Quincy Adams, now enfeebled and fearing death. Adams confessed that he no longer had the strength to work effectively in Congress and was anxious that Giddings now take on all responsibilities of leadership. Giddings felt deeply touched as he "looked the good old patriot in the face and saw the tears glistening in his eyes. . . ." He left "Father Adams' " room with firm resolve to carry out his dear friend's commission[32] and to save the Whig party by returning to his work for antislavery fusion.

Shortly after his talk with Adams, Giddings released an unusual letter to the Ashtabula *Sentinel*. In it he declared that by virtue of the annexation of Texas and the Mexican War the Union had been dissolved. Here was a device which he hoped would stun the Whigs into some sober second thoughts, for at first glance his ideas appeared quite extreme. But Giddings was advocating, as he always would, union and reform, not a separation of the states.

He argued that the original Union of 1789 had been nullified

by the entrance of "foreign, slaveholding" Texas. The founding
fathers had intended the Union to check just that sort of "arbitrary
and tyrannical power" which had been used in the annexation
and which Texas itself embodied as a slave state. Since the federal
government now operated as a tyranny rather than a republic, the
people of the free states could, if they wished, ignore federal law
and refuse to send delegates to Congress.

So far Giddings' pronouncements sounded quite radical, but at
the last moment he backed away from endorsing disunion. Whig
representatives should not stay home or refuse the oath of office,
he declared. Rather, they must inform the people, "unveil to their
view the crimes and corruptions of a profligate administration
..." so that public opinion would one day return the Union to its
original condition of freedom. Giddings, with his typically conservative logic, was appealing that the Union be recaptured, not dissolved, through antislavery action.[33]

Although his ideas were clear enough to most people in the Reserve,[34] Giddings had chosen an ill-advised tactic which affronted
one of the most deep-seated loyalties of the average American, his
devotion to the national compact. A superficial reading of the "dissolution letter" left an impression of the worst sort of "ultraism."
Hostile editors and politicians wishing to diminish Giddings' influence found themselves furnished with a potent weapon. The
Democrats accused him of treason, charging that he was secretly
conniving with Garrisonian agents in the Reserve like Marius
Robinson, Parker Pillsbury, and Stephen S. Foster. These individuals worked constantly to diminish the influence of Liberty men
who had parted with William Lloyd Garrison's perfectionism in
1840.[35] Such accusations undoubtedly had a stronger impact upon
Whig minds than Giddings' fuzzy call for reform.

The "dissolution letter," however, did have a more plausible
rationale behind it, for its feigned radicalism just might aid union
between the Whig and the Liberty parties. At the behest of John
P. Hale, Giddings had left Congress in mid-July, before the end of
the session, to aid the process of coalition in New Hampshire. During his ten-day stay, he had basked in the plaudits of many audi-

ences and had delivered a well-received address to the state legislature. But more important, Giddings also had been given a chance to observe at first hand the dynamics of fusion.[36] When he arrived home in mid-August to get re-elected, the letter was in print, and he felt even more impressed with the benefits of inter-party cooperation.

Immediately, he informed Liberty men that he would never again vote for a slaveholder, not even for Henry Clay, and would bolt to a third party if the Whigs did not nominate a Northerner for president in 1848.[37] He also announced that the "dissolution letter" would constitute his campaign platform.[38] Prospects for political change were further enhanced by the establishment of the *True Democrat* in Cleveland. It was edited by an unequivocating antislavery Whig, Edward S. Hamlin, and the new paper quickly proved the equal of the conservative *Herald*. Also encouraging Giddings' hopes for fusion was the Whig gubernatorial nominee William Bebb's apparently unapologetic stand for repeal of Ohio's segregationist "Black Laws." Times had never seemed better for reunifying antislavery men. Giddings felt that perhaps Ohio could even be made the pivot of a national movement.[39]

By early August Giddings was deep in correspondence with Salmon P. Chase, the most astute Liberty party manipulator in Ohio and long a believer in broadening that organization's basis of support.[40] Giddings initially proposed an informal meeting between Ohio's influential third party leaders, Samuel Lewis, Leicester King, Edward Wade, Chase himself, and a like number of Whigs drawn from Giddings' antiwar coterie in Washington. Dropping his shop-worn arguments that Whig economic programs were antislavery measures, he suggested a broad agenda in which fiscal questions would be irrelevant. Such issues should neither separate the two groups nor be permitted to keep away antislavery Democrats who might wish to join. "The day has come when party claims must sit loosely upon us," Giddings observed.[41]

Chase proved a hard man to convince. He was justifiably suspicious that Giddings meant to capture Ohio's antislavery leadership for the Whigs rather than to create a broader third party.

117

He also disagreed with Giddings' contention that economic questions were not so important as the growing crisis over slavery. Chase's sympathies in such matters lay with the Democrats; he was an inveterate free-trader and anti-bank man. Also, his deep opportunistic instinct told him that the surest path to political preferment lay within dissident elements of the Democratic party.[42]

Chase's posture, coupled with a sudden reversal on the part of William Bebb concerning his position on repealing the "Black Laws," shattered Giddings' plans. And his attempt to secure his nomination by the local Liberty party convention in addition to the Whig endorsement proved fruitless, as Edward Wade and others rejected the idea emphatically.[43] Giddings was forced to take the stump against two opponents in the 1846 elections, and, as usual, he beat them both handily.[44] But antislavery politicians still remained divided in a time of crisis, and Giddings deplored the "bigotry, intolerance and self-will among those who profess to be abolitionists both Whigs and Liberty men." [45]

In November, 1846, Giddings felt he had good reason for his petulance. Just after he had left Washington in July, an obscure, slovenly Pennsylvania Democrat named David Wilmot had offered an amendment to a war appropriations bill which declared that all lands conquered from Mexico must be kept free of slavery. After it had passed in the House, the Senate had refused to act on the measure, and the "Wilmot Proviso" had expired, but only momentarily.[46] The "free soil question" was to confuse and inflame American politics for the next fifteen years. One day it would plunge the nation into bloody sectional warfare and into an ultimate reckoning with slavery itself. Giddings, not forseeing this first event but anxious for the second to take place, vowed to Charles Francis Adams that the Wilmot Proviso would be offered again, as soon as Congress convened in December. Antislavery sentiment was clearly increasing, and Giddings thought it a crime that its partisans were unwilling to unite. He was convinced that Northern solidarity was essential in the upcoming crusade for free soil or an immediate end to the Mexican War.[47]

118

NOTES

1 U.S. *Congressional Globe*, 28th Cong., 2d Sess., XIV, 7; Giddings, *History*, 195, 237–38; JRG to LMG, December 15, 1844, Giddings MSS.

2 JRG to LMG, December 15, 1844, Giddings MSS (quotation). Giddings was "certain" that Southerners and "doughfaces" were in complete control of affairs, admitting that "we are to be at their mercy." JRG to JAG, December 13, 1844, Giddings MSS.

3 Giddings, quoted in Richard H. Sewell, *John P. Hale and the Politics of Abolition* (Cambridge, 1965), 44. This fine political biography gives a complete account of Hale's career as reformer and politician.

4 Chaplain W. Morrison, *Democratic Politics and Sectionalism, The Wilmot Proviso Controversy* (Chapel Hill, 1967), 5–7.

5 JRG to James A. Briggs, January 5, 1845, Briggs MSS, WRHS (quotation); JRG to James A. Briggs, January 15, 1845, James A. Briggs MSS, OHS (quotation); JRG to Seth M. Gates, January 2, January 6, 1845, Gerrit Smith-Miller MSS, SUL.

6 JRG to JAG, January 5, 1845, Giddings MSS.

7 U.S. *Congressional Globe*, 28th Cong., 2d Sess., XIV, Appendix, 342–47.

8 JRG to David Lee Child, January 21, 1845, Child MSS, BPL (quotation); U.S. *Congressional Globe*, 28th Cong., 2d Sess., XIV, Appendix, 219, 345.

9 JRG to David Lee Child, January 21, 1845, Child MSS, BPL.

10 U.S. *Congressional Globe*, 28th Cong., 2d Sess., XIV, 194; JRG to "Dear Child," January 25, 1845, Giddings MSS (quotations).

11 U.S. *Congressional Globe*, 28th Cong., 2d Sess., XIV, 372.

12 *Ibid.*, Appendix, 363.

13 *Ibid.*, Appendix, 363–64.

119

14 *Ibid.* (text), 250–56; Adams, *Memoir of Adams,* XIII, 162–63.

15 JRG to JAG, December 7, 1845, Giddings MSS.

16 U.S. *Congressional Globe,* 29th Cong., 1st Sess., XV, 60–65. For Giddings' depressed outlook see JRG to Son, December 16, 1845, Giddings-Julian MSS, LC.

17 Thurlow Weed to JRG, January 3, 1846, Giddings MSS.

18 JRG to Oran Follett, July 16, 1845, in Hamlin, "Follett Papers," 27–29; Lewis Tappan to JRG, December 19, 1845, Giddings MSS.

19 Frank Otto Gatell, *John Gorham Palfrey and the New England Conscience* (Cambridge, 1963), 121–43; David H. Donald, *Charles Sumner and the Coming of the Civil War* (New York, 1960), 130–83.

20 *Ibid.*

21 JRG to Oran Follett, February 18, 1845, in Hamlin, "Follett Papers," 21–22 (quotation); JRG to James A. Briggs, December 20, 1845, Briggs MSS, WRHS (quotation). Giddings explained his motives fully in a letter to JAG, January 31, 1846, Giddings MSS.

22 Giddings, *Speeches,* 148–63.

23 John C. Calhoun to Thomas Clemson, January 23, 1846, in J. Franklin Jameson (ed.), "The Correspondence of John C. Calhoun," *Annual Report of The American Historical Association,* 1899 (Washington, 1900), 678–79; Edward Stanley to Willie P. Mangum, January 27, 1846, in Henry Thomas Shanks (ed.), *The Papers of Willie Person Mangum,* 5 vols. (Raleigh, 1950–1956), IV, 162. For Giddings' protest see U.S. *Congressional Globe,* 29th Cong., 1st Sess., XV, 236, and Adams, *Memoir of Adams,* XIII, 236–37.

24 JRG to JAG, January 23, 1846, Giddings MSS.

25 JRG to JAG, January 25, 1846, Giddings MSS (quotation); JRG to James A. Briggs, January 20, 1846, Briggs MSS, WRHS (quotation). For the co-ordinated press attacks against the Ohio and Massachusetts conservative Whigs see JRG to James A. Briggs, January 31, 1846, Briggs MSS, WRHS and the Boston *Courier,* January 28, 1846, JRG Scrapbook, 1846, Giddings MSS.

26 John P. Hale to JRG, April 5, 1846, JRG to JAG, February 12, 1846, Giddings MSS; JRG to JAG, March 21, 1846, Giddings MSS (quotation); JRG to James A. Briggs, April 6, 1846, Briggs MSS, WRHS (quotation).

[27] JRG to JAG, May 1, May 9 (quotation), 1846, JRG to LWG, May 10, 1846, Giddings MSS.

[28] U.S. *Congressional Globe,* 29th Cong., 1st Sess., XV, 782–83, 795; JRG to JAG, May 13, 1846, Giddings MSS.

[29] For the plan to establish a speaking schedule see JRG to LWG, May 17, 1846; quoted material comes from JRG to JAG, May 12, 1846. Both letters are in Giddings MSS.

[30] Giddings, *Speeches,* 177–201; U.S. *Congressional Globe,* 29th Cong., 1st Sess., XV, Appendix, 641–45.

[31] JRG to James A. Briggs, June 26, 1846, Briggs MSS, WRHS.

[32] JRG to LWG, June 7, 1846, Giddings-Julian MSS, LC.

[33] JRG to O. P. Brown and L. A. Hamilton, June 3, 1846, reprinted in the Ashtabula *Sentinel,* July 13, 1846.

[34] Albert Gallatin Riddle to JRG, July 4, 1846, Giddings MSS; Painesville *Telegraph,* July 22, 1846.

[35] Cleveland *Plain Dealer,* July 8, 1846.

[36] JRG to LWG, July 12, July 19, 1846; JRG to LMG, July 17, 1846, Giddings MSS; New Hampshire *Democrat and Freeman,* July 26, 1846; Portland *Advertiser,* July 25, 1846, JRG Scrapbook, Giddings MSS; New Hampshire *Democrat and Whig,* reprinted in the Ashtabula *Sentinel,* July 26, 1846.

[37] Theodore S. Foster to James G. Birney, August 1, 1846, in Dumond (ed.), *Letters of James Gillespie Birney,* II, 1024–26. According to this letter Joshua Leavitt encouraged Giddings and other antislavery Whigs in their protestations against the nomination of a Southern candidate for 1848. See also JRG to Salmon P. Chase, October 30, 1846, Chase MSS, HSP.

[38] JRG to JAG, July 26, 1846, Giddings MSS.

[39] Smith, *Liberty and Free Soil Parties,* 93; Holt, *Party Politics in Ohio,* 244–45; JRG to JAG, June 19, June 28, 1846, Giddings MSS; JRG to Salmon P. Chase, September 28, 1846, Chase MSS, HSP.

[40] Joseph Rayback, "The Liberty Party Leaders of Ohio, Exponents of Antislavery Coalition," *Ohio Archaeological and Historical Quarterly,* LVII (May, 1948), 161–78; Reinhard Luthin, "Salmon P. Chase: Political Career Before the Civil War," *Mississippi Valley Historical Review,* XXIX (January, 1943), 517–40.

[41] JRG to Salmon P. Chase, August 3, August 31, October 30 (quotation) , 1846, Chase MSS, HSP.

[42] Salmon P. Chase to JRG, August 15, September 4, 1846, Giddings MSS; JRG to Salmon P. Chase, September 18, 1846, Chase MSS, HSP.

[43] Holt, *Party Politics in Ohio*, 245; JRG to Salmon P. Chase, October 30, 1846, Chase MSS, HSP; Painesville *Telegraph*, September 2, 1846.

[44] Ashtabula *Sentinel,* October 19, 1846.

[45] JRG to Salmon P. Chase, November 23, 1846, Chase MSS, HSP.

[46] Charles Buxton Going, *David Wilmot, Free Soiler: A Biography of the Great Advocate of the Wilmot Proviso* (New York, 1924) , 94–98.

[47] JRG to Charles Francis Adams, November 11, 1846, Adams Family MSS, MHS; JRG to Salmon P. Chase, November 23, 1846, Chase MSS, HSP.

Chapter 7

WAR, WINTHROP,
AND THE
WILMOT PROVISO

·‹ ›·

1846-1847

James K. Polk, like many Democrats, was worried and nervous in the winter of 1846. Van Burenites like Jacob Brinckerhoff and David Wilmot had willingly wrenched the issue of slavery in the territories out of its purely "theoretical" context in order to make opportunistic gains at the administration's expense. Even more unnerving was the carping of the Whigs, antislavery and otherwise, as they piled up political capital with the war question while looking ahead to the 1848 elections. The Democratic ascendancy seemed imperiled and so did the continuance of section peace.[1] Polk's concern was justified on both counts. The events of 1847 opened deep sectional schisms in both major parties, and in this process Joshua Giddings began to play the most significant role of his political career.

The president dealt with his fears directly in his annual message to Congress by presenting all the hackneyed assertions available to a party leader in domestic trouble because of a warlike foreign policy. He dismissed the issue of slavery in the territories as an implausible abstraction, while castigating Giddings and his friends for opposing the war. Their extremism gave "aid and comfort" to the Mexican enemy, Polk averred, and even bordered on treason.[2] Giddings' reaction to Polk's charges was purely visceral, and he immediately "led off in order to give the doughfaces an example" by delivering an unrestrained rebuttal. In an hour-long speech he reminded Congress of the "un-Christian" nature of aggressive war and its consequent duty to refuse to vote supplies. While calling for an immediate end to hostilities and the withdrawal of all American troops, he insisted that Polk's message was a huge sophistry designed to mask the real cause of the war—the South's insatiable appetite for more slave territory.[3]

In quick order, Giddings' clique of antiwar Whigs followed up the initial attack. Charles Hudson, a Massachusetts "Conscience" man, and Joseph M. Root from Ohio presented strongly worded critiques of the administration and the war effort.[4] Meanwhile, able and rotund Preston King, leader of the New York Van Burenites, introduced a motion to attach the Wilmot Proviso to an appropriations bill. His attempt failed in the House by a single vote.[5] Such incidents symbolized the growing tensions within both parties which Polk's message, far from quieting, had only helped to exacerbate.

Whig leaders hardly welcomed imminent splits within their party, for as Polk's Democratic consensus continued to degenerate, the opposition's prospects for presidential victory grew. Recollections of General William Henry Harrison's 1840 victory made many consider the slaveholding war hero Zachary Taylor an attractive Whig contender. Memories of Henry Clay's 1844 defeat by the Liberty party also made most Whigs nervous about further fragmentations over the slavery question. The "Conscience" Whigs, Giddings, and several other mavericks had already told everybody that they would not support a slaveholder for president. Something had to be done to drive the dissidents back into line.

While privately making it clear to Giddings that he was badly out of step with party policy on the war,[6] the Whig leaders attempted in one stroke to humble the "Conscience" group in Massachusetts and the antiwar faction in Congress. Giddings was sure that he was "sustained by a majority of the Whigs" and that those who opposed him would soon "find themselves under the necessity of *backing* out." [7] But this roseate analysis was quickly blasted on January 8, 1847. Robert C. Winthrop, now a familiar nemesis to Giddings, delivered a biting reply to his doctrine of total opposition to the war.

He tore into Giddings' assertion that voting against all supplies was a practice sanctioned by common law through the actions of Burke, Fox, and Chatham in the English Parliament during the American Revolution. Instead, Winthrop charged, Giddings was acting very much like Timothy Pickering and the old Federalists who came close to treason during the War of 1812. According to Winthrop, Giddings' behavior only encouraged the Mexicans to fight harder by creating the illusion that American opinion was divided. In so doing, he concluded, Giddings and his friends were not in line with official Whig policy and should not be mistaken for legitimate party spokesmen. "We cannot be too perfectly united in a determination to defend our country," [8] Winthrop intoned.

Predictably, the speech did nothing to chasten the antislavery Whigs; Giddings took it as a personal affront,[9] and the "Conscience" men in Massachusetts were furious. Winthrop seemed to personify all that was keeping the party from reforming itself "But for him we should all be united in opposition . . ." to the war, wrote Charles Sumner hotly, as he sent along detailed advice about how best to rebut Winthrop's "subtle but unsound" efforts. The Boston *Whig*, now the "Conscience" Whigs leading newspaper, ran long editorials initiated by Charles Francis Adams, praising Giddings' independence and condemning Winthrop as a "doughface." Meanwhile Winthrop's main organ, the Boston *Atlas*, picked up the onslaught against the antiwar Whigs where it had been dropped in the House.[10] Winthrop, in short, had only solidified the connection between the nation's two largest sources of antislavery Whig leadership, the urban Boston of Charles Sumner and Giddings' rural Western Reserve. Because of Winthrop's choice of targets, Giddings suddenly found himself almost as deeply involved in Massachusetts politics as he was in those of his own state. At Giddings' request, one of his most devoted congressional allies, Columbus Delano, delivered a stern rebuke to Winthrop which followed many of Sumner's suggestions.[11]

Despite the developing ties between himself and the Boston antislavery clique, Giddings found some of his opinions at variance with those of his new friends. His hopes still resided entirely with the Whig party, which he thought could at least rally around the Wilmot Proviso if not around a total withdrawal of American forces from Mexico. He might agree with Charles Sumner's eager call for "fraternization" among Whigs, Liberty men, Democrats, and even Garrisonians. But Giddings cautiously avoided endorsing Charles Francis Adams' idea that antislavery Whigs organize a convention to declare in advance their intention to bolt if Taylor should be nominated. Adams' warning to Giddings that his "main dependence" on the Whig capacity for self-reform would prove delusive in "the pinch" did nothing to cure the Ohioan of his optimism.[12] Ever since 1838 he had deemed himself a loyal Whig, assuming that his sectional agitation was beneficial to his party. He could not suddenly cast aside this belief and realize instead that maintaining moral consistency could dictate abandoning Whiggery. To Giddings, such a recognition would have amounted to a premature admission of failure, and he was not one to give up easily. Long after most of his associates had decided to bolt, Joshua Giddings was still determined to reform the Whig party. Duty demanded that he attempt, until the last possible moment, to save the Whigs from accommodating the "slave power." Occasionally, he warned Whigs of a permanent split unless the party voted down all war supplies or helped to enact the Proviso. But such threats were meant to coerce the party in the right direction, rather than to stand as a promised course of action. He still looked forward to dividing the Democrats along

126

sectional lines and absorbing the entire North into the Whig organization.[13]

Superficially at least, prospects in Congress bore out Giddings' expectations, for all branches of Whiggery, as well as the Northern Democrats, displayed an ever greater hostility to the war. In January, 1847, Alexander Stephens, the talented, fiery Whig leader from Georgia, introduced resolutions calling for peace with Mexico and no annexations of territory. This suggestion, prompted by Southern fears over the creation of new free states, was defeated by an eleven-vote margin. Giddings found himself acting with the party's most fervent apostles of slavery, Robert Toombs, Henry A. Wise, and J. R. Ingersoll.[14] Even more cheering, however, was the performance of Thomas Corwin, Ohio's eloquent junior senator and recognized spokesman of moderate Whig opinion. On February 11 the "Ohio ploughboy" delivered an electrifying three-hour speech against the Mexican War which sent waves of gratification through antislavery ranks.

"If I were a Mexican I would tell you," Corwin thundered, " 'Have you not room in your own country to bury your dead men?' " The war was an unjust, aggressive American act, he declared. Corwin dwelled long upon the sectional perils behind the acquisition of any new lands and the consequent need to make immediate peace without sequestering a single inch of Mexican soil. It was the most emphatic antiwar speech yet heard from a major Northern politician.[15]

Thomas Corwin, however, was the farthest thing from a "Conscience" Whig. Like Robert Schenck and Joseph Vance, Corwin feared the conquest of Mexico, for it would visit intolerable stresses upon the Union over whether or not to extend slavery. It was the possibility of disunion, not the expansion of slavery, which worried him to the point of decrying the war so dogmatically. Besides, the Whig party, to which he was undyingly loyal, just might break apart under severe sectional pressure, an event which Corwin fervently wished to avoid.[16]

127

But most antislavery Whigs, hardly aware of Corwin's motives, welcomed him as the savior of the party. Giddings believed his speech maintained "every position all young Whigs occupy," while Charles Francis Adams felt it would "probably be a marking point in the country's history." Both were certain Corwin had become the man who could wrench the nomination from the slaveholding Taylor, and neither paid much attention to the perceptive misgivings of Charles Sumner. He alone was certain that no antislavery Whig candidate could receive the united support of the party. Even Henry Wilson, by far the most tough-minded and politically oriented of the "Conscience" Whigs, threw himself behind Corwin's nomination. Meanwhile, the Ashtabula *Sentinel* ran up the senator's name as the preferred choice.[17]

As if Corwin's speech were not enough, still another event gladdened Giddings' heart—the bipartisan performance of Northern representatives on the Wilmot Proviso question. In early February, Preston King and Jacob Brinckerhoff had attached the Proviso as a rider to a three-million-dollar war appropriations bill, touching off two weeks of torrid debate. Initially, Giddings had cared little about whether or not it actually passed, feeling that its "moral effect" would be to show up "doughfaces" in both parties and that, this being done, "the people will discard those who go for slavery."[18] But in placing a great deal of faith in the Proviso's purgative power, Giddings made a bad mistake. He misread not only the motives of its backers but also the explosive sectional appeal the Proviso carried by linking racism and political opportunism with anti-Southern feeling. More than anything else, the measure included equal hatreds for the American Negro and James K. Polk. As such, it embodied a dynamic which Giddings would not have liked, had he understood it.

The Proviso itself was largely the product of several years' feuding between the Polk administration and the Van Burenites. Problems included patronage quarrels, tariff disagreements, personal animosities, and clashing ambitions, as well as differing views on the issue of slavery in the territories.[19] The earliest and most fervent sponsors of the Proviso, King, Wilmot, Brinckerhoff, and John A. Dix, a New York senator, had also been among the loyal supporters of the war effort. Each had avoided completely Giddings' leadership in trying to end it by choking off its supplies.[20] None of these Democrats except John P. Hale, an utterly independent figure in politics, shared the deep moral revulsion to the war felt by Giddings, Charles Sumner, and some other Whigs. Furthermore, most Van Burenites were ardent expansionists, but only in the name of saving the West from Negroes. This was what the Proviso was designed to do. "I would preserve for free, white labor," David Wilmot once explained, "a fair country, a rich inheritance, where the sons of toil, of my own race and color, can live without the disgrace which association with negro slavery brings upon free labor." Or, as Preston King later clarified, "If slavery is not excluded by law, the presence of the slave will exclude the laboring white man." [21]

Such beliefs were hardly in accord with convictions which led Giddings to champion the abolition of the discriminatory "Black Laws" in Ohio, to preach (and practice) the doctrine of aiding fugitive slaves once they had reached the free states, and to insist on equal legal justice for free blacks. The Negro might not be the complete political equal of the white man, Giddings felt, but equity dictated that "he who murders a black man shall be hanged . . . he who robs the black man of his liberty or property shall be punished like other criminals." His greatest objection to popular sovereignty, whereby the electorate of each new territory should decide whether to admit slavery, was simply that the process was undemocratic. Negroes themselves would have no voice in deciding if they were to be enslaved or freed. He always protested homestead laws and territorial constitutions which excluded or legislated against Negroes.[22]

The Wilmot Proviso's appeal as a political lever and an outlet for racism constituted its most profound tragedy. After 1846 the demand to end slavery's expansion was to attract an ever wider following, allowing Northern society, ridden with Negrophobia at every level, finally to confront the question of slavery, albeit

129

obliquely.[23] Giddings, with his qualified but genuine humanitarian concern for the condition of the American Negro, only occasionally glimpsed this fact. He could never admit that as the antislavery movement gained recruits it became progressively and permanently less altruistic. Instead, he interpreted each new group of free soil adherents as representing but another phase of the "moral revolution" which would surely bring the mass of Americans to his own position. Giddings' faith in the conversion experience thus obscured his political vision, while his inability to endorse immediate abolition left him only partially confronting the excruciating question of slavery. No ante-bellum American, however, completely reconciled politics and moral issues, and few were even half so successful as Giddings himself. In a deeper sense, his predicament represented his own generation's most tragic dilemmas. Only by recourse to armed conflict would the nation finally come to terms with these confusing problems.

But for the moment, perhaps, hardbitten Joshua Leavitt saw matters more clearly when he admonished his Liberty party followers to beware the supporters of the Wilmot Proviso. They were content with "the continuance of *slavery as it is*," he warned. "What have we to do with the movements of the Wilmot Proviso men?" he asked. "Plainly nothing." A year later, in 1848, Joshua Leavitt was to discover that his own reform career had been permanently compromised by the forces of expediency and antiabolitionism which generated the demand for "free soil." [24] Joshua Giddings' inability to fathom fully the contradictions in antislavery politics was typical, not unique, in the national experience.

Giddings revealed the full extent of his unawareness when he finally joined in the debate on Preston King's interjection of the Wilmot Proviso. He had already heard Jacob Brinckerhoff argue for the measure in an openly racist fashion, while disclaiming any unpatriotic opposition to the war itself.[25] But instead of noticing this unsavory twist, Giddings opened his speech by rejoicing in the unity shown by Northern Whigs and Democrats on sectional questions. Since slavery and freedom were "necessarily at war with each

130

other," it was about time Northern men of both parties began standing "shoulder to shoulder for human rights."

Giddings did not voice his warm welcome to the Van Buren Democrats, however, on the basis of their cry for expanding America's "free soil." Instead, he argued that the Proviso should be passed simply to deny the South its war aims. If Congress decreed that all lands open to conquest were to be forever free, if the government exercised its constitutional obligation to legislate for the "life, liberty and the pursuit of happiness" of all men, Southerners would suddenly become more willing to leave all occupied areas in Mexican hands. To Giddings, the Wilmot Proviso simply represented a means to coerce the Southerners into making peace. Besides, the interests of reform would be far better served if the federal government left such lands under free Mexican law to serve as a haven for fugitives. Since the moral and legal right of the slave "to use violence to regain his freedom" was "unquestionable," any government interested in legislating for humanity must take steps to insure the protection of such individuals. A good place to begin, Giddings vowed, was for Congress to make sure by enacting the Proviso that Mexico kept all of its lands.[26]

When the speechmaking finally ended, the House passed the war appropriation, Proviso and all, by a strictly sectional vote, 115–106. The Senate struck out the rider, then approved the bill and sent it back to the House for concurrence. The House assented 115–81, and on March third the Wilmot Proviso was laid to rest for the moment.[27] Giddings was desolate on this last day of the session as he watched many Northern congressmen change their minds and vote for the unrestricted appropriations. "Let their names go to the ends of the *earth as traitors to freedom*," he told Charles Francis Adams.[28] David Wilmot or Jacob Brinckerhoff might have chosen identical words to express their feelings, but they would have hardly meant the same thing. As antislavery feeling in the North gained momentum, Giddings' political influence began increasing. But, at the same time, many of his new

colleagues were far less kindred spirits than had been Theodore
Weld, Seth Gates, or old William Slade.

Such subtleties, however, disturbed Giddings little during the
long congressional vacation between March and December, 1847.
The Whig party still remained his major concern, and he initiated
a final effort to unify antislavery opinion behind his new presidential hope, Thomas Corwin. Giddings had reason to feel optimistic about his chances for success. The increasing activity of
antislavery Whigs and Democrats in Ohio now overshadowed the
appeal of local Liberty party organizations. At the same time,
Ohio's third party leaders acted ever more anxious to give their
organization greater inclusiveness.[29] These heartening omens, as
well as Corwin's overwhelming popularity in northern Ohio,
prompted Giddings to reconsider Charles Francis Adams' earlier
proposal. Giddings now agreed that antislavery Whigs should
hold conventions to emphasize Zachary Taylor's unacceptability.
If the party could be shown that its antislavery wing was in
earnest, Whig leaders would abandon Taylor and make Corwin
their nominee.[30]

After discussing this idea with Ohio Whigs, Giddings broached
it to the eccentric sage of the *New York Tribune,* Horace Greeley.
"I do not think much is to be gained by agitation," wrote back
the editor, observing that Corwin was far more "timid" than his
famous speech had led Giddings to believe. Greeley guaranteed
that Corwin would "become panicked if openly touted by the
Free Soilers as an alternative to Taylor." [31] But Giddings paid no
attention to Greeley's predictions. He traveled around the Reserve
organizing outdoor rallys, lauding Corwin, and assuring audiences: "Sooner should this arm fall from its socket and my
tongue cleave to the roof of my mouth than I will vote for Zack
Taylor for President." [32] He posted a stream of letters to leading
newspapers in Ohio and Massachusetts calling on Northern men
to stand firm at least on Henry Clay's original doctrines from the
election of 1844, while denouncing the idea of Taylor's candidacy
as a palpable absurdity. "The Whigs of Ohio with almost unani-

mous voice will adhere to the position taken by Mr. Corwin in his speech," Giddings promised.[33]

Giddings, continuing his desperate efforts to resuscitate the Whigs, twice made trips to the East. Heeding pleas for help from his old friend Seth Gates, as well as those of John P. Hale, he made speaking tours through upstate New York and in New Hampshire, addressing "the masses of *all* parties. . . ." His message, couched in appeals to tradition, was always the same; he stressed the need for Whigs to return to "first principles" by nominating Corwin and, by passing the Proviso, to end a war which the founding fathers would have opposed. Audiences received him warmly, "and no one who heard," Gates reported, "went away advocating . . . Taylor's claims. . . ." [34]

Meanwhile, in New York State, the Democratic party was experiencing the first spasms of an open split. In the state convention, resolutions endorsing the Wilmot Proviso, introduced by Preston King and others of the "Barnburner," or anti-Southern, faction, were voted down by the conservative majority. John Van Buren, the son of the former president, and David Wilmot himself led the radicals out of the convention, and in a separate meeting endorsed a program of "Free Labor, Free Speech and Free Men." The material for Giddings' long-desired Northern party was slowly solidifying, but the Ohioan felt initially suspicious of the Barnburners. "They seek power and know that to attain it they must take an anti-slavery ground," he wrote perceptively. "I have no confidence in the sincerity of the leading Locos of New York." [35] Sumner's glowing reports of the doings in that state, however, soon caused Giddings' faith in the conversion experience to override his better judgment. Perhaps the New York dissidents had suddenly seen the sinfulness of slavery. He gradually began getting excited about the prospect of welcoming the Barnburners into a Corwin-led Whig party.[36]

But Thomas Corwin proved uncooperative, bearing out to the letter Horace Greeley's predictions. The Ohio senator grew ever more uneasy about the unsolicited aid Giddings was giving him, fearing that he was being used against his will to defeat Zachary

Taylor, the Whig's best prospect for president. To correct such false impressions Corwin delivered a speech in Carthage, Ohio, in which he disavowed the Wilmot Proviso, called it a "dangerous issue," and appealed for party unity.[37] Gamaliel Bailey, anxious to amalgamate the Liberty party with other dissident politicians, hurriedly retracted his newly founded *National Era*'s endorsements of Corwin. Charles Sumner reported that the "conscience" men all over the Bay State were "much disheartened" by the "Carthage speech." [38] Giddings, shocked by the sudden desertion of his one great hope for Whig solidarity, made lame excuses for Corwin's behavior,[39] while sending off a letter pleading with the senator to change his mind.

Giddings' attempt to save Thomas Corwin differed little from his treatment of Henry Clay during the election of 1844. Corwin's reply to Giddings' letter made very clear his opposition to both the Wilmot Proviso and to any effort to run him for president, saying that the Whig party would split on sectional issues if agitation continued. Giddings, in turn, tried to put up the best front he could by rationalizing the "Carthage speech." Meanwhile he argued that Corwin would still be a suitable candidate if sufficiently encouraged.[40] Joshua Giddings was still determined, at any cost, to remain a Whig. He would continue to feel this way until the day that the national convention finally nominated Zachary Taylor.[41]

The plain fact was, however, that the Whig party had no candidate whom Giddings could accept and was lapsing into a condition which he thoroughly deplored. Every report from out of state indicated Taylor's growing popularity.[42] The party's insistence upon leaving Mexican territory in Mexican hands looked worthless. Without the added insurance of the Proviso, Giddings felt certain that the Southern Whig appetite for slave territory would overcome any hostility to further annexations. It was also unmistakable that the party as a whole thought in Thomas Corwin's terms, and time was running out as the 1848 elections came ever closer.[43] Giddings decided to make one last attempt to save the party by contriving a direct confrontation between the antislavery wing and the "doughfaces" over "repealing all laws of Congress which support slavery...." [44]

The Thirtieth Congress was to be evenly divided, and a balance of power was available to anyone daring enough to seize it. Here was a chance to force the party into a reckoning with itself. The contest for Speaker of the House promised to be a close one, a fact quickly noticed by Giddings and his Massachusetts comrades. In the early fall, Giddings had tried to solidify backing for the strongly antiwar Hoosier, Caleb B. Smith.[45] But as winter set in, it became obvious that Robert C. Winthrop, Giddings' archetype "doughface," was winning the party's endorsement. "Mr. Winthrop *cannot be speaker*," Giddings vowed to Charles Francis Adams; "I plan to say to our friends at once 'we shall go for [no] man who is not pledged so to arrange the committees as to secure reports in favor of withdrawing our troops from Mexico.'" [46]

These firm promises evoked warm responses in Boston, for over the summer Winthrop had again proven his ability to repress "Conscience" Whig efforts to capture the state organization. In the state convention Charles Francis Adams, Charles Sumner, and others had introduced resolutions endorsing the Wilmot Proviso. Winthrop had led a successful effort by the "Cotton" Whig majority to table this declaration.[47] The conservative congressman seemed even more to be standing athwart the political prospects and antislavery principles of the various "Conscience" Whigs, who certainly had ample reasons for encouraging Giddings' Speakership strategies. Winthrop was "*secretly* favoring" the Taylor movement, Charles Francis Adams reported. "Do what you can for union" with the Barnburners, counseled Sumner. "At all events extricate us from our present uncomfortable position of political association with those who really hate us [more] than they hate the Locofocoes. . . . I hope this may be [done] *in the organization* of the House." [48] In his last quest for reformed Whiggery Joshua Giddings was soon to find himself acting as the congressional arm of antislavery politicians all over the North, while also giving vent to his long-accumulating hatred of Robert C. Winthrop.

Giddings would not be alone, however, as he nervously set out early for Washington to save his party by utterly defying it. Although his Massachusetts friends had vetoed his plea that Sumner and Adams set up an anti-Winthrop lobby in the Capitol,[49] Giddings was soon to be joined by scholarly John G. Palfrey, an original "Conscience" Whig, who carried the highest credentials as Massachusetts' most recently elected antislavery congressman. "He is true as steel," Sumner had guaranteed. Palfrey's reputation and two brief meetings with him had already convinced Giddings that the new representative would "enter Congress with no doubtful character," and prove an invaluable friend in the upcoming struggle to "defeat Winthrop and break the present dynasty of our Whig party." [50]

NOTES

[1] Morrison, *Democratic Politics and Sectionalism*, 3–20; Arthur M. Schlesinger, Jr., *The Age of Jackson* (Boston, 1950), 451–53.

[2] U.S. *Congressional Globe*, 29th Cong., 2d Sess., XVI, 7–10.

[3] JRG to JAG, December 20, 1846, Giddings MSS (quotation); U.S. *Congressional Globe*, 29th Cong., 2d Sess., XVI, Appendix 54–59.

[4] JRG to Charles Francis Adams, December 26, 1846, Adams Family MSS; MHS; U.S. *Congressional Globe*, 29th Cong., 2d Sess., XVI, Appendix, 48–52, 84–86.

[5] U.S. *Congressional Globe*, 29th Cong., 2d Sess., XVI, 105.

[6] JRG to Charles Francis Adams, December 23, 1846, Adams Family MSS, MHS.

[7] JRG to LWG, December 27, 1846, Giddings MSS.

[8] U.S. *Congressional Globe*, 29th Cong., 2d Sess., XVI, 144–45; Julian, *Giddings*, 202.

[9] JRG to Charles Francis Adams, January 8, 1847, Adams Family MSS, MHS; JRG to J. W. Taylor, January 9, 1847, James W. Taylor MSS, NYHS.

[10] Charles Sumner to JRG, January 14 (quotation), January 21, 1847, JRG to JAG, January 18–19, 1847, Charles Francis Adams to JRG, January 16, 1847, Giddings MSS.

[11] JRG to Charles Sumner, February 1, 1847, Charles Sumner MSS, cited by permission of the Harvard College Library (hereinafter HL); U.S. *Congressional Globe*, 29th Cong., 2d Sess., XVI, Appendix, 313–17; Julian, *Giddings*, 203–4.

[12] Charles Sumner to JRG, January 22, 1847 (quotation), Charles Frances Adams to JRG, December 16, 1846, Giddings MSS (quotation); JRG to Charles Francis Adams, December 23, 1846, Adams Family MSS, MHS.

[13] JRG to Horace Greeley, December 24, 1846, Giddings-Julian MSS, LC; JRG to Seth M. Gates, January 25, 1847, Gerrit Smith-Miller MSS, SUL; JRG to JAG, January 15, 1847, Giddings MSS.

[14] U.S. *Congressional Globe,* 29th Cong., 2d Sess., XVI, 239–40.

[15] *Ibid.,* Appendix, 237–46.

[16] Norman Graebner, "Thomas Corwin and the Election of 1848," *Journal of Southern History,* XVII (February, 1951), 162–79.

[17] JRG to Charles Sumner, February 11, 1847, Sumner MSS, HL (quotation); Charles Francis Adams to JRG, February 22, 1847, Giddings MSS (quotation); Charles Sumner to JRG, February 25, 1847, in Edward L. Pierce (ed.), *Memoir and Letters of Charles Sumner,* 4 vols. (Boston, 1877–1893), II, 141; Henry Wilson to JRG, February 24, 1847, Giddings MSS; JRG to Charles Francis Adams, February 26, 1847, Adams Family MSS, MHS; Ashtabula *Sentinel,* April 19, 1847.

[18] Going, *Wilmot,* 161–63; U.S. *Congressional Globe,* 29th Cong., 2d Sess., XVI, 303; JRG to David Lee Child, January 27, 1847, Child MSS, BPL (quotation).

[19] Morrison, *Democratic Politics and Sectionalism,* 3–18; and Eugene F. Berwanger, *The Frontier Against Slavery: Western Anti-Negro Prejudice and the Slavery Extension Controversy* (Urbana, Illinois, 1967), *passim.* Berwanger, however, mistakenly attributes to Giddings strong colonizationist sentiments.

[20] For voting patterns, see U.S. *Congressional Globe,* 29th Cong., 2d Sess., XVI, 166, 230, 273.

[21] Wilmot and King, quoted in Schlesinger, *The Age of Jackson,* 451–52. For an excellent discussion of "free soil's" racist overtones, see Morrison, *Democratic Politics and Sectionalism,* 71–73. Gilbert Hobbes Barnes and Dwight L. Dumond have both oversimplified greatly the process by which anti-Southern feeling generalized throughout the North. Both writers assert that the abolitionists' moral protests on behalf of the slave led directly to the Republican party's stand for "free soil." Such a view overlooks the roles of racism and opportunism operant in Northern politics, which made most opinion heavily antiabolitionist. See Barnes, *Antislavery Impulse,* 191–97, and Dwight L. Dumond, *Antislavery Origins of the Civil War of the United States* (Ann Arbor, 1939), *passim.*

[22] U.S. *Congressional Globe,* 35th Cong., 2d Sess., XXVIII, 346 (quotation); 29th Cong., 2d Sess., XVI, 445.

[23] For provocative inquiries into the ante-bellum North's deep animus toward the Negro, see Leon F. Litwack, *North of Slavery: The Negro in the Free States, 1790–1860* (Chicago, 1961), *passim.;* Winthrop Jordan, *White Over Black: American Attitudes Toward the Negro, 1550–1812* (Chapel Hill, 1968), *passim.* These studies also cast grave doubts, by implication, on the interpretations of Barnes and Dumond.

[24] *Emancipator,* June 16, 1847 (quotation); Filler, *Crusade Against Slavery,* 189. Filler, in this broad history of the antislavery movement, offers the most sensitive treatment of the dilemmas of the political reformer in the nineteenth century.

[25] U.S. *Congressional Globe,* 29th Cong., 2d Sess., XVI, Appendix, 377–79.

[26] *Ibid.,* Appendix, 454–57.

[27] *Ibid.,* 556, 573.

[28] JRG to Charles Francis Adams, March 3, 1847, Adams Family MSS, MHS.

[29] Smith, *Liberty and Free Soil Parties,* 116–17.

[30] JRG to Charles Francis Adams, April 16, 1847, Adams Family MSS, MHS.

[31] JRG to Horace Greeley, April 16, 1847, Giddings-Julian MSS, LC; Horace Greeley to JRG, April 24, 1847, Giddings MSS (quotation).

[32] *National Era,* June 10, 1847.

[33] Draft of JRG letter for publication in the Boston *Whig,* JRG to Charles Francis Adams, April 26, 1847, Adams Family MSS, MHS (quotation); Ashtabula *Sentinel,* June 14, July 5, August 2, 1847; *Ohio State Journal,* reprinted in the *Emancipator,* August 30, 1847.

[34] JRG to Seth M. Gates, August 2, 1847, Gerrit Smith-Miller MSS, SUL (quotation); Boston *Whig,* September 24, 1847, JRG Scrapbook, 1847, Giddings MSS; Ashtabula *Sentinel,* September 13, October 4, 1847; Seth M. Gates to Charles Francis Adams, September 14, 1847, Adams Family MSS, MHS (quotation); John P. Hale to JRG, June 8, 1847, Giddings MSS; Concord *Democrat and Freeman,* July 28, 1847, JRG Scrapbook, 1847, Giddings MSS.

[35] JRG to Oran Follett, July 26–27, 1847, in Hamlin, "Follett Papers", 30–34.

[36] Charles Sumner to JRG, November 1, 1847, Giddings MSS; JRG to

Charles Sumner, November 8, 1847, Sumner MSS, HL; JRG to Seth M. Gates, October 28, 1847, Gerrit Smith-Miller MSS., SUL.

[37] Cleveland *Herald,* September 28, 1847.

[38] *National Era,* September 30, 1847; Charles Sumner to JRG, October 1, 1847, Giddings MSS.

[39] JRG to Charles Sumner, October 8, 1847, Sumner MSS, HL.

[40] Thomas Corwin to JRG, August 18, October 12, 1847, Giddings MSS.; JRG to Charles Sumner, October 18, 1847, Sumner MSS, HL; JRG to Charles Francis Adams, October 25, 1847, Adams Family MSS, MHS.

[41] JRG to Charles Sumner, November 8, 1847, Sumner MSS, HL; Charles Francis Adams to JRG, November 2, 1847; Charles Sumner to JRG, November 1, 1847, Giddings MSS.

[42] Caleb B. Smith to JRG, May 21, 1847, Giddings MSS.

[43] JRG to Charles Francis Adams, August 12, 1847, Adams Family MSS, MHS; JRG to Oran Follett, July 26–27, 1847, in Hamlin, "Follett Papers," 30–34.

[44] JRG to Charles Francis Adams, November 11, 1847, Adams Family MSS, MHS.

[45] Caleb B. Smith to JRG, September 3, 1847, Robert C. Schenck to JRG, November 20, 1847, Giddings MSS.

[46] JRG to Charles Francis Adams, October 25, November 11, 1847, Adams Family MSS, MHS (both letters quoted) .

[47] Gatell, *John Gorham Palfrey,* 140–41; Charles Sumner to JRG, October 1, 1847, Giddings MSS.

[48] Charles Francis Adams to JRG, November 28, 1847, Charles Sumner to JRG, December 1, 1847, Giddings MSS.

[49] JRG to Charles Francis Adams, October 25, November 11, 1847, Adams Family MSS, MHS; Charles Francis Adams to JRG, November 28, 1847, Giddings MSS.

[50] Charles Sumner to JRG, November 1, 1847, Giddings MSS (quotation) ; JRG to Charles Sumner, October 8, December 4, 1847, Sumner MSS, HL (both letters quoted) .

Chapter 8

THE
ACCIDENTAL
ORGANIZER

·《 》·

1848

John G. Palfrey arrived in Washington on December 4, the day of the Whig nominating caucus for the Speaker. Giddings met him at the train station, thankful for having one man on whom to rely. They carefully avoided attending the conclave, for neither man wished to appear obliged to support the party's choice of Winthrop. Instead, they spent their time drawing up a set of conditions to which Winthrop would have to agree if he wanted the bolters' votes. Late that afternoon Amos Tuck, a newly elected New Hampshire representative and friend of John P. Hale, agreed to join the venture. Meanwhile, Giddings worried about losing "influence" by "partially separating" from the party but comforted himself with the thought that he held "important cards." [1]

On December 5 Palfrey presented the bolters' demands. Winthrop must promise to organize House committees to help bring an end to the war, report bills to abolish slavery in the District of Columbia, repeal the 1793 fugitive slave law, and obstruct the extension of slavery. Giddings hoped Winthrop would be willing to

141

bargain, but the Massachusetts conservative quelled such optimism, writing Palfrey that the demands were out of the question. Now there was no backing out; even the pleas of old John Quincy Adams, who supported Winthrop on purely sentimental grounds, could not change the mavericks' minds.[2]

The balloting began the next day, December 6. Rumors of revolt filled the corridors of the Capitol, and when Giddings and Palfrey walked to their seats the gallery was already jammed.[3] On the first ballot, Winthrop was only three short of a majority as Giddings and Tuck "wasted" their votes on James Wilson of New Hampshire and Palfrey voted for Charles Hudson, a mildly antislavery Whig from Massachusetts. This pattern held on the second round, Winthrop gathering two new supporters. On the third try, with Winthrop lacking only one vote, Isaac Holmes of South Carolina walked out of the hall and handed the Whigs the election.[4]

Although Palfrey acted in a gentlemanly fashion by congratulating Winthrop on his victory, Giddings said nothing, waiting to be "bitterly assailed" for apostasy. If the Whigs attacked him, "I think Winthrop will regret it," he predicted ominously.[5] Palfrey wondered how to mute the inevitable recriminations, but Giddings was preparing to repel whatever criticisms came his way. He was sure that the party could be kept together "only in one way; that is, to get up the question of slavery in every possible shape, and thereby [to] compel northern Whigs and southern Whigs to take their positions." [6] Attempts to save Whiggery through a direct moral crisis were only beginning.

The Whig presses in Washington, Ohio, and Massachusetts were quick to give Giddings his opening. The Cleveland *Herald,* the Boston *Atlas,* and the *National Intelligencer* reprinted in unison an editorial from the *National Whig,* a newly founded Washington Taylorite sheet. It described the bolters as having "intellects so entirely obfuscated by the madness of Abolitionism, that they can neither see nor feel what is due to themselves, or to the party to which they profess to belong, but of which they are the mere putrid excrescences." [7] "They talk about reading me out of the Whig

church," Giddings chuckled, "ain't it smart . . . ?" Meanwhile, Palfrey, "reeked [sic] fore and aft like a crippled ship of war" by the
Whig journals, bore himself bravely. Giddings grew ever more
respectful of this quiet Cambridge intellectual who was trying his
best "to play the statesman." [8]

As the attacks mounted, Giddings advanced to the next phase of
his plan to renovate his party by confrontation. During the last
week of December he drew up a lengthy defense of his refusal to
vote for Winthrop. He addressed it to the Cleveland *Herald*, the
newspaper in the Reserve most hostile to his decision to bolt. After
waiting over a week, the *Herald* printed Giddings' self-justification,
which amounted to a detailed condemnation of Robert Winthrop's "proslavery" career. Aiding Winthrop's election would
have been "an act of moral perjury . . . ," Giddings explained, because during the Whig caucus, prior to the vote declaring war
against Mexico, Winthrop had urged all his colleagues to support
hostilities. Giddings charged further that Winthrop, on the floor
of the House, had continued to cajole members into supporting
the war before voting himself "to strike the most fatal blow ever
aimed at American liberty." [9]

Giddings made his accusations without consulting any of his
friends in Massachusetts. None of his letters to Charles Sumner or
Charles Francis Adams before December 25 mentioned these
charges, except for one to Adams on December 7, which hinted
vaguely that Winthrop would find himself in trouble if the Whig
press attacked the bolters.[10] Giddings acted on his own as he
opened the most significant public squabble of his tempestuous
political career.[11]

Ohio's orthodox Whigs sneered at Giddings' indictment of
Winthrop. The Cleveland *Herald* declared Giddings' general behavior betrayed "a little too much JUDAS" for anyone to believe
his charges. The Conneaut *Reporter* editorialized in a similar
fashion. Meanwhile, every antislavery newspaper in Ohio, led by
the Ashtabula *Sentinel*, now operated by Giddings' son Joseph,
applauded the bolters' votes while giving full credence to the

143

allegations.[12] "Can party allegiance relieve a man from the discharge of moral obligations?" queried the *True Democrat*.[13] A chasm was opening among the Ohio Whigs over Giddings' indictment, and it did not take long for the split to race across state boundaries, carrying with it the potent forces of party disruption.

On January 15 Charles Francis Adams' Boston *Whig* reprinted Giddings' bill of particulars verbatim, and on the 27th the Boston *Atlas*, in Winthrop's name, branded every word a lie: "*Mr. G. and the* [editors of the Boston Whig] *are all wrong. We challenge either of them to prove what they have asserted.*" [14] Conservative newspapers in the Reserve immediately repeated these contrary allegations word for word, though the Boston *Courier* joined the forces of the "Conscience" men by defending Giddings. The other influential "Cotton" journal of greater Boston, the *Daily Advertiser,* took sides with Winthrop.[15] By late January, Whigs in Ohio and Massachusetts were dividing into two hostile camps. Giddings' charges had become a major issue, forcing Northern Whiggery to take its stand, one way or the other, on slavery questions.

Giddings was completely astounded by Winthrop's denial of his accusations, for there was no doubt in his mind about their accuracy.[16] The sincerity of his assertions is not hard to prove. There had been a Whig caucus on the war vote in 1846, for, despite the *Atlas'* denial, Giddings had mentioned it at the time in a letter to his son.[17] Furthermore, in February, 1847, nine months before the issue of Winthrop as Speaker arose, Giddings had written to David Lee Child, one-time editor of the *National Anti-Slavery Standard* but now largely retired from active life, "I suppose it to be generally known that Mr. Winthrop advocated the policy of voting for the war both in public and in private." [18] There is no reason to believe that Giddings, always a proud guardian of his own integrity, consciously lied either in February, 1847, when there was no reason to do so, or in January, 1848, when policy and falsehood might have served each other better. Winthrop's denial in the *Atlas* was obviously designed to purge the "Conscience" Whigs forever from the party by casting the worst possible light on their association with Giddings.

The tactic was a most effective one, for Giddings could not easily meet the *Atlas'* challenge to prove his contentions. Any Whig who substantiated him would be a traitor to the party, and all saw this fact clearly. Charles Sumner correctly reported that the "whole matter" was being used "as an instrument to weaken our position" and pleaded for Giddings to confront the conservatives with evidence.[19]

After trying without success to make Winthrop admit privately to the charges, Giddings set about to collect testimony.[20] But as he interviewed various congressmen he quickly discovered "much confusion in the recollections of those who were present" when the war vote was taken.[21] The Taylorite strategy was proving difficult to overcome, but Giddings hardly felt beaten. "I have no fears that I shall finally loose [sic] in this conflict," he assured his son Joseph. "I am a believer in the omnipotence of truth and believe it as impossible to overthrow . . . as it would be to overturn the throne of the Deity himself." [22]

As Giddings search for proof, he wrote articles in his own defense for the *True Democrat*, the *Sentinel*, and the Boston *Whig*, imagining himself coordinating a bitter struggle for control of the party.[23] He never realized that by his actions he was actually solidifying the antislavery Whigs of Ohio and Massachusetts in favor of third party fusion with the Barnburners and Liberty men.

While assembling his evidence against Winthrop, Giddings also cast about for another presidential hopeful, who would lead the Whigs into the nomination of a Northerner. Early in the session, Giddings had spent an hour in conversation with Supreme Court Judge John C. McLean, an Ohioan of high stature in the Whig party, and had come away much impressed with the politically ambitious justice's private views on slavery. After a warm initial endorsement of McLean from Charles Francis Adams, Giddings began hoping that Taylor could be unhorsed.[24] His remarkable optimism, which thoroughly astounded Palfrey and Charles Francis Adams, continued to make him pursue his vain

145

plans. Meanwhile, the necessity of leaving the party became ever more apparent to most of his associates. But as Palfrey once observed astutely to Charles Francis Adams, this trait was "invaluable" to Giddings "in bearing him up during the wars at Washington." [25] Convinced that he and McLean together could yet save the Whig party, Giddings decided to switch the battle site from the newspapers to the halls of Congress. While he searched for evidence against Winthrop, he began to publicize sectional issues in the House as vigorously as he could.[26]

There seemed to be no end of promising subjects. Polk had announced that more men and money were needed to liquidate the war, and there were always those unexpected events which forced the House into discussions of slavery. Having Palfrey as an ally proved more than helpful. The two men quickly developed a friendship which never abated over the years. Giddings found that conversation with Palfrey on any subject was "a feast," and that the quiet scholar's devotion to conscience matched his own. He and the mild professor made "a very good pair," Giddings decided. "He knows nothing about politicks, but is exceedingly interesting on morals, religion and science." Giddings felt "honored to call him my friend," and Palfrey reciprocated these warm feelings.[27]

The issues Giddings concentrated upon were the Mexican war and slavery in the District of Columbia, and he began without hesitation by presenting a petition from eighteen citizens of the District praying the abolition of the slave trade in their city. He moved to refer this request to the Judiciary Committee with instructions to report on the constitutionality of all District laws by which men were defined as property. Although his motion passed by one vote, nothing further came of the proposal. But Giddings was not discouraged, for bills brought forward by other antiwar congressmen to abolish the internal and District slave trades failed by only six and sixteen votes, respectively.[28] On January 15, 1848, the Ohio congressman made one of his

146

most strenuous efforts to rid Washington of the practice of selling human beings.

The case concerned the strong-armed kidnapping of a free Negro by three thugs engaged in the slave trade. The men had forced their way into the Negro's room, had beaten and shackled him, and had sold him at a local auction. Giddings offered a set of resolutions which combined a genuine desire for reform with hatred of Winthrop. He called for the creation of a special five-man committee to investigate the case, while at the same time recommending that this body also look into the best way of abolishing the District slave trade.[29] His insistence on a special committee, he explained privately, was "an imputation to Robert C. Winthrop": his resolutions were designed to take the matter out of the hands of the Committee on the District of Columbia, where it rightfully belonged, for he felt Winthrop had staffed this committee in a proslavery manner.[30]

Although Giddings' suggestions were voted down, he persisted in bringing them up again, taking time out only to cast the lone negative vote in the House against resolutions thanking Generals Zachary Taylor and Winfield Scott for their "indomitable skill, valor and good conduct" during the Mexican war. Giddings instead moved for the House to honor Albert Gallatin for his essays on pacifism,[31] but he was not content to let his opposition to the war rest here. On February 22 he spoke for an hour on the latest military appropriations bill. The speech represented Giddings' last effort to salvage his party. The tactic he chose was to frighten the Whigs by forecasting massive Northern disaffections unless the party deserted Zachary Taylor. Giddings still believed and would guarantee privately that "Taylor will not be the candidate"; Ohio would "furnish the next [nominee]. . . . It will be Corwin [!] or McLean."[32]

Slavery was now the only important national issue, he warned the House, and party lines were becoming ever more "obscure and uncertain whenever the subject is pressed." Keeping alive the dispute with Winthrop, Giddings predicted that the Whig

147

future was dark indeed unless the party ceased voting for war funds and never again elected a Speaker who supported American aggression and the slave trades while promoting the payment of slave claims. If the party refused to enact the total divorce of the federal government from slavery, and unless it denounced Taylor as "one whose hands are dripping with human gore," the Barnburners, antislavery Whigs, and Liberty men would be forced to band together in an independent effort. The coalition, he warned with a prophetic accuracy of which he was totally unaware, would form *"the germ of a party which will, at no distant day, become dominant in this nation."* [33]

Of course, neither Giddings' threats nor his general exertions did anything to forestall Taylor's nomination. Instead, as his agitations continued to make headlines, old political abolitionists with whom he had long ago severed all ties began to notice him again. Memories of his effective opposition to James G. Birney's presidential attempts in 1840 and 1844 still rankled many Liberty party leaders. Salmon Chase, Gamaliel Bailey, and other third party men from the old Northwest had told Giddings of their eagerness to fuse with other bolters.[34] Nevertheless, Joshua Leavitt, Henry B. Stanton, Lewis Tappan, and other veterans of political abolitionism continued to regard antislavery protestations within the two major parties with extreme skepticism. The programs of Giddings, Sumner, and the Barnburners all seemed too limited. "OUR WORK IS MORE RADICAL, OUR AIM IS HIGHER," Leavitt had emphasized in 1847 while warning his readers to disregard the inviting rumors of fusion.[35]

Having for so long written off the antislavery Whigs as opportunists, many Liberty men simply had not believed that Giddings and the rest would bolt if Taylor got the nomination. "Let me be plain and say that I regard your position . . . very much like that on the Temperance question of the Clergyman who apologizes for rumselling, or the deacon that keeps a respectable rumselling hotel," Henry B. Stanton had snapped at Giddings in late 1847. Stanton, an original antislavery rebel from Lane Seminary,

148

had at this time replaced Joshua Leavitt as editor of the *Emancipator* and now spoke for large portions of the Liberty party. He had been certain that Giddings would barter principle for party once the Whig presidential convention had tapped "Old Zak." [36]

But such Liberty leaders began changing their minds as they watched Giddings defy his party on the Speakership and battle manfully for the abolition of slavery in the District of Columbia. While Stanton waited for Giddings to present his evidence against Winthrop to the *Atlas*, he penned a second letter apologizing for the earlier tongue lashing: "I feel still more disinclined to come into conflict with you, knowing as I do that we agree on more points than we differ in." [37] Lewis Tappan, who knew little about politics but was an expert on moral consistency, was one of the most bitter and constant Liberty party critics of the antislavery Whigs. Yet he acted even more friendly than Stanton in assuring Giddings that his "course this session" had "greatly endeared" him "to the friends of Human Rights." "Giddings has improved wonderfully in his *tone* and *temper* since 1844," enthused another Liberty man.[38] While Giddings' struggle with Winthrop continued to make ever more permanent the divisions among the Northern Whigs, his activities were also causing an important segment of Liberty party opinion to re-evaluate its position. Many third party men soon discovered themselves far more favorable toward union with the dissident antislavery groups within the two major parties.

In the meantime, the Whig newspapers in Ohio and Massachusetts continued to batter at one another while awaiting Giddings' proof. "Things are rapidly coming to an issue, and the feeling on our side . . . grows firmer," Charles Francis Adams reported.[39] By early March the testimony was in Sumner's hands, which itched for the first opportunity to make it public.[40] The sudden death of John Quincy Adams, however, put the entire controversy into abeyance, for none wished to revive it during the period of mourning.[41] Probably no one save Adams' own

149

family agreed more completely with this opinion than did Giddings.

After his dearest friend had collapsed on the floor of the House on February 22,[42] Giddings remained constantly at his bedside, wiping the perspiration from Adams' forehead and massaging the old man's hands. While Adams was slowly and quietly slipping away, Giddings grieved more deeply than he ever would again: "I am incapable of business and will appropriate my time to watch the exit of my dying friend." Adams expired on February 23. Winthrop's petty and inexcusable act of purposely overlooking Giddings in appointing the congressional funeral entourage mattered very little compared to the "departure of one who was dear to me, and whose friendship gave me more pleasure than that of any other man." [43]

The Boston *Atlas* shook Giddings out of his bereavement on March 17 by publishing the long-awaited proof. The evidence took the form of five letters from Northern Whig congressmen, each of whom bore witness to as many of Giddings' allegations as he honestly could. All agreed a Whig caucus had met, and only one writer could not place Winthrop in attendance. After that, testimony became a bit more uneven. Robert Schenck, one of the fourteen who voted against the war, could not remember anything else, and four of the other witnesses were not certain whether Winthrop had made a formal speech in favor of hostilities. But Erastus D. Culver, another antiwar Whig, was emphatic that Winthrop had told the caucusing Whigs "we must not oppose the measure; that *policy* would require us to support it." All but Schenck confirmed that Winthrop had circulated among the members on the floor of the House, urging them to vote for the declaration of war. Columbus Delano remembered Winthrop's arguments "very well," and Luther Severance of Maine, a member of the 1843 insurgency, judged Giddings "unquestionably correct" in this part of his indictment. One colleague had given A. Robert McIlwaine of Ohio "distinctly to understand" that Winthrop had been trying his best to influence undecided

Whigs.[44] The evidence, while not airtight, was very damaging to the *Atlas'* blanket denial of every word in Giddings' charges.

The *Atlas,* however, put on a bold front by attacking Giddings' personality rather than his evidence. The paper's editorial called him a victim of "seeming monomania which distracts, if it does not paralyze his reason and conscience." With the damning testimony confronting him, editor James Shouler chose the word "frivolous" to hide behind. As Giddings rightly judged, "the Atlass' [sic?] reply is a total failure. . . . I call it all twaddle." [45]

"Twaddle" or not, the entire controversy reopened. The newspapers of Boston and the Reserve assumed their previous positions, and the streams of invective flowed again. Giddings felt fully vindicated and was anxious to let the matter rest. He instructed Joseph to keep the *Sentinel* out of the fray.[46] The bitter rejoinders lasted for another month, and by this time the party had completely polarized. The Whigs in the Reserve were ready, if necessary, to follow Giddings and the Massachusetts minority *en masse* into a third party.

But Joshua Giddings still believed that bolting would not be necessary. As late as April and May, with the national convention to meet in June, Giddings had not rid himself of his chronic optimism. He felt certain McLean was "the most promising candidate . . . ," and that if he were nominated he could easily draw the Barnburners and Liberty men into the Whig party. He even experienced a momentary spasm of support for Henry Clay, which he quickly stifled.[47]

Salmon Chase, however, was of a far different mind than Giddings. Since mid-1847 this talented Liberty party manipulator had been casting his lines in every direction, trying to induce fusion between the Liberty men, the Barnburners, and the antislavery Whigs. While pressuring the Liberty party's presidential nominee, John P. Hale, to step aside in favor of a candidate with broader appeal, the persuasive Chase had begun coordinating strategy with Sumner in Massachusetts, Preston King of the Barnburners in New York, and Giddings in Washington.[48]

In Giddings, Chase found a most uncooperative coadjutor. Chase finally revealed a plan to organize a bolters' convention in Ohio, which would coincide with others already being arranged in Massachusetts and New York State. Giddings refused to lend his name to the list of sponsors, for he felt "sanguine in the belief that the Whigs will nominate no man for President whose sentiments are not known to be opposed to extending slavery." [49] Chase, no doubt marveling at Giddings' naïveté, proceeded to assemble a third party organization in Ohio which he himself could dominate. Giddings' persistent hopes for Whig reformation were now beginning to deprive him of Ohio's Free Soil party leadership.

While Giddings was forfeiting his dominance in his native state, he continued to lead antislavery agitation in Congress. In mid-April, the case of the Schooner *Pearl* plunged Washington into two days of rioting, and Giddings put himself in the center of the controversy. On April 17, Captain Daniel Drayton and his mate, William Sayres, both root-and-branch abolitionists, cast off their ship from the Washington wharves, carrying seventy-eight slaves bound for freedom. Giddings had full knowledge of this risky enterprise beforehand and was anxious for its success. But the *Pearl* became windbound on Chesapeake Bay and was captured by the navy and brought back to Washington. The slaves were quickly sold, Drayton and Sayres being sent to the District jail.[50]

The next day, Giddings demanded that Congress investigate why the two men were imprisoned, for neither man was charged with a specific crime. That evening proslavery mobs gathered in the streets, hoping to lynch Drayton and Sayres and to burn down the offices of Gamaliel Bailey's *National Era*. Giddings found several notes threatening his life under his boarding house door. He put on his coat, collared two associates, and began pushing his way through the hostile throng in front of the jail. It was an admirable display of courage, typical of Giddings. For the "first time" in his congressional career he entertained "some doubts whether blood would not flow before it was all over," as he offered legal help to Drayton and Sayres while the mob pressed in behind him. But, by standing up to the Southerners, he emerged, as usual, untouched.[51]

On April 20, John P. Hale and John G. Palfrey again thrust the issue before Congress, introducing in the Senate and House sets of resolutions similar to those Giddings had put forth. Each called for an investigation of police practices within the District, while protesting the threats against Giddings and Bailey. It took five days of bitter debate to table these proposals. Giddings kept the issue inflamed by delivering a speech which affirmed his belief that the *Pearl* Negroes had the "same right to liberty as any Congressman." When the clamor finally ended, Giddings felt satisfied that "the whole affair has thrown forward the cause of humanity more than any other incident for years," and also that "we shall have no more mobs here for some time to come." [52]

Mobs, however, were not among the major preoccupations of Americans in May and June, 1848. Presidential politics instead overshadowed all else as the Whigs trooped to Philadelphia and the Democrats to Baltimore to select their contenders. The results were anything but pleasing to antislavery men. Lewis Cass, the corpulent old war hero of 1812, received the Democratic endorsement on a platform of "popular sovereignty." This doctrine opened to possible slavery all lands taken from Mexico by the recently ratified Treaty of Guadaloupe-Hidalgo. Preston King, Samuel J. Tilden, and Martin Van Buren repudiated Cass and left the convention in disgust. The Whigs served antislavery men no better. On the fourth ballot General Taylor, despite his total lack of political experience, won out over his contenders on the strength of his "availability." The convention adopted no platform at all. Henry Wilson led the antislavery Whigs down the aisle and out the door.

Salmon Chase issued a call for a nonpartisan state convention to be held in Columbus, and the Barnburners put forth an announcement of a bolters' meeting in Utica. The Massachusetts "Conscience" Whigs proclaimed that a similar gathering would convene in Worcester, and Gamaliel Bailey advised all Liberty men to share in these various deliberations. "We are ripe and ready . . . for any movement that looks like a fusion of parties," reported one of Giddings' local operatives. People in the Reserve were "ready to pronounce a valedictory to the dead and roten [sic] carcass of the National Whig party," and the Free Soil movement was beginning. Giddings rushed home for a week's stay, announced that no "true" Whig could support Taylor, and supervised the local protest meetings which swept northern Ohio.[53]

The Ohio fusion convention was slated for June 21, and Salmon Chase had already seen to the details. The Liberty men were to meet separately. After an appropriate span of time, Chase planned to lead his party into a "spontaneous" alliance with the other bolters, whose gathering was to be held right next door. The joint assembly was then to repudiate Taylor and Cass and issue a call for a national nominating convention to be held in Buffalo. The whole proceeding worked exactly this way,[54] and Chase dominated every moment of it. Giddings' refusal to participate in the pre-convention planning now left him second to Chase in Ohio's antislavery leadership. It made little difference that Giddings, despite reservations about the political consequences and his lack of oratorical polish, had already decided to pass up the Columbus convention in favor of helping his friends in Massachusetts.[55]

At ten o'clock in the morning on June 28 the heavy wooden doors of Worcester City Hall in Worcester, Massachusetts, swung open, and 5,000 boistrous delegates and spectators jammed into the seats. Giddings, flanked by Henry Wilson, Charles Allen, Charles Francis Adams, and Sumner, sat at the speakers' table. A resolution endorsing Giddings' actions in Congress was the first agenda item, and it passed unanimously. The Ohioan then rose to deliver a stirring keynote address which "fully met the expectations of his friends." The delegates rejected Taylor and Cass with a chorus of groans and adopted resolutions calling for a national convention to meet in Buffalo on August 9.[56] But

Giddings' triumphal tour of the Bay State was just starting.

His next stop was Lowell, Massachusetts, which Giddings judged "the hardest place in all New England to start the ball of freedom." Here he addressed two thousand listeners at an outdoor rally. Cheers thundered after every paragraph and drowned out the scattered hisses of the "Hunkers." [57] In Boston's spacious Tremont Temple the audience received Giddings with frenzied ovations. Loud cries for "Giddings!" seemed to "rend the very heavens" as seven thousand people jumped to their feet, waved hats and handkerchiefs, and gave him nine hearty cheers. Identical scenes of tumult took place in Lynn and Springfield, and local conventions all over Massachusetts passed unanimous resolutions praising his conduct and character. Giddings, deeply touched, felt "amply compensated for all the toil and anxiety" he suffered in public life, for thousands of "virtuous citizens" were casting aside party and prejudice to "declare for freedom and humanity." [58]

The full significance of Giddings' endless wars with the "Cotton" Whigs had finally been revealed. Antislavery Whigs were completely aroused, and large portions of the Liberty party now acted much more friendly toward fusion because Giddings gave it his approval. The *Emancipator,* hoping to force the Buffalo convention into accepting John P. Hale as its nominee, endorsed Giddings for vice president. "These are the men, and the only prominent men that represent the anti-slavery sentiment of the country." The reputations and principles of Giddings and Hale, Stanton vowed, "are our tower of strength. . . ." Joshua Leavitt welcomed Giddings in a warm speech, promising that Liberty men "would never again be separated from him." [59] In the six months since he had chosen not to vote for Robert Winthrop, he had tried his best to save the Whigs from the "slave power." But because of his activities, no man had done more, albeit unwittingly, to galvanize the third party movement than had Joshua Giddings.

The great question of the presidential nomination now confronted every antislavery man. At their Utica convention, the Barnburners had endorsed Martin Van Buren. Liberty men, however, remained loyal to their nominee, John P. Hale. Among the antislavery Whigs opinion split over whether to support Van Buren or to push John C. McLean to the head of the ticket, for Hale's popularity was far too limited. Furthermore, Van Buren's record on slavery questions was anything but spotless. While president, he had endorsed the gag rule, slavery in the District of Columbia, and the restriction of abolitionist literature in the Southern mails. Leavitt, among others, was positive that Van Buren had "not a hair changed" since the 1830's.[60]

At first Giddings promised to back Van Buren "heart and soul," so long as the platform proved sufficiently antislavery.[61] But as opposition to the "little magician" mounted he began having second thoughts. When Van Buren refused in July to make a clear statement of his opinions on sectional questions, Giddings started thinking that any other nominee would make a better showing in Ohio.[62] He made straightway for the chambers of John C. McLean to convince the judge to contest Van Buren, or at least to accept the vice presidential nomination. "In either case," Giddings implored, "you will perceive that you must of course stand first at the next Presidential election, when we all believe we shall undoubtedly triumph." [63] McLean remained aloof. To the dismay of many "Conscience" Whigs and Liberty men, Van Buren encountered little opposition. When the Buffalo convention opened on August 8, Salmon P. Chase, McLean's principal booster, had no choice but to withdraw the judge's name.[64] From this point on the Barnburners dominated every decision of the gathering.

Giddings was only one of many who had to choke down their distaste as the "Red Fox of Kinderhook" took the nomination and content themselves instead with a platform pledging "free soil" as only one item of a partial denationalization of slavery. Certain Liberty party leaders simply could not stomach either the limited doctrines of the new party or the note of expediency on which it was being formed. Gerrit Smith, William Goodell, and F. Julius LeMoyne, recognizing that joining the Buffalo convention meant the trading of moral purpose for votes, left the proceedings to form a fourth party. Their "Liberty League," based on the doctrine that the Constitution sanctioned abolition, was to remain active through the election of 1860. It preserved the scruples of its adherents while acting, along with the Garrisonians, as a repository for the untarnished ideal of emancipation.

Joshua Leavitt claimed at the time that the Liberty party had not died in Buffalo but had simply been "translated" into something larger without loss of principle. His statement was sincere but wrong. Several of the most high-minded political abolitionists, such as James G. Birney, soon dropped out of sight, smothered by professional politics. Others like Henry B. Stanton, who in 1847 had so vehemently chastised Giddings for lack of principle, were to discard their own antislavery ethics in pursuit of political careers.[65]

But for Giddings the Free Soil party represented an advance in position, not a retreat. Unlike other antislavery Whigs such as Horace Greeley or Ben Wade, Giddings had finally chosen to cut all ties with his old party. Despite the opportunistic nature of the proceedings, Free Soil doctrines did far less violence to his beliefs than they did to those of Joshua Leavitt or Gamaliel Bailey. Futhermore, he was stoutly to defend a most radical interpretation of this platform in the same manner that he had always proclaimed the Whig party to be an antislavery enterprise. Despite Joshua Leavitt's pronouncements to the contrary, organized abolitionism in politics had expired. Still Joshua Giddings remained uncompromised in his mission to denationalize slavery with high-minded moral arguments. In this manner he was to avoid the pitfalls of Henry B. Stanton's later career.[66]

Nevertheless, the convention's choice of Charles Francis Adams for the vice-presidency did little to reconcile Giddings to Van Buren. The *Sentinel* could only promise that the Reserve would sacrifice all its "deep seated prejudices," for "whatever may be said against Mr. Van Buren, (and there is much) it can never

157

be charged that he ever violated a pledge or abandoned his friends." If, like Charles Sumner, Giddings felt he was "marching to Zion" via Free Soil, he began the trip with serious misgivings.[67]

By July 20 the *National Era* gave up trying to report political events in Ohio. "We could not find room enough for even brief notices of all the Free Soil meetings," it explained. "The people there seem to be cutting loose *en masse* from the old party organizations." [68] If anything, the tempo had picked up considerably by the time Giddings arrived at home and took to the stump. By one estimate, an average of two Free Soil rallies a day took place from early August until the day of the presidential election.[69] The enthusiasm proved contagious. Giddings, relieved that the people had received the nomination so cheerfully, soon was predicting Van Buren to carry the Reserve with greater ease than had Harrison in 1840.[70]

The Whig organization within the District vanished. Thomas Corwin, addressing a lethargic audience in Cleveland on the merits of Taylor, was startled to hear unexpected applause. He looked up just in time to see his effigy, hanging from a tree, go up in flames.[71] The local conservatives were astounded when the Whig congressional convention passed a resolution that no candidate should be nominated who was "not a true Whig" and then voted unanimously for Giddings to run again.[72] The few remaining Whigs, led by Benjamin Wade, forced themselves to coalesce on the local level with the hated Democrats. Together they nominated one Bushnell White to oppose Giddings. The Conneaut *Reporter* and the Cleveland *Herald* joined with the Cleveland *Plain Dealer* in endorsing White. Their campaign slogan was "Between White and Giddings no *white* man would hesitate for a moment." [73]

Meanwhile, Giddings plunged into one of the most exhausting campaigns of his life, for the Taylor men opened an intensive canvass. "Everything that can put three words together is on the stump," Ben Wade declared. Horace Greeley issued a circular to Reserve voters castigating the Free Soilers. Wade, anticipating Giddings' defeat, reported with satisfaction that "all the famous heads of the Whig Party from the state of New York, this state, and Kentucky . . ." had planned extended appearances in Ohio.[74] Giddings also spoke in nearly every center of population, traveling sixty miles and making at least three two-hour orations a day. He appeared in almost every southern and central Ohio town, occasionally pairing himself with Thomas Corwin for debates. Giddings even allowed his enthusiasm to carry him to Columbus, where he met with the Whig State Committee and proposed with a completely straight face that they declare the party's demise and "go in for free soil." [75]

The results of the state elections in October foreshadowed disaster for Taylor in Ohio. The Democrats won small pluralities in both chambers of the state legislature, but fourteen Free Soilers held the balance of power in the House. Seabury Ford, the lackluster Whig gubernatorial nominee, was elected by a slim margin only because the Free Soilers had chosen not to run a candidate of their own. Giddings campaigned on the assertion that the Whig party had abandoned its "true principles" by nominating Taylor. Orthodox constitutionalism now resided exclusively in the doctrines of the Free Soilers, Giddings maintained. His own position had not changed a bit; the Whigs were the real deviators. The farmers and mechanics of the Reserve, no less suspicious of innovation in 1848 than they had been in the 1830's, agreed overwhelmingly with Giddings' appeals to tradition. He carried every county in his district and defeated his coalition opponent by over 3,000 votes. Further west, Giddings' antiwar ally, Joseph M. Root, also succeeded in obtaining a congressional seat as a Free Soiler.[76]

In November, Van Buren carried the Reserve, Lewis Cass triumphed in Ohio, and the Whig party in the state received a blow from which it never fully recovered.[77] Nationally, Van Buren garnered not one electoral vote, but Free Soil defections in New York swung the state and the nation to Zachary Taylor. A handful of Free Soil congressmen were elected. The white-hot issue

159

of extending slavery into the expanses taken from Mexico had now begun to polarize America's political opinion. The next sessions of Congress promised to magnify sectional hostility rather than to arrest it.

NOTES

[1] Gatell, *John Gorham Palfrey*, 140; JRG to Charles Sumner, December 4, 1847, Sumner MSS, HL (quotation); JRG to Seth M. Gates, December 4, 1847, Gerrit Smith-Miller MSS, SUL; JRG to LWG, December 5, 1847, Giddings MSS; JRG to Charles Francis Adams, December 7, 1847, Adams Family MSS, MHS.

[2] JRG to LWG, December 5, 1847, Giddings MSS; John G. Palfrey to Robert C. Winthrop, December 5, 1847, Robert C. Winthrop to John G. Palfrey, December 5, 1847, in Robert Charles Winthrop, Jr. (ed.) *A Memoir of Robert C. Winthrop* (Boston, 1897), 68–70; JRG to Charles Sumner, December 26, 1847, Sumner MSS, HL.

[3] Gatell, *John Gorham Palfrey*, 144.

[4] *Ibid.*, 144–45; U.S. *Congressional Globe*, 30th Cong., 1st Sess., XVII, 2–3; Winthrop, *Memoir of Robert C. Winthrop*, 71–72.

[5] Gatell, *John Gorham Palfrey*, 145; JRG to Charles Francis Adams, December 7, 1847, Adams Family MSS, MHS (quotation).

[6] *Ibid.;* JRG to Charles Francis Adams, December 15, 1847, Adams Family MSS, MHS (quotation).

[7] U.S. *Congressional Globe*, 30th Cong., 1st Sess., XVII, 23–24; *National Intelligencer*, December 16, 1847; Cleveland *Herald*, December 22, 1847; *National Whig*, quoted in the Cleveland *True Democrat*, December 23, 1847.

[8] JRG to LMG, December 26, 1847, Giddings MSS.

[9] Cleveland *Herald*, January 5, 1847.

[10] JRG to Charles Francis Adams, December 7, 1847, Adams Family MSS, MHS.

[11] This point is mentioned, for David Donald in his *Charles Sumner and the Coming of the Civil War*, 160–161, presents a different view of the controversy. He sees Sumner as the instigator of the quarrel, the

161

source of the initial public attack upon Winthrop, and the person largely responsible for the editorial war which followed. Actually, Giddings' charges against Winthrop had been circulating in Ohio papers for ten days before Sumner had them rerun in the Boston *Whig*, and there was no reason for Sumner not to believe Giddings. After all, Giddings had already seen fit to put his accusations in the press.

12 Cleveland *Herald*, January 12, 1848; Conneaut *Reporter*, January 6, 1848; Ashtabula *Sentinel*, January 17, 1848; Painesville *Telegraph*, January 19, 1848.

13 Cleveland *True Democrat*, January 10, 1848.

14 Boston *Whig*, January 15, 1848, Boston *Atlas*, January 27, February 3, 1848, in JRG Scrapbook, 1848, Giddings MSS (quotation); Charles Francis Adams to JRG, February 17, 1848, Giddings MSS.

15 Cleveland *Herald*, February 9, 1848; Boston *Atlas*, January 29, February 3, February 18, 1848, Boston *Daily Advertiser*, February 17, February 19, 1848, in JRG Scrapbook, 1848, Giddings MSS.

16 JRG to Charles Sumner, January 28, 1848, Sumner MSS, HL; JRG to JAG, January 22, 1848, Giddings MSS.

17 JRG to JAG, May 13, 1846, Giddings MSS.

18 JRG to David Lee Child, February 13, 1847, Child MSS, BPL.

19 Charles Sumner to JRG, February 3, 1848, Giddings MSS. Charles Francis Adams also exhorted Giddings to "begin gathering up paper" against Winthrop in order to "strip off the covering" of "equivocation" to which the Speaker had resorted. Charles Francis Adams to JRG, February 10, 1848, Giddings MSS.

20 JRG to LMG, February 6, 1848, Giddings MSS; JRG to Robert C. Winthrop, February 7, 1848, Robert C. Winthrop MSS, MHS; Robert C. Winthrop to JRG, February 7, 1848, reprinted in the Cleveland *True Democrat*, March 28, 1848.

21 JRG to JAG, January 25, 1848, Giddings MSS.

22 JRG to JAG, February 11, 1848, Giddings MSS.

23 JRG to JAG, February 11, February 17, 1848, Charles Sumner to JRG, February 11, 1848, Giddings MSS.

24 JRG to Charles Francis Adams, December 7, 1847, Adams Family MSS, MHS; JRG to JAG, January 12, 1848, Charles Francis Adams to JRG, December 8, 1847, Giddings MSS.

[25] John G. Palfrey to Charles Francis Adams, December 20, 1847, Adams Family MSS, MHS.

[26] JRG to LMG, February 20, 1848, Giddings MSS.

[27] JRG to LWG, January 30, 1848, Giddings MSS; Palfrey told his wife regarding Giddings that "I have scarcely known the man whom I so entirely respect and esteem. With perfect firmness and some impetuosity, he has rare gentleness and a delicacy of character, all sustained by an enlightened and fervent piety. He looks rough, but the mildest elements are mixed up in him, and he fears God and nothing else." Palfrey, quoted in Gatell, *John Gorham Palfrey*, 165.

[28] U.S. *Congressional Globe,* 30th Cong., 1st Sess., XVII, 60, 64, 73, 82.

[29] *Ibid.,* 179–80.

[30] JRG to JAG, January 18 (?) , 1848, Giddings MSS.

[31] U.S. *Congressional Globe,* 30th Cong., 1st Sess., XVII, 268, 304, 308; *Emancipator,* February 16, 1848. Garrisonian abolitionists on the Reserve, as well as antislavery Whigs, were deeply impressed with Giddings' handling of the kidnapping case. Radicals felt that the issue was "sufficiently near to . . . the contracted vision of even an American Congress." Garrisonians hoped that "Giddings will not let the matter rest . . . but will improve all possible opportunities to bring it up again and again, and to try to infuse into some of the members as much love for freedom as he has himself. . . ." Giddings complied, and the radical abolitionists' keen (and subsequently overlooked) interest in politics had contributed to effective action. *Anti-Slavery Bugle* (Salem, Ohio) , February 4, 1848.

[32] JRG to LMG, February 20, 1848, Giddings MSS.

[33] U.S. *Congressional Globe,* 30th Cong., 1st Sess., XVII, Appendix, 380–83.

[34] Salmon P. Chase to JRG, February 29, 1848, Giddings MSS.

[35] *Emancipator,* October 13, 1847.

[36] Henry B. Stanton to JRG, November 15, 1847, Giddings MSS (quotation) ; *Emancipator,* October 20, November 24, 1847.

[37] Henry B. Stanton to JRG, December 11, 1847, Giddings MSS.

[38] Lewis Tappan to JRG, April 12, 1848, Giddings MSS (quotation) ; William Chaplin to Gerrit Smith, March 25, 1848, Gerrit Smith-Miller MSS, SUL (quotation) .

[39] Charles Francis Adams to JRG, February 17, 1848, Giddings MSS.

[40] JRG to LWG, March 5, 1848, Charles Sumner to JRG, March 13, 1848, Giddings MSS. Contrary to David Donald's assertion (see Donald, *Sumner,* 161), Sumner was not at all disappointed with Giddings' evidence and did not find it lacking in conclusiveness: "I am anxious not to lose the chance of its publication in the Atlas [sic]," he wrote to Giddings. Sumner did not feel he was about to be caught in a lie, although Donald alleges the opposite.

[41] *Ibid.*

[42] Donald, *Sumner,* 161.

[43] JRG to LMG, February 22, 1848, Giddings MSS; JRG to LWG, February 27, 1848, Giddings MSS (both letters quoted).

[44] Boston *Atlas,* March 17, 1848, JRG Scrapbook, Giddings MSS.

[45] Boston *Atlas,* reprinted in the Cleveland *Herald,* April 5, 1848; JRG to JAG, March 19, 1848, Giddings MSS (quotation).

[46] Boston *Atlas,* reprinted in the Cleveland *Herald,* April 5, April 19, 1848; Cleveland *True Democrat,* March 28, April 3, April 20, April 21, 1848; Painesville *Telegraph,* April 19, 1848; JRG to JAG, March 19, 1848, Giddings MSS.

[47] JRG to Seth M. Gates, April 27, 1848, Gerrit Smith-Miller MSS, SUL (quotation); JRG to David Lee Child, May 27, 1848, Child MSS, BPL; JRG to JAG, March 19, April 15, 1848, Giddings MSS; JRG to Salmon P. Chase, March 16, 1848, Chase MSS, HSP.

[48] Salmon P. Chase to JRG, February 29, 1848, Giddings MSS; Charles Sumner to Salmon P. Chase, February 19, 1848, Salmon P. Chase to John P. Hale, June 15, 1848, Salmon P. Chase MSS, LC.

[49] JRG to Salmon P. Chase, April 7, 1848, Chase MSS, HSP.

[50] Giddings, *History,* 273–75.

[51] *Ibid.;* U.S. *Congressional Globe,* 30th Cong., 1st Sess., XVII, 641; JRG to LWG, April 20, 1848, Giddings MSS (quotation).

[52] U.S. *Congressional Globe,* 30th Cong., 1st Sess., XVII, 649, 652–55, 658–59, 667–70; Giddings *Speeches,* 220–49, (quotation); JRG to Seth M. Gates, April 27, 1848, Gerrit Smith-Miller MSS, SUL (quotation); JRG to JAG, April 25, 1848, Giddings MSS (quotation).

[53] Charles Sumner to JRG, June 8, 1848, Giddings MSS; JRG to JAG,

June 12, 1848; Albert Gallatin Riddle to JRG, June 12, 1848, Giddings MSS (quotation) ; Painesville *Telegraph,* June 21, 1848.

[54] Cleveland *True Democrat,* June 27, 1848; *National Era,* June 29, July 6, 1848; Ashtabula *Sentinel,* July 1, 1848.

[55] JRG to JAG, June 18, June 28, 1848, Charles Sumner to JRG, June 23, 1848, Giddings MSS; JRG to Charles Francis Adams, June 17, 1848, Adams Family MSS, MHS.

[56] *New York Tribune,* reprinted in Cleveland *True Democrat,* July 4, 1848 (quotation) ; *Emancipator,* June 28, July 5, 1848.

[57] JRG to LMG, June 29, 1848, Giddings-Julian MSS., LC.

[58] JRG to LWG, July 2, 1848 (quotation) , Boston *Whig,* July 3, 1848, JRG Scrapbook, 1848, Giddings MSS.

[59] *Emancipator,* July 5, 1848.

[60] Joshua Leavitt to JRG, July 6, 1848, Giddings MSS (quotation) ; *National Era,* July 13, 1848.

[61] JRG to JAG, June 23, 1848, Giddings MSS (quotation) ; JRG to JAG, June 30, 1848, Giddings-Julian MSS, LC; JRG to Seth M. Gates, July 8, 1848, Gerrit Smith-Miller MSS, SUL.

[62] JRG to Charles Sumner, July 23, 1848, Sumner MSS, HL.

[63] John G. Palfrey to Charles Francis Adams, July 24, 1848, Adams Family MSS, MHS; JRG to John McLean, July 13, 1848, McLean MSS, LC (quotation) .

[64] Smith, *Liberty and Free Soil Parties,* 141.

[65] Oliver Dyer (ed) , *Phonographic Report of the Proceedings of the Free Soil Convention at Buffalo* (Buffalo, 1848) , 1–29; Smith, *Liberty and Free Soil Parties,* 138–42; Gatell, *John Gorham Palfrey,* 170–71; Sewell, *John P. Hale,* 102–3. For Leavitt's observations and the future course of Stanton's career see Filler, *Crusade Against Slavery,* 189. Filler best captures the delicate mixture of idealism and opportunism present at the convention.

[66] See JRG, speech at the Buffalo convention, Buffalo *Commercial Advertiser,* reprinted in the Ashtabula *Sentinel,* August 19, 1848.

[67] Ashtabula *Sentinel,* August 12, 1848; Donald, *Sumner,* 167.

[68] *National Era,* July 20, 1848.

[69] Smith, *Liberty and Free Soil Parties,* 143.

70 JRG to Thomas Bolton, August 20, 1848, Giddings Miscellaneous MSS, NYHS.

71 Cleveland *True Democrat*, September 15, 1848.

72 Ashtabula *Sentinel*, August 22, 1848.

73 Conneaut *Reporter*, September 6, 1848; Cleveland *Herald*, August 16, September 6, 1848; Cleveland *Plain Dealer*, September 13, 1848 (quotation).

74 Benjamin F. Wade to Caroline Wade, October 27, 1848, Benjamin F. Wade MSS, LC (quotations); Cleveland *Herald*, October 25, 1848.

75 JRG to JAG, October 2, October 8, October 10, October 11, 1848, Giddings MSS; JRG to Seth M. Gates, October 12, 1848, Gerrit Smith-Miller MSS, SUL (quotation).

76 For this recurring theme of Whig conservatism, see the reprint of JRG's speech on the Buffalo convention, in the Cleveland *True Democrat*, September 28, 1848. For election results, see Ashtabula *Sentinel*, October 14, 1848; Cleveland *Herald*, October 18, 1848; Cleveland *True Democrat*, November 1, 1848.

77 Cleveland *Herald*, November 15, 1848.

Chapter 9

DISCORDS,
DIVISIONS, AND
COMPROMISES

·◄ ▷·

1849-1850

Outgoing president James K. Polk indulged in wishful think-ing but also spoke for many Americans during December, 1848. His last annual message to Congress pleaded for sectional har-mony on territorial questions, calling the extension of slavery an "abstract rather than practical" issue. California and New Mex-ico should be admitted immediately under the terms of popular sovereignty, thus avoiding all needless rancor.[1] Seldom would a presidential recommendation be offered more in vain.

As soon as enough members arrived in Washington, Giddings brought the antislavery congressmen together at Mrs. Sprigg's. Among the planners were Palfrey, Amos Tuck, Wilmot, Joseph M. Root of Ohio, and two New York ex-Barnburners, Daniel Gott and A. R. McIlwaine. The gatherings annoyed some of Giddings' conservative fellow boarders, including Abraham Lin-coln of Illinois. Lincoln, a loyal Taylor supporter in the recent election, never quite adjusted to sharing quarters with so radical a man as Giddings. Early in the session a dinner table discussion of slavery questions degenerated into name-calling and "ill-humor." Giddings and Lincoln tried to soothe hurt feelings, but Giddings concluded that the future "Great Emancipator" had rather timid ideas about how to deal with the South. Despite such bickering with Taylor men, the antislavery circle was in "fine spirits" when Congress opened on December 4. They had drawn up several sets of resolutions against slavery and the slave trade within the District and had made careful plans to reintroduce the Wilmot Proviso.[2] The sectional passions Polk had hoped to smother were about to erupt with unusual virulence.

On December 13 John G. Palfrey began the antislavery offensive by introducing a resolution to abolish slavery and the slave trade within the District of Columbia. As soon as this motion was tabled after a lengthy debate, Joseph M. Root seized the floor, demanding that the Wilmot Proviso be applied to New Mexico and California. Following Giddings' call for yeas and nays, Root's measure passed on a purely sectional vote, 106–80.[3] Although this resolution was subsequently reconsidered and put down, it was clear from the opening days of the session that Giddings was directing a well-coordinated congressional machine, designed to turn the crisis over the territories into an antislavery victory.

Giddings' leadership was fully appreciated by the conservatives. They snubbed him on the streets and "looked daggars [sic]" at him in the House. Every "contemptable [sic] doughface," he told a friend, acted anxious "to hang me or send me to the penitentiary for life." Giddings, acting "perfectly indifferent" to such idle threats, pushed ahead on December 18 by offering his own measure to end servitude within the District.[4] He introduced a bill calling for a plebiscite in which "all male inhabitants" would vote for "slavery" or "liberty." Patrick W. Tomkins of Louisiana demanded to know if Negroes, free and enslaved, would be allowed to vote. Giddings replied that as he "looked abroad upon the family of man," he saw "no distinctions" among people which justified giving one man "the control of another's liberty." The bill was defeated amidst loud threats and cries of indignation.[5]

As Giddings expected, the conservatives acted "rabbid [sic]" over the plebiscite bill, but far more puzzling were the responses of his Free Soil friends. Wilmot made a special point of telling Giddings that Negro suffrage was completely out of bounds. Even Gamaliel Bailey's *National Era* castigated the bill as too extreme. When Giddings protested Bailey's lack of support, the old political abolitionist explained that his need to "maintain his own position" among the Free Soilers had forced him to oppose the measure. Giddings complained of Bailey's "want of confidence" without ever realizing the deepest implications of this incident.[6] He had experienced his first encounter with the racism and political compromise inherent in the Free Soil party. But equally important, for the first time in his career, Giddings found himself in a more radical position than Bailey and many other ex-Liberty men. To be sure, his own doctrines had not changed at all. Yet the ideals of political abolitionism, which Bailey had always espoused, were melting away before the burning issue of free soil. Bailey adjusted by compromising. Giddings stood fast and began occupying a more extreme position on the narrowing political spectrum. Edward S. Hamlin's newly founded Free Soil paper, the *Ohio Standard,* reprinted an article which put the matter succinctly. Many third party men, it said, believed that Giddings' "misguided zeal" over Negro rights drew attention from the "practical question" of keeping slavery out of the territories.[7]

Giddings, however, was not given to reflecting on such matters. Instead, he felt hopeful about victory over the South. If the assault on slavery and the slave trade in the District were stepped up, he began to believe the major parties could be "blown Sky high," and enough votes then could be mustered to denationalize slavery forever. Giddings offered this opinion to Daniel Gott, a New York representative, on the morning of December 21. Ten minutes later Gott reappeared in Giddings' room, resolutions in hand, ready to abolish the slave trade in

169

Washington. Giddings approved them, and that afternoon, to the delight of every antislavery man, they passed, 99–88.[8]

Giddings' "emotions were such that no language could describe them," while Palfrey judged the victory "the strongest blow ever dealt against Slavery in this House." Neither man's belief in the power of moral conversion allowed him to realize that it was, for the moment, bad political form for any Northerner publicly to endorse the slave trade. But it was only a matter of time before, in Palfrey's words, the "screws of the party" were applied. The resolutions were reconsidered and defeated.[9] One final attempt to end the District slave trade, a conservative formula offered on January 8 by Abraham Lincoln, was never even brought to a vote. This final setback bothered Giddings little, for he had approved Lincoln's plan only grudgingly because of its strong tinge of gradualism.[10] The assault on slavery in the District ran out of momentum, but its effect upon the South had been deeply upsetting. John C. Calhoun and several associates, shaken by the agitation and fearing Northern domination of Taylor's administration, resolved to read an ultimatum to the North threatening secession if Southern demands went unsatisfied.[11] It was a response far exceeding the piecemeal reforms which Giddings and his friends had been attempting.

Rumors of Calhoun's plan had circulated in Washington for several weeks, sending Wilmot and other Free Soilers into a cold sweat. When the Pennsylvanian aired his fears to Giddings, the Ohioan replied grimly that "the more we assail them [the Southerners] the less likely they will be to assail us." Threats of secession were "the merest humbug." [12] His opinion had not altered when, over the signature of forty-eight Southern congressmen, Calhoun's "Address to the People of the Southern States" was released to the press and printed in the *Congressional Globe* on January 15.[13]

Giddings read that the South preferred secession to slavery's exclusion from the territories and that American history was but a series of unwarranted aggressions by the North upon the

170

Southern labor system. He judged the "Address" a "very weak paper, destitute of power," and at the behest of Palfrey and others he began drawing up a reply. Calhoun's ultimatum, Giddings believed, was simply a maneuver designed to force the North into capitulation. He always read into slaveholders' promises of secession some of his own tactical methods. He was sure that Southern men employed such warnings only to make moment-to-moment gains and to convince the nation of the justness of slavery. Giddings was also certain that the Southerners' promises were basically insincere. The cries of disunion were Southerners' last weapons, complete bluffs and preludes to defeat. "They will submit," he predicted. "When this is done we will commence legislating for freedom and not for slavery." [14] Throughout his career Joshua Giddings never took seriously Southern vows to secede.

Giddings delivered his speech as a point-by-point refutation of Calhoun's "Address." He had no wish to launch epithets at either its author or signers, he announced, and the rebuttal lived up to these purposes. If the government "failed to secure and encourage oppression," which, according to Giddings, was Calhoun's real complaint, this fact provided "the best of all possible reasons for continuing the Union." Calhoun's assertions that Northern agitation disturbed slavery in the South amounted to a vindication of free speech, Giddings announced. Here was a sure sign that "justice is beginning to assert her rights, the voice of humanity is being listened to." If slavery was jeopardized, so much the better, for the nation was shaking off its lethargy. Calhoun's protests against the Northerners who attacked slavery were "superfluous," for it was "any good Christian's duty to be aware of sin." Moral men who opposed a system "based on torture and coercion" which "degrades, brutalizes and murders" human beings were facing facts, no matter how painful they were. Finally, Giddings rebuked Southerners for demanding that slavery be allowed in the territories by paraphrasing the words of the Declaration of Independence. Human governments were instituted to secure for all men the inalienable

171

rights to life, liberty, and the pursuit of happiness, Giddings maintained. Extending slavery into California and New Mexico was subversive of the Constitution, "at war with the principles of justice, and opposed to the dictates of humanity. . . ." In basic assumptions about the nature of man and government, he told his Southern listeners, "we start in different directions and while we travel we shall, of course, increase the distance between us." [15]

As Congress entered the last days of the session, however, its concern became sectional adjustment, not Giddings' and Calhoun's calls for national crisis. The territorial question remained deadlocked until February, when the Senate passed and sent to the House Isaac P. Walker's solution, opening the territories on the basis of popular sovereignty. Giddings, expecting "the enemies of freedom to triumph," advocated inaction. He feared that president-elect Zachary Taylor, recently arrived in Washington, was giving all his support to the Walker amendment. The measure would surely pass if allowed on the floor. In the next Congress, Giddings reasoned, Free Soilers would be more numerous and "better able to contend with the slave power." [16]

When this tactic failed and the House took up the amendment, Giddings tried obstruction. He led the Free Soilers in choruses of objections, quorum demands, and irrelevant motions designed to run the House out of time. Wild debate and threats of violence, including one by a drunken Virginian against Giddings, characterized the proceedings until the last day of the session. On this day, March 4, while Robert W. Johnson of Arkansas and Orlando B. Ficklin of Illinois bloodied each other's noses, the House rejected the Walker amendment. Giddings felt the burdens of anxiety lighten and considered the outcome a "significant defeat" for the South.[17] The House adjourned with the question of extending slavery no nearer resolution.

While Washington was passing through scenes of chaos, the Ohio state legislature also experienced tumultuous times in which Giddings was deeply involved. Whigs and Democrats, evenly divided in the House, were practically at war with one another over disputed elections in Salmon Chase's Hamilton County, which had been split into two districts by a blatant Whig gerrymander in 1848. Each newly created district sent two pairs of "duly elected" representatives to Columbus, and the arguments over which ones would be seated had moments of violence matching Johnson's and Ficklin's passage at arms. Under such conditions the Free Soilers, who held the balance of power, were perfectly situated to control the selection of a United States senator.[18]

Giddings and Chase both appreciated the situation and were eager to obtain the Senate seat. But they pursued far different strategies. Giddings hoped not only to obtain election but to use the contest to strengthen the independent position of Ohio's Free Soil organization. He advised the eight third party men who held the balance of power in the House not to make any concessions to the Whigs or Democrats. Such political dealing, he feared, would compromise Free Soil principles, and he wanted no one to "sacrifice . . . the paramount interests of humanity" just to secure his election. Besides, Giddings believed that if the Free Soilers stood firm the party could greatly increase its strength. In a prolonged stalemate, one of the larger organizations might capitulate to Free Soil demands, elect Giddings, and as a body adopt the third party affiliation. If this tactic did not work Giddings hoped that Free Soil independence might "drive the old hunkers of both parties to unite" on a senatorial choice. He was sure that such an outcome "would do more for our party than the election of any free soil man," for antislavery-minded Whigs and Democrats alike would finally realize the corrupt nature of the major parties. They would defect in massive numbers to the Free Soil standard, and both old organizations would dissolve.[19] No matter what the contingency, Joshua Giddings

173

had a plan which linked the senatorial election to a moral revolution in Ohio politics. His strategy, though politically unfeasible, did insure that the Free Soilers would not weaken themselves by compromising. Were he to obtain the Senate seat, he would be obliged to serve only his conscience, not the wishes of coalitionist "hunkers."

Salmon Chase showed no such concern about either his or the Free Soil party's integrity. He was anxious for national office and was in a position to logroll for it, for he had many contacts in Columbus among the Democrats, whose party he had always admired. By virtue of his eminence in Free Soil leadership Chase easily shattered the unity which Giddings hoped to preserve. In late December, 1848, two Free Soilers, Norton Townshend and James F. Morse, suddenly began voting to seat the Democratic representatives from Hamilton County. By early January they had thrown their weight behind every measure favorable to the Democrats in organizing the House. A Democratic Speaker and Clerk, each a good friend of Chase, were elected by two votes, those of Townshend and Morse. The rest of the Free Soilers who thus far had followed Giddings' advice read the deviators out of the party.[20]

Giddings, with only the fuzziest idea of what was happening, sat in Washington and fretted in his diary about the reports from Columbus: "Our members are without experience and I fear [they] will be overreached by expert politicans and designing demagogues." [21] But his wrath was directed not at Townshend or Morse but toward Nathaniel Chaffee, a Free Soiler from Ashtabula who tried dealing with the Whigs to secure Giddings' election. Giddings was completely "disgusted" at Chaffee's "want of principle" and vowed that he would "never for one moment" allow himself to be sent to the Senate under such conditions.[22] Giddings in Washington never really grasped the Byzantine nature of events taking place in the state legislature.

While Giddings was "far from . . . giving up" his chances, he noted the rancor at Townshend and Morse and moved quickly to heal developing splits within the party. The *Sentinel,* acting on his orders, denied any ill will toward the two deviant Free Soilers, saying that each would be able to justify his vote.[23] Giddings' concern for unity was completely at odds with his senatorial hopes. By trying to soothe Free Soil strife through the *Sentinel* he appeared to be indirectly endorsing Chase by defending the acts of Townshend and Morse. This dilemma, Giddings' dogged insistence upon preserving principle, and Chase's close supervision over events in Columbus left no doubt as to the outcome. In late January and early February, 1849, a quick series of deals between Townshend, Morse, and the Democrats sent Chase to the Senate. Democrats were elected to strategic judgeships with the aid of the two Free Soilers. The Democrats, in turn, repealed Ohio's obnoxious "Black Laws" and voted as a bloc along with Townshend and Morse for Chase.[24] The clear-headed pragmatist had bested the seemingly confused moralist who actually knew what was best for his party.

Giddings, accepting defeat tastefully, assured Palfrey and Sumner that Chase could "do more in the Senate than I" for the antislavery cause,[25] and graciously offered the new senator the use of his room at Mrs. Sprigg's boarding house while Chase was finding permanent lodgings in Washington.[26] But if Giddings treated Chase with courtesy and praised his qualities to others, he also felt uneasy about the repercussions of the election. Townshend and Morse were being vilified as crypto-Democrats by the Free Soil presses in the Reserve, and the statewide organization was collapsing because of events in Columbus.[27] Although Chase stood as the undisputed leader, Giddings was intent on repairing the damage before the party completely disintegrated. As soon as they arrived home in early March, he discovered that this task would prove far more difficult than he had expected. Salmon Chase himself seemed bent on destroying the Free Soil structure by merging it with the Democrats.

The apportionment of Hamilton County became Chase's vehicle for fusion; he started insisting that Free Soilers work to

175

repeal this Whiggish inequity. Were the Free Soilers to cooperate, Chase assured Giddings, "the Democrats would aid
us in consummating every free soil measure. . . ." To induce
Giddings' support of such measures, Chase even promised him
the next available Senate seat.[28] The only thing Chase neglected to make clear was that by uniting the Free Soilers and
the Democrats he would greatly strengthen his own shaky political base in Ohio.

Giddings politely refused to listen. The vast majority of Reserve Free Soilers had recently been Whigs, and most would
rather return to their old party than be even partially associated
with the "locofocos." Widespread criticisms of Townshend and
Morse for supporting "old hunker Democrats" had already
driven this point home. Giddings much preferred a policy of
keeping the Free Soilers aloof from all Whig and Democratic
squabbles. The third party, he told Chase, should "stand on
the Buffalo Platform, disregard former party sympathies," and
"let bygones be bygones." [29]

The *Sentinel* flatly demanded that the other Free Soil papers
stop attacking Townshend and Morse. At the same time Giddings
organized a special state convention in Cleveland which would
redeem the two apostates, smother the Hamilton County question, and cement party unity. Concurrently, James A. Briggs,
Giddings' friend and new editor of the Cleveland *True Democrat,* ran editorials attacking all fusion attempts as "nefarious
schemes designed . . . to end the existence of the Free Soil Party."
Chase, however, continued to push ahead, again inviting Giddings to join in the "glorious mission" of "rejuvenating" the
Democrats.[30]

To Chase, as to the vast bulk of Free Soilers, the party was
simply a temporary device for political gain. Since 1848 David
Wilmot, Preston King, and others of the ex-Democratic faction
had agreed with this position. Henry Wilson and some other
"Conscience" Whigs also looked to the Free Soil organization as
a vehicle for personal preferment. But ever since the Buffalo convention, Joshua Giddings had interpreted the nature of the

party in a far different manner. His need to feel politically loyal, which he had always satisfied through his antislavery agitation, had not at all diminished after he had abandoned the Whigs. His conviction that party decisions and moral considerations should be inextricably connected had not abated either. Politics, to Giddings, still consisted of appealing to the national conscience. Therefore, he adamantly opposed Chase's programs of compromising Free Soil principles through cooperation with the Democrats. Instead, Giddings insisted that the party must act as a permanent, independent, evangelical institution. Fusion would destroy the organization's identity and rob it of distinctive moral power. The party, he insisted, had but "one mission[:] . . . to *correct public opinion.*" Free Soilers, he argued, should not try "at present to control political action," for some day the message "shall become understood, our numbers shall increase and our influence shall strengthen." Only after "public sentiment shall be so far enlightened as to sustain our action . . ." would political considerations replace moral conversion in Giddings' mind as the rationale for an antislavery party.[31] Chase, the exponent of political victory, and Giddings, the unselfish converter of human consciences, quickly became locked in a quiet but bitter struggle over the nature of antislavery politics and the future of the Free Soil party. Chase was destined temporarily to win this contest, while Giddings preserved only his integrity.

Senator Chase did not attend Giddings' Free Soil "reunion" convention on May 2 when it met in Cleveland. Therefore, although Townshend and Morse shared the platform with Giddings and other ex-Whigs, this symbolic display of unity contained little real substance. Nevertheless, resolutions were unanimously adopted defining the Hamilton County question as "of minor importance . . . to men pledged to the principles of Human Freedom." Everyone exchanged handshakes, and Giddings, acting as president, made a conciliatory speech imploring Free Soilers to ignore partisan issues and behave like "a band of brothers." He then convinced the delegates to pass a resolution calling

177

for a national convention to meet on July 13 in Cleveland. The convention's purpose would be to preserve party harmony in every Northern state. Although it had been difficult to make the participants vote for evangelism instead of fighting with each other, Giddings felt that at least a tenuous equilibrium had been achieved.[32] He looked forward to the national convention, at which moral purpose would again confront the politics of pragmatism.

But the struggle between coalition and independence, the conflicting strategies of Chase and Giddings, was decided well in advance of the convention. In every Free Soil stronghold Chase's type of activity won out. In June the New York Barnburners allowed their deep instincts of expediency to override their anti-slavery convictions. Reunion meant patronage, and soon Preston King and David Wilmot inched their way back into the Democratic party. Former Liberty party man Henry B. Stanton also followed along in search of office. By August the process was completed. Free Soil politics in Vermont, Indiana, and elsewhere followed the Barnburners' example. In Massachusetts, Free Soil willingness to barter principle for office ultimately destroyed nearly all of John G. Palfrey's faith in the political process. Chase meanwhile continued his efforts in Ohio. Many ex-Whig Free Soilers noted their dwindling influence and quickly retreated toward their old affiliation.[33]

By mid-July, when nominations for the off-year elections were made, nearly every county in Ohio had a Free Soil platform which announced fusion with the Democrats. Even the party's name was changed, with "Free Democracy" being substituted for "Free Soil." Only a handful of independent souls, most of them left over from the Liberty party, resolved to salvage integrity in politics and continued to stand by Giddings' insistence on independence.[34] Although he scarcely sensed it, Joshua Giddings was already being left behind by many politicians within the antislavery movement. Its members were growing too amoral, too sophisticated, and too hardnosed to accommodate him. But, at the same time, Giddings' insistence on preserving principle left him at the head of a small group willing to press the public with moral issues. The methods of the old Liberty party, if not its programs, were now remanded to Joshua Giddings' care.

Giddings' July national convention in Cleveland proved a pathetic affair. John Van Buren and other Free Soil Democrats were kind enough to give complimentary speeches. Chase consented to attend, and warm letters of varying sincerity were read from Lewis Tappan, Horace Mann, Charles Francis Adams, Sumner, and Palfrey.[35] But the convention did nothing to retrieve Free Soil. Gamaliel Bailey, now forsaking completely his old commitments, judged fusion in Ohio honorable because the "work of reformation" was beginning "in the right place." In the meantime, the Democrats swept the state and the Free Soilers' vote plummeted to forty per cent of its 1848 showing. Only in Giddings' district did an independent Free Soil ticket run successfully.[36]

Giddings' summer efforts had netted him nothing save continued political security on the Reserve, but his complaint to Sumner that Chase was "unfit to lead a party"[37] was not wholly justified. Part of the problem was also that political antislavery now made gains by disregarding its principles. In many ways it was Giddings who ultimately proved "unfit" to lead in the day-to-day maneuvers of antislavery politics.

Free Soil cooperation with Whigs and Democrats did not carry over into national affairs, however, for, when the fateful Thirty-first Congress opened in December, the territorial problem of slavery had become even more tangled. California bulged with settlers and had applied for statehood with a constitution prohibiting slavery. Texas threatened war over boundary disputes with New Mexico. John C. Calhoun again talked of secession as Robert Toombs and Alexander Stephens, the leading voices of Southern Whiggery, promised to bolt the party unless it agreed to underwrite the unlimited expansion of slavery. If such men made good their promise, Free Soilers and several sympathizers would hold the balance of power in the House.[38]

179

The Free Soil Representatives had long foreseen this possibility and had organized in advance. Charles Allen of Massachusetts, Barnburners Wilmot and King, Amos Tuck of Vermont, Giddings, and Joseph M. Root had all agreed with Sumner long before the caucusing that "there must be a *breakup* of parties on the choice of a speaker at the next session." The *Sentinel* even advised the Whigs and Democrats to avoid the dangers of protracted struggle by nominating candidates pledged to denationalize slavery.[39]

Neither party followed Giddings' counsel. The Whigs renominated Robert C. Winthrop, and Robert Toombs led six Southerners out of the caucus after resolutions affirming Congress' duty to extend slavery were defeated. The Democrats selected jovial, skillful, and moderate Howell Cobb of Georgia.[40] Meanwhile, nine Free Soilers met at Mrs. Sprigg's and "solemnly pledged" to "stand by the enduring principles of truth and justice" by voting for David Wilmot. Giddings hoped that the Free Soil example would show the way to Whigs and Democrats "who hang between heaven and h........, not knowing what to do or how to act." As always, he felt that Northern men from major parties could be convinced to abandon their allegiances and adopt Free Soil ties. "At any rate," he reported, there was "a Glorious Confusion" in the ranks of the major parties, and he was emphatic that "old organizations must be broken up and new associations formed...."[41]

It took sixty-three ballots to elect a Speaker. Neither Cobb nor Winthrop could secure a majority as the bolting Southerners wasted their votes and the Free Soilers stood behind Wilmot. A few Northern Whigs and Democrats also began to stray, casting ballots for Horace Mann of Massachusetts or handsome, club-footed Thaddeus Stevens, a Pennsylvanian. Mann and Stevens, although not Free Soilers, were both reputed to hold advanced antislavery views. Neither had the endorsement of their party's caucus, and Giddings was doubtless heartened to see such a weakening of Whig and Democratic allegiances. Cobb and Winthrop soon withdrew from the election in favor of a long series

180

of trial candidates, none of whom could make any headway.[42]

This was just the sort of struggle Giddings loved. As the balloting dragged on amidst welters of proposals, objections, threats, and rebuttals, the Free Soilers sat up late at Mrs. Sprigg's, mapping strategy. Each day seemed to have "advanced the cause more than any other," as neither party could come close to a majority. Every ballot made Giddings surer that the Whig and Democratic organizations were being "knocked into pie." The Free Soil group itself struck Giddings as a fraternity of heroes. Charles Allen was "a *man*, the noblest of his race," while Joseph M. Root acted "firm" and Amos Tuck constantly rallied "under his devotion to the cause." If only enough Northern men could be goaded into converting and voting for Thaddeus Stevens or David Wilmot, "the old babel of slavery" would "begin to reel and totter like a drunken man." [43]

Although Giddings' predictions of a congressional conversion were overly enthusiastic, there was "babel" to spare as the balloting progressed from stalemate to stalemate. Robert Toombs and Alexander Stephens gave speeches which threatened violent disunion. In a prelude to their remarks, William Duer of New York called Virginia's Richard Meade a secessionist and a liar. Meade let out a string of curses and made after his accuser. Giddings sat in his seat and "laughed at a scene which from twelve years' service here" seemed rather pedestrian. He "anticipated no bloodshed," and there was none. The fracas was just another sign that the Speakership contest had begun "to assume the character of a strife between *freedom* and *slavery*." [44]

But, instead of causing party breakups, the Speakership impasse led to compromise. After an incident which found "fire-eating" Southern secessionists and Free Soilers supporting the same candidate on the basis of contradictory promises,[45] the Whigs settled the issue. They assumed the Free Soilers would end their obstructionism if faced with the prospect of a Southern Speaker, so on December 21 Winthrop was drafted to return to the race against the Georgian Cobb, who had also been put up again. Before the sixty-first ballot the Whigs introduced, by

181

pre-arrangement, a resolution declaring that only three more votes would be held. If neither Cobb nor Winthrop received a majority, the leader after the last balloting would be declared Speaker on the basis of his plurality. Once Giddings' objections had been beaten down, the House adopted the "plurality rule." But the Free Soilers blasted Whig hopes by supporting Wilmot to the last, and after the sixty-third ballot, Cobb was declared the winner, 102–100.[46] The Free Soilers had assured the election of a Southern Speaker and at the same time brought down upon themselves the wrath of national Whiggery.

Giddings took it upon himself to justify the Free Soilers' strategy by repeating all his old allegations against Winthrop and declaring that Whig and Democratic policies were enough alike to make meaningless the differences between their nominees. He maintained that the Whigs, not the Free Soilers, were responsible for Cobbs' election; the "plurality" rule had been their idea. Furthermore, the Whig party had enjoyed a majority in the House for two years under Winthrop, but the slave trades and slavery within the District had remained untouched. Whigs should have known that Free Soilers who "hate oppression and detest crime" would never support a nominee who had sustained "these continental iniquities." [47] Winthrop, red-faced and furious, listened to these explanations and tried unsuccessfully to stumble through an impromptu rebuttal. Giddings' one-time friend and fellow antiwar Whig during 1846 and 1847, Robert Schenck of Ohio, filled in by accusing Giddings of "intolerant and fanatical" sectionalism. He charged Giddings with preaching disunion while acting as a congressional agent for radical abolitionists like William Lloyd Garrison and his disunionist circle. Whig presses all over the nation carried on in similar veins.[48]

Giddings, for once, could not pretend that he was oblivious to the attacks. The vituperations hurt him deeply, and he felt he was the object of an "extensive plan concerted and put into action to crush a poor individual. . . ." For a moment, he even longed to retire, "to step aside and leave the stage for younger and more able managers. . . . Twelve years of turmoil, strife and bitter persecutions" had left him longing for "rest and repose." But, despite his depression, his conscience and combative personality had to be served. To "retreat under the hot fire" of slaveholders and "doughfaces" was unthinkable.[49] Besides, the day of reformation might be near after all. He was certain that "a few weeks" of further agitation would reveal that the Speakership impasse had already separated the Northern wings of both parties "a great degree from Southern dictation." [50] As usual, his optimistic outlook saved him from disillusion. But legislators were already talking of sectional compromise on the slavery question. Giddings' promise to apply the Wilmot Proviso to the territories and to "press the slave question is [its] various aspects" meant little as Congress set about to preserve sectional harmony.[51]

On December 31 Joseph M. Root offered resolutions applying the Wilmot Proviso to all territory taken from Mexico at the conclusion of the war by the treaty of Guadaloupe-Hidalgo, and the House buried the proposal for six weeks before rejecting it. An attempt by Giddings to affix the Declaration of Independence to all territorial bills was defeated by fifteen votes.[52] The nation's attention had shifted instead to the Senate. On January 29, 1850, the aging Kentuckian Henry Clay offered an inclusive plan to settle all outstanding sectional grievances.

He proposed that California be admitted with her free constitution. New Mexico and Utah, which were also applying for territorial status, should be allowed to enter under the terms of popular sovereignty. Congress should settle the Texas-New Mexico boundary dispute by allowing the federal government to assume the debts of the "Lone Star" state in exchange for an end to all her territorial claims. By Clay's formula, slave trading, but not slavery, in the District of Columbia was to be suppressed. To compensate for this concession to the North,

Southerners would be granted a new, far harsher fugitive slave law and guarantees that Congress would never abolish the interstate slave trade.

Once the plan was broached, the titans of American politics took their respective stands in the Senate and conducted eight months of debate and complicated political dealing. Taylor and a minority of Northern Whig senators opposed Clay's package with their own policy of admitting all territories as quickly as possible while making no concessions to Texas on boundaries. William Seward, New York state's most powerful Whig, assumed leadership in this faction. Seward, like Giddings, had made his way into the Whig party through Antimasonry, but, unlike the Ohioan, he espoused sectional convictions in a compelling, if erratic, fashion. Seward's allies included Free Soilers Chase and Hale plus maverick Democrats like Hannibal Hamlin of Maine. Hamlin, a Cass supporter in 1848, would, like Seward, wait until 1854 before endorsing an anti-Southern party. At that later date Giddings would consider both men timid conservatives. That Hale's and Giddings' sympathies momentarily lay with Seward and Hamlin was a dramatic indication of the depth of sectional feeling within the nation in 1850. Fire-eating followers of John C. Calhoun refused to entertain any thought of Southern concession and spoke at length of the possibility of secession. A large number of senators from both parties, led by Stephen A. Douglas of Illinois, followed Clay's lead rather than Seward's or Hamlin's. Douglas, an expert legislative tactician and a man of unfathomable ambition, spoke for many politicians when he pleaded that the nation avoid forever its moral dilemmas by enacting Henry Clay's proposals.[53]

Giddings, of course, judged the compromise plan to be, "as usual, all on one side" and utterly rejected Clay's idea that "our government was founded as much for the promotion of slavery as of freedom." But his hope that the bipartisan support of the Douglas Democrats and the Clay Whigs would drive the Taylorites and Democrats like Hannibal Hamlin into the Free Soil party was very naïve.[54] Besides, the proceedings were completely

184

out of his hands. The House had lost initiative and was content to rivet its attention on the Senate, where the free soil question was being decided. Daniel Webster, to the disgust of antislavery men everywhere, pleaded eloquently for compromise with his "Seventh of March" speech. Four days later, William Seward replied and electrified the nation. In his oration he denounced any accommodation with the South over the territories by appealing to a "higher law" than the Constitution itself. Such strong language undoubtedly excited Giddings. Many Americans began to anticipate, or fear, a "moral revolution" of some kind. Attempts to reach a settlement continued to occupy the Senate until August.

In the meantime, Giddings tried hard to exploit the nation's sudden concern over free soil, hoping to expand it to encompass more humanitarian reforms. In May he spoke against an amendment to an Oregon land grant bill which restricted Negroes from homesteading in the new territory. This proposal, Giddings insisted, was "not only destitute of reason but . . . absolutely *wrong.*" What sane man preferred to allow boorish white settlers into the territory merely on the strength of their "pale faces" while denying that men of "dusky hue" might have higher moral worth? Free Negroes had long established themselves as equal citizens by fighting in the Revolution and the War of 1812. Rather than submit to "groveling, narrow prejudices," the House should remember that "*all* mankind is made in God's image" and legislate accordingly. After a number of vulgar, racist jokes at Giddings' expense, the House passed the amendment and continued to bide its time with meaningless speeches.[55] A joint effort by Giddings and Thaddeus Stevens to abolish the District slave trade while securing certain legal rights for Washington's free Negroes was stifled before reaching the floor.[56] The nation was far too preoccupied with discussing the compromise measures to countenance such diversions.

On July 9 Zachary Taylor suddenly died. Millard Fillmore, a supporter of Clay's compromise, assumed the presidency, and Northern opposition to Clay's formula quickly collapsed. Giddings fully appreciated the blow, for "Old Tai" had been a "great fighter...," but Fillmore was "in favor of the Compromise or anything else that will relief [sic] him from ... responsibility." "Strange as it may seem," said the *Emancipator,* "antislavery men have more reason to regret his [Taylor's] death than have any other class of men." [57]

These observations were correct. It took only a short time for the supporters of compromise to marshal their forces. Stephen Douglas, in conjunction with Fillmore, Webster, and Clay, succeeded in breaking Clay's package down into individual bills, the first of which passed the Senate on August 9, Meanwhile, Douglas worked through his lieutenants, Lynn Boyd of Kentucky, John McClernand from Illinois, and Speaker Howell Cobb, to pave the way in the House. Die-hard Southerners like Robert Toombs agreed to vote for the compromise measures just as the Senate passed the Texas boundary bill and sent it to the House.[58]

This measure embodied one of Clay's most controversial proposals, for ten million dollars' worth of Texas bonds were to be assumed by the federal government. In exchange, Texas should drop its claims on New Mexican soil. The whole arrangement threatened to become a major sticking point; it smacked of fiscal corruption, and the price was high. Texas bondholders were lobbying vigorously for federal assumption of the bonds, and one could make a plausible case that bribery, and not the passion of sectionalism, was the principle motive behind the measure. This bill became the test case for the rest of the compromise in the House. Should it be accepted, Douglas' House machine would easily pass the other measures as the Senate sent them down.[59] Not surprisingly, Giddings decided to make the bill the focus of his rhetorical effort. In desperation he hoped that his words would stiffen the backbones of the Taylor Whigs, dispirited after the loss of their leader.

On August 12 Giddings obtained the floor and rejected Texas' territorial claims. The disputed area had never been under Texan sovereignty; Texas simply had no legal title to it. To those who feared Texas would secede if not compensated, Giddings replied that if the ten million dollars were paid to get Texas *out* of the Union, he "might perhaps vote for it." The state had embroiled the nation in trouble ever since annexation. "Now shall we crown her series of outrages upon the free States by paying her ten million dollars . . .?" Texan threats of secession were the ravings of "stock-jobbers and gamblers in Texas script" who wished to rob honest laborers of their hard-earned funds by frightening a lily-livered Congress. "The cry of dissolution has been the *dernier resort* of southern men for fifty years," Giddings declared. Threats of secession had been repeated so often that even "nervous old women" and "lovesick girls" back in Ashtabula County laughed at the idea. Rather than submit to verbal blackmail from Texas slaveholders, Congress should cease its "political effeminacy" and refuse either one dollar or one acre. He closed with an appeal to the anticompromise Taylor Whigs to reassert their collective manhood by blocking this bill and the rest of the compromise proposals.[60]

Giddings felt he had "made a impression." The "Whigs of the Old Taylor stripe" seemed infused with new resolve. With their help he even dared contemplate the defeat of the bill,[61] but as usual he overestimated the potency of words upon the consciences of his hearers. Douglas' House machine worked perfectly, and the Texas bill passed by a small majority. By mid-September the House had ratified the rest of Clay's measures, while the Free Soilers looked on helplessly.[62]

Fillmore eagerly signed each bill into law, while Clay proclaimed on the floor of the Senate, "There is, I believe, peace now prevailing throughout all our borders. . . . I believe it is permanent." [63] Meanwhile, Joshua Giddings published a letter to his constituents telling them to ignore the "unconstitutional" Fugitive Slave Law, for it denied presumed runaways the protection of habeas corpus, jury trials, and the right to give evidence, while demanding that Northerners help in enforcement. If it were obeyed, America would become "a nation of slave-hunters and slave-catchers," Giddings warned in the *Sentinel*. "We cannot be Christians and obey it." [64] Moral issues could not be obfuscated,

187

and no elected official in American politics was more finely tuned to the stark human anomaly of slavery than Joshua Giddings. Instead of smarting under this bitter defeat, he felt that the United States could descend to "no lower depth of infamy" and must, perforce, begin self-regeneration. The nation would soon discover the immoral consequences of its capitulation.[65] Several years were to pass before Clay's boasts proved hollow, but antislavery men like Giddings were anxious from the first to make his predictions false ones.

NOTES

1 U.S. *Congressional Globe,* 30th Cong., 2d Sess., XVIII, 4–6.

2 JRG Diary, December 4, December 15, 1848, Giddings MSS. Later on in the session Lincoln lost his tact, disagreeing with Giddings' and Palfrey's objectives. After Palfrey had introduced some antislavery resolutions in the House, Giddings reported that Lincoln and another messmate "were both very insulting after the adjournment." JRG Diary, December 13, 1848, Giddings MSS.

3 U.S. *Congressional Globe,* 30th Cong., 2d Sess., XVIII, 38–39.

4 JRG Diary, December 3, December 18, 1848, Giddings MSS (both entries quoted) ; JRG to Albert Gallatin Riddle, December 16, 1848, Albert Gallatin Riddle MSS, WRHS (quotation) .

5 U.S. *Congressional Globe,* 30th Cong., 2d Sess., XVIII, 55–56.

6 JRG Diary, December 17 [18], December 25, December 26, December 27, 1848, Giddings MSS.

7 Undated clipping of the *Ohio Standard* in JRG Scrapbook, 1849, Giddings MSS.

8 JRG Diary, December 20 [21], 1848, Giddings MSS (quotation) ; U.S. *Congressional Globe,* 30th Cong., 2d Sess., XVIII, 83–84.

9 JRG Diary, December 20 [21], 1848, Giddings MSS (quotation) ; Palfrey, quoted in Gatell, *John Gorham Palfrey,* 181; U.S. *Congressional Globe,* 30th Cong., 2d Sess., XVIII, 107–8; *National Era,* January 18, 1849.

10 JRG Diary, January 8 [9], January 9 [10], 1849, Giddings MSS; U.S. *Congressional Globe,* 30th Cong. 2d Sess., XVIII, 212–16.

11 Nevins, *Ordeal,* I, 223.

12 JRG Diary, December 21, 1848, Giddings MSS.

13 Nevins, *Ordeal,* I, 222.

14 *Ibid.*; JRG to LMG, January 17, 1849 (quotation), JRG to LWG, January 28, 1849 (quotation), JRG Diary, January 28, 1849, Giddings MSS.

15 U.S. *Congressional Globe,* 30th Cong., 2d Sess., XVIII, Appendix, 124–29.

16 JRG to LMG, February 25, 1849, Giddings-Julian MSS, LC (quotation); JRG to JAG, February 26, 1849, JRG Diary, February 24, February 26, 1849 (quotation), Giddings MSS; JRG to Readers," *Western Reserve Chronicle,* March 14, 1849.

17 JRG to JAG, March 4, 1849 (quotation), JRG Diary, March 3, March 4, 1849, Giddings MSS.

18 Smith, *Liberty and Free Soil Parties,* 162–64.

19 JRG to Thomas Bolton, November 14, 1848, Giddings MSS (quotation); JRG to Albert Gallatin Riddle, November 25, 1848, Riddle MSS, WRHS (quotation); Ashtabula *Sentinel,* December 2, 1848.

20 Smith, *Liberty and Free Soil Parties,* 165–68.

21 JRG Diary, January 4, 1849, Giddings MSS.

22 *Ibid.,* January 2, 1849.

23 JRG to JAG, January 23, 1849, Giddings MSS (quotation); Ashtabula *Sentinel,* January 6, 1849.

24 Smith, *Liberty and Free Soil Parties,* 169–72.

25 JRG Diary, February 23, 1849, Giddings MSS; JRG to Charles Sumner, February 25, 1849, Sumner MSS, HL (quotation).

26 JRG to Salmon P. Chase, March 3, 1849, Chase MSS, HSP.

27 *Western Reserve Chronicle,* February 28, 1849; Cleveland *True Democrat,* March 1, 1849.

28 Salmon P. Chase to JRG, March 6, 1849, Giddings MSS.

29 JRG to Salmon P. Chase, March 14, 1849, Chase MSS, HSP (quotations). See also Samuel Lewis to JRG, March 20, 1849, Giddings-Julian MSS, LC.

30 Ashtabula *Sentinel,* March 24, 1849; JRG to James A. Briggs, March 27, 1849, Briggs MSS, WRHS; JRG to Salmon P. Chase, March 28, April 12, 1849, Chase MSS, HSP; Cleveland *True Democrat,* April 12, 1849 (quotation); Salmon P. Chase to JRG, April 23–24, 1849, Giddings MSS (quotation).

[31] JRG to Salmon P. Chase, May 6, 1849, Chase MSS, HSP.

[32] Cleveland *True Democrat,* May 3, May 4, 1849; *National Era,* May 17, 1849 (quotation) ; JRG to Salmon P. Chase, May 6, 1849, Chase MSS, HSP.

[33] Smith, *Liberty and Free Soil Parties,* 178–81; Preston King to JRG, September 19, 1849, Giddings MSS; Gatell, *John Gorham Palfrey,* Chaps. 12–13.

[34] Smith, *Liberty and Free Soil Parties,* 178–81.

[35] *National Era,* July 26, August 2, 1849; Cleveland *True Democrat,* July 12, July 13, 1849.

[36] *National Era,* September 20, 1849 (quotation) ; Smith, *Liberty and Free Soil Parties,* 182; Ashtabula *Sentinel,* October 13, 1849.

[37] JRG to Charles Sumner, October 19, 1849, Sumner MSS, HL.

[38] Nevins, *Ordeal,* I, 250–51.

[39] Joseph M. Root to JRG, June 12, October 13, 1849, Preston King to JRG, September 19, 1849, Giddings MSS; *National Era,* November 15, 1849; Charles Sumner to JRG, July 3 (quotation) , July 30, 1849, Giddings-Julian MSS, LC; Ashtabula *Sentinel,* December 1, 1849.

[40] *National Intelligencer,* December 6, 1849; Holman Hamilton, *Zachary Taylor, Soldier in the White House* (Indianapolis and New York, 1951) , II, 242–45.

[41] JRG to Editor, Ashtabula *Sentinel,* December 15, 1849; New York *Evening Post,* reprinted in the *Emancipator,* December 13, 1849; JRG to LWG, December 2, 1849, Giddings MSS (quotations) ; JRG to John G. Palfrey, December 4, 1849, John Gorham Palfrey MSS, HL.

[42] Hamilton, *Zachary Taylor,* 244–245.

[43] JRG to JAG, December 8, December 12, December 15, 1849, Giddings MSS (all letters quoted) .

[44] U.S. *Congressional Globe,* 31st Cong., 1st Sess., XIX, 23, 27–30; JRG to GRG, December 14, 1849 (quotation) , JRG to JAG, December 8, 1849 (quotation) , Giddings MSS.

[45] JRG to Editor, Ashtabula *Sentinel,* January 5, 1850; *National Era,* December 20, 1849; *National Intelligencer,* December 13, 1849; Joshua Leavitt to JRG, December 15, 1849, JRG to LMG, December 16, 1849, Giddings MSS.

46 For full references to debates and votes on the Speakership see U.S. *Congressional Globe*, 31st Cong., 1st Sess., XIX, 1–66; for the plurality rule see 63–65.

47 *Ibid., Appendix,* 35–40.

48 *Ibid.* (text), 80, Appendix, 40–43 (quotation); "Washington Correspondence," *Ohio State Journal,* January 7, 1850; Boston *Atlas,* January 3, 1850, JRG Scrapbook, 1850, Giddings MSS.

49 JRG to Henry Fassett, January 5, 1850, Giddings MSS.

50 JRG to Albert Gallatin Riddle, December 30, 1849, Giddings MSS.

51 JRG to JAG, January 20, 1850, Robert S. Pierce MSS, WRHS.

52 U.S. *Congressional Globe*, 31st Cong., 1st Sess., XIX, 91, 276–77.

53 For a brilliant, brief treatment of the 1850 Compromise, see Holman Hamilton, *Prologue to Conflict: The Crisis and Compromise of 1850* (Lexington, 1964), *passim.* Also useful is Filler, *Crusade Against Slavery,* 199–200; Glyndon G. Van Deusen, *William Henry Seward, Lincoln's Secretary of State, the Negotiator of the Alaska Purchase* (New York, 1967), 113–34.

54 JRG to Charles Francis Adams, January 30, 1850, Adams Family MSS, MHS (quotation); JRG to JAG, January 30, February 3, 1850, Giddings MSS.

55 U.S. *Congressional Globe*, 31st Cong., 1st Sess., XIX, 1690–93.

56 The undated draft of this proposal is found in the Thaddeus Stevens MSS, LC. It is written in Giddings' hand and was amended by Stevens. This session was the only logical time at which it could have been introduced, for this was the only session in which Stevens served while the District slave trade operated.

57 JRG to LWG, July 14, 1850, Julian MSS, ISL (quotation); JRG to JAG, July 22, 1850, Giddings MSS (quotation); *Emancipator,* July 18, 1850.

58 Hamilton, *Prologue to Conflict,* 133–50; William Y. Thompson, *Robert Toombs of Georgia* (Baton Rouge, 1966), 63–76; U.S. *Congressional Globe*, 31st Cong., 1st Sess., XIX, Part II, 1555–56.

59 Hamilton, *Prologue to Conflict,* 155; Nevins, *Ordeal,* I, 342–43.

60 U.S. *Congressional Globe,* 31st Cong., 1st Sess., XIX, Appendix, 1224–28.

[61] JRG to JAG, August 15, August 22, 1850, Giddings MSS (both letters quoted).

[62] Nevins, *Ordeal*, I, 342–44.

[63] Clay, quoted in Sewell, *John P. Hale,* 139.

[64] JRG to Editor, Ashtabula *Sentinel,* September 21, October 5, 1850.

[65] JRG to Editor, Ashtabula *Sentinel,* September 14, 1850.

Chapter 10

THE
CONSERVATIVE
ASCENDANCY

•◄ ▶•

1850-1853

The Compromise of 1850, accepted grudgingly by most congressmen at first, quickly became an object of veneration. National politicians, shaken by their recent flirtation with sectional disruption, vowed that the Compromise measures amounted to a "final solution" of slavery questions. The abiding desire to avoid conflict also determined party behavior in Ohio, as continued fusion with the Democrats nearly extinguished the state's Free Soil organization. Elections in the spring of 1850 for delegates to a state constitutional convention completed the merger in every Ohio district except one, that of Joshua Giddings. Here, as in 1848, Whigs and Democrats united against the Free Soilers but made a poor showing. Giddings had carefully nurtured his independent local party, warding off all possible splits and compromising all jealousies between his local supporters. He felt no uneasiness in the summer of 1850 about attempting re-election without dealing with either old organization.[1]

After the ballots had been counted, the results announced the ruin of Ohio's third party as an independent reform movement. Giddings alone succeeded as an independent representative, and the Free Soil nominee for governor, Samuel Lewis, polled only one-third of Van Buren's 1848 total.[2] As Giddings traveled from Jefferson to Washington in December, 1850, he had only two goals in mind. The national conscience had to be reawakened to the enormity of its compromises between human freedom and slavery, and the Free Soil party had to be re-established. Both problems, being interconnected, required the same approach—agitation. At age fifty-five, Joshua Giddings decided to begin his career all over again.

Symbolic of his fresh start was Giddings' move out of Mrs. Sprigg's rooming house after thirteen years as a loyal renter. He selected as his new messmates "first rate free-soilers" like Charles Durkee of Wisconsin and Charles Allen of Massachusetts. But Giddings' favorite among his fellow boarders was George Washington Julian, an earnest young representative from Indiana. Julian had admired Giddings long before coming to Congress. He had found substantiation for his own antislavery convictions by reading reprints of the older man's speeches, and he was destined for a vigorous and successful career in the Free Soil party. Later on, Giddings' example was significant for Julian's most important activities during the Civil War and Reconstruction. The two men became fast friends and later on relatives by marriage; in 1861, Julian took Giddings' youngest daughter, Laura Ann, as his wife. Julian was to spend his last years writing a laudatory biography of his mentor.[3]

Despite the camaraderie established within Giddings' little circle, all other congressmen carefully avoided contact with the antislavery partisans. David Wilmot, Preston King, and other ex-Barnburners never stopped by to discuss strategy, for it was no longer in their interest to be identified with sectionalism. For the first time since 1841 Giddings was unable to gather at least eight colleagues around him. This scarcity of followers was a clear indication that the fire of reform in national politics had nearly died out. Congress now wanted, more than anything else, to ignore the question of slavery. "Their plan is to stifle all debate and all agitation," Giddings reported, "but I have had too much experience in this work to be headed off course by such miserable evasions." [4] Millard Fillmore unwittingly gave Giddings a chance to redeem this promise and to hurl defiance at the conservatives, for the president defended the Fugitive Slave Law in his annual message. Giddings' reply, made on December 9, signaled the beginning of an arduous personal campaign to retrieve the antislavery movement from its lowest ebb since 1830. His astounding tenacity and carefully cultivated political independence equipped him perfectly for the job.

Fillmore had promised to use all his powers to enforce the Fugitive Slave Law, even to the point of calling out federal troops. "This taunting menace should never have been addressed to free men," Giddings announced, for no morally upright Northerner would obey the law, no matter how many "swiss guards of slavery" Fillmore might deploy. By passing the fugitive bill, Congress had overstepped the limits of civil government in order to "usurp powers that belong only to God," for the statute commanded "the perpetuation of crimes that no human act can justify." Good Christians "faced with the choice of whether to obey God or the oppressors of mankind" would obviously follow "the higher law of kindness, benevolence and humanity. . . ."

The President had stated further that the Compromise measures would restore sectional harmony if all Americans would only support them. "Vain advice," Giddings warned, "Agitation will never cease until the [Fugitive Slave] law ceases. While such crimes are authorized by statute, the American people will not keep silent." Neither would he stop disturbing Congress until slavery was completely separated from the federal government.[5]

Giddings had become the first national politician to break the new "conspiracy of silence" surrounding slavery, and the "hunkers" acted "perfectly rabid, *hydrophobic*," [6] just as they used to during the early gag rule debates. "Never was a set of poltroons so alarmed as they were at my speech," he judged proudly. "Our cause is going forward here." [7] All the old techniques of the early 1840's were working again; the conservative presses responded to Giddings' rhetoric by putting slavery questions back into the headlines. The Washington *Globe* called Giddings' views "unpalatable and erroneous," the Boston *Atlas* branded him an anarchist, and the Cleveland *Herald* said that his conduct was disgraceful. Congressmen of both parties signed their names to well-publicized agreements which upheld the Compromise measures and "outlawed" agitation.[8] Giddings' old optimism began to quicken as he noted this display of uneasiness.[9] But he had no allies to help push sectional issues back into the forefront. Even his messmates, Allen, Durkee, and Julian, often refused to speak up, and the New York Free Soilers remained content to associate with their Democratic friends. Once Giddings even read a short lecture on the floor of the House to former antislavery men for keeping their "lips sealed in relation to the Fugitive Law during the entire session...." [10]

In mid-February, Henry Clay delivered a racist philippic in the Senate against an integrated mob of Boston abolitionists which had rescued a runaway named Shadrach from the custody of federal marshals, commissioned under the Fugitive Slave Law.[11] Giddings, in turn, castigated Clay's "bad taste" on the floor of the House. The rescuers, Giddings maintained, were defying tyranny, just as the Sons of Liberty had done at the Boston Tea Party. When John Mason of Virginia interrupted to ask if Giddings endorsed mob violence and civil disobedience, the Ohioan replied that his decision depended strictly on whether or not the slave and his rescuers had a good chance of winning in a "clear field and a fair fight." [12] As incidents like the Shadrach case became increasingly frequent after 1851, Giddings continued to channel their popular impact into the halls of Congress. The process was little different than during the petition campaigns of ten years before, when Giddings had first helped link abolitionist projects to debates in the House of Representatives.

But agitation, as always, meant little to Giddings without a stable party behind him to act as a sounding board for his evange-

197

lism. A perceptive conservative observer, noting Giddings' activities, cautioned that "the fortunes and destinies of the party arrayed against Fillmore" had been committed to Giddings' keeping. Friends of the Compromise would do well to keep track of the Ohio congressman, for his activities were of "very great importance" to those wishing the end of sectional politics.[13] This warning was accurate, for Giddings designed his verbal exercises as preludes to his painstaking and successful effort to rebuild the defunct Free Soil party.

As he made his way back to Jefferson in March, Giddings paid scant attention to developments in the Ohio legislature. Nominal Free Soilers again held the balance of power in the House, and Thomas Corwin had vacated his Senate seat. Salmon Chase was anxious that Giddings be selected for the spot with Democratic help, in order to control his last leading opponent of permanent fusion,[14] but Giddings was hardly interested in Chase's overtures. He sent out the customary advice that no Free Soiler should barter for his election, while confiding with candid accuracy to a friend that he lacked the brains and ambition to act effectively in the Senate.[15] When the legislature finally chose his old enemy Benjamin Wade, Giddings grudgingly endorsed him and let the matter drop,[16] for he had preserved to the last his political independence from Chase. Now he was perfectly situated to begin rejuvenating the Free Soil party in time for the state elections of 1851 and the 1852 national contest, no matter what course Ohio's senior senator might pursue.

Despite his humiliating failures in 1849 to preserve the party through a series of conventions, Giddings adopted the same approach a second time. The decision took a good bit of courage and also meant a summer of hard labor. But he was aided considerably by the unpopularity of the Fugitive Slave Law, which had led to open defiance of civil authorities by abolitionists in Boston, Syracuse, and other places. The measure caused even Gamaliel Bailey to recall the merits of moral suasion and to reexamine his position on fusion.[17] Furthermore, the new state constitution, a product of Democratic legislators, was distasteful to some antislavery men, for it denied suffrage to free Negroes. Giddings' Ashtabula *Sentinel* wasted no time in pointing out that this "outrage on a valuable class of people" might not have happened, had the Free Soilers spurned the false promises of the "locos." Now the *Sentinel* insisted that the party acknowledge its errors and reorganize. "The old issues of tariffs, sub-treasury and banks have lost their charm. The *right of man to himself, to his life, his intellect, his liberty* is . . . of higher importance." [18] The issue of Negro suffrage in a free state, for one of the few times in ante-bellum history, had become a political club in the hands of its supporters.

Giddings was deeply in earnest while making these appeals on behalf of the Negro in Ohio. In his campaign to rebuild the Free Soil party he did not exploit this issue simply to get support from people of reform opinions. Yet, it must be emphasized that Giddings never once endorsed total Negro equality on either a national basis or throughout the free states only. The reasons for his confusing stance can be only partially reconstructed. Doubtless, prejudice entered into his thinking, a natural consequence of a society ridden with Negrophobia. Although he never revealed open racism in his letters, he did view the black man in a paternalistic way, often referring publicly to the panting fugitive" who simply needed to be fed, clothed, and taught the rudiments of religion by the kindly white. Giddings admired outstanding Negroes of his day, like Frederick Douglass and Charles Remond, and was unabashed in praising their high qualities to others. Yet Douglass and Remond represented to Giddings what some Negroes might become if sufficiently uplifted by white philanthropy. With such views, Giddings was obviously unwilling to sponsor unreserved equality for every man in the nation.[19]

Furthermore, Giddings' antislavery doctrines, which denied immediate abolition, were far too narrow to sustain any federal legislation for complete political freedom. His belief in the right of each state to regulate its own institutions led him to his program to denationalize slavery but not to abolish it. He would argue

199

that Ohio should repeal its discriminatory laws but that the people of New York or South Carolina were free to make their own decisions in such matters.

Nevertheless, Giddings did not balk at endorsing unqualified Negro freedom for fear of political harm. He gained no popularity by demanding in Congress that the federal government end restrictive practices for which it was solely responsible. Fellow representatives always responded with curses and abusive laughter, and the Northern press issued distasteful editorials about his love for "niggers." By opposing Ohio's segregationist constitution in 1851, Joshua Giddings was not just looking for an issue on which to rally the Free Soil party. Although not living up to modern "liberal" creeds, he saw in white America injustices that most citizens were anxious to defend and to perpetuate.

While the *Sentinel* broadcasted its calls for Free Soil reformation, Giddings held private meetings with local associates to advance the same program. Old friends like Edward Wade, Ephriam Brown, and John Hutchins had proved their worth by helping to keep fusion out of the Twentieth District. By early April all three men had agreed with Giddings' plan to organize a statewide rally to reassert the policy of "standing firmly upon our independent organization." They rebuffed coldly Chase's attempt to turn the proposed convention into a coalition meeting,[20] and a month later Giddings presided over a district gathering in Painesville. He offered a strong set of resolutions which called for a total revamping of the party. He also announced that he had planned an organizational meeting, which would be held in Ravenna on June 26 without formal delegations.[21] A movement which soon reached national proportions had its roots in this modest beginning.

Despite a painful spill from his wagon which cost him two broken ribs and a week in bed, Giddings was on hand to preside over the Ravenna meeting.[22] Unlike the 1849 fiasco, this enterprise proved a brilliant success. When the old "apostates," Townshend, Morse, and Chase, again shared the platform with Ohio's leading independents, Samuel Lewis, Edward Wade, and Joshua

200

Giddings, the display of unity was real. Every one of the two thousand spectators cheered loudly when the band played a funeral dirge for Daniel Webster, and they glowed with the spirit of party brotherhood as Giddings brought forward a sweeping set of sixteen resolutions and the convention adopted them unanimously.

Giddings' platform pledged the party to every imaginable antislavery measure, short of immediate abolition or disunion. The entire Compromise of 1850 was to be repealed in favor of complete denationalization of slavery. Were there any Whigs and Democrats in America with acceptable antislavery principles, the Free Soilers would welcome them into the organization. But the third party itself would never bow to either of the old "corrupt" organizations. The delegates judged nefarious the state constitution's discriminatory clauses and demanded their repeal. Finally, all agreed with Giddings' motions to schedule a state nominating convention in Columbus for August 21 and a national "consultative" convention to meet in Cleveland and prepare for the 1852 campaign.[23] "We think no one [who was] present there will entertain further fears of the Free Soilers going over to the other parties . . . ," enthused the *Sentinel,* and even Chase had to admit he had a "glorious time," despite his discomfiture over the glaring absence of Democratic overtones in the resolutions.[24]

As the aroused Free Soilers prepared for their state gathering, the Whigs and Democrats picked their gubernatorial nominees, Samuel Vinton and Reuben Wood. Neither was as "worthy of the confidence of our people as . . . Hope H. Slatter, the great slave-dealer of Washington city . . . ," said the *Sentinel,* which had become the guiding spirit of the party and could afford to editorialize uncharitably. A complete slate of independent candidates had to be brought forward by the upcoming state convention.[25]

The delegates promptly obeyed, and the leading figures at the Columbus meeting illustrated the dramatic shift Giddings had wrought in the leadership of Ohio's third party. Chase did not appear, and Giddings was chosen by acclamation to act as president, an honor which he richly deserved. Remaining space on the speakers' platform was reserved for old warriors like Samuel Lewis from Liberty party days and for Free Soilers such as Joseph M. Root and Albert Gallatin Riddle, all of whom had avoided Chase's influence back in 1849. Giddings' keynote speech announced that the days when "ambition lures off the well meaning or blinds the selfish . . ." were over, for "justice reigns above and will rule below, and the power of man cannot blot it out." Samuel Lewis, the embodiment of moral earnestness, accepted the nomination to stand for governor on a platform in which antislavery pronouncements completely outshone the few remaining tinges of locofocoism. "We no longer believe," declared one resolution, "that the encroachments of slavery . . . will be checked by either of the two great parties [which] . . . depend for their very existence on the smiles of the South." [26] The convention's final act was to call again for a national meeting to be held in Cleveland on September 24. Giddings did not wish the spirit of reform to stop at state boundaries, for through the Cleveland convention he now planned to "let the country know that we are not disbanded, and do not intend to disband." [27]

As Giddings began planning for the Cleveland meeting, the state campaign began. The Whigs quickly discovered that besides the Democrats they had a united Free Soil party with which to contend. In a laughable effort to destroy third party unity Benjamin Wade released a letter to prove that Giddings was plotting through his series of conventions to dupe Free Soilers into backing Texas Senator Sam Houston for president of the United States! [28] More significant, however, was the reaction of Salmon P. Chase. In the space of five months Giddings had abruptly seized control of Chase's party by transforming it. Suddenly, Chase's fusionist power bloc had dissolved, and his only hope for political survival was to become a Democrat.

He did so on September 11, when he published a statement in the *National Era* announcing his support of Reuben Wood for governor over Samuel Lewis.[29] But this revelation, far from betokening the "nadir" of the third party, as some historians have claimed,[30] represented a benchmark in the Free Soil metamorphosis. Gamaliel Bailey, now Giddings' firm ally, rejoiced at Chase's hurried exit, declaring that "Messrs. Root, Lewis and Giddings, with the large body of voters they represent," would "exert far more influence . . ." than they had in elections since 1848. He was right.[31] While the Democrats swept the state, the Free Soilers carried the Reserve with ease and polled three thousand more votes than they had the previous year.[32] In Ohio the party's existence was again secure, without the spectre of Salmon P. Chase to threaten it.

While the campaign wore on, Giddings divided his time between a strenuous speaking schedule and planning for the Cleveland convention.[33] He sent invitations to his Massachusetts friends, as well as to George W. Julian, Charles Durkee, and countless other Free Soilers. But Giddings had broader objectives than just a normal meeting, for he decided to include men with far purer antislavery positions than those which the Free Soil party boasted. He now hoped to use his new reputation as party leader to fulfill his lifelong desire for antislavery unity. The third party's sense of moral direction had obviously vanished in the years since 1848. Giddings wished not only to restore, but to give wider dimension to the reform impulse in politics. Through the Cleveland convention he planned, as he informed Julian, to make the Free Soil party "embody the entire antislavery force of the entire United States." [34]

To achieve this difficult objective, Giddings turned to the only abolitionist groups in America which had managed to preserve their integrity while remaining in direct contact with politics. Gerrit Smith, William Chaplin, William Goodell, and F. Julius LeMoyne, all veterans of the 1830's, received invitations to attend Giddings' Cleveland convention. These men, constituting a faction of the old Liberty party, had all spurned the Free Soilers' anti-abolitionist programs in 1848 in favor of fourth party action. Their Liberty League perpetuated the principles of political abolitionism by habitually running Smith for governor of New York or for the presidency, depending on which office was

open. Lewis Tappan, whose consistency in the antislavery movement was unique in the 1850's, also received a request to join
the Cleveland convention. Tappan, while operating on the fring-
es of Smith's Liberty League, was trying to foster the old spirit of
the pre-1840 abolitionist movement, in which he had exercised
powerful leadership. Cassius Clay, although a far more tarnished
warrior than Tappan or Goodell, also agreed to participate. Clay's
Negrophobia accounted for much of his hatred of slavery, but
still he had taken to the perilous habit of heading emancipationist tickets in Kentucky.[35]

Giddings' attempt to organize such a disparate collection of
people and positions proved no simple job, for Gerrit Smith insisted on absorbing everyone into his own faction as a precondi-
tion of his appearance. Cassius Clay was anxious to come, but
only if Smith had nothing to do with the affair. As it turned out,
Smith sent representatives but chose to stay home while Clay attended. Charles Sumner and the other Massachusetts men finally
decided not to participate, for they were attempting fusion with
the Democrats and wanted no association with a broadly based
independent party.[36]

Regardless of the difficulties, the Cleveland convention was
constructive as well as innately interesting. Delegates came from
every Northern state except Massachusetts and New Hampshire.
George W. Julian and Charles Durkee, down-to-earth Free Soil
politicians, mingled easily with Lewis Tappan, the penultimate
of evangelical reform. Even Ohio's newest Democrat, Salmon
Chase, could not resist showing up. During the proceedings he
completely duped the bemused Tappan with "sincere" avowals
of loyalty to the cause. F. Julius LeMoyne chaired the convention, Samuel Lewis and Cassius Clay made stirring speeches, and
Giddings composed resolutions which Tappan, as vice-president
of the convention, eagerly seconded. The delegates approved an
ambitious antislavery platform which failed to endorse only immediate abolition, while approving internal disarmament and
the prohibition of "ardent spirits." At Tappan's behest, a nation-

al committee was appointed to organize each state for the presidential convention of 1852.[37]

Despite the odd assortment of participants, Giddings had successfully laid the foundation for the Free Soil campaign of the following year. Apart from the noticeable absence of the Massachusetts representatives, the national party had been given a much-needed dose of altruism as well as a fresh organization. Without the help of men like Tappan and LeMoyne, Giddings' efforts would have been far less successful. These individuals, discounted by many historians as ineffectual in the 1850's, brought to the national convention the spark of idealism at the core of nineteenth-century reform movements. These men of advanced views supplied Giddings, Julian, Durkee, and other politicians with a moral criterion against which to measure the Free Soilers' more limited and necessarily more pragmatic actions. Because of his summer successes Giddings felt mellow enough to overlook the snubs of his Massachusetts friends. On his way back to Washington he stopped over in Boston to commend publicly Charles Sumner on his recent election to the Senate. For one of the few times in his life, he congratulated himself on being a "practical" politician. The Free Soil party was again revived and ready to compete in 1852. Furthermore, he had disproven the arbitrary distinction between "realistic" politics and "radical reformers," which was to be largely the invention of later historians.[38]

Despite Giddings' fruitful summer, there was no quick transference of renewed antislavery zeal from the state level to Washington. Kentucky Democrat Lynn Boyd scored a crushing bipartisan victory in the contest for Speaker,[39] and his election constituted the first fruits of identical pledges ratified in the Whig and Democratic caucuses to crush all agitation. Such dealings reminded Giddings of "the crew of a sinking ship who, when they saw the vessel going down . . . all with one consent *clung to the anchor. . . ."* [40] Benjamin Wade was dealing in irrelevancies by observing that Giddings had less an idea of major party strategies than if he "spent his time in the uttermost parts of Oregon." It was clear enough to Giddings that Whigs and Democrats still wanted to hear nothing of slavery.[41] But the advent of Louis Kossuth in Washington gave Giddings his first chance to spoil such plans.

Kossuth, the exiled leader of Hungary's abortive 1848 revolution, had already achieved heroic stature in American eyes before Fillmore decided to invite him to visit the capital. But, once Kossuth had arrived in Washington, the warm welcome for him became involved with George Washington's "nonintervention" doctrine and unreasonable Southern fears that the dashing Hungarian noble sympathized with abolition.[42] Even before Kossuth arrived, William R. Smith of Alabama tried to amend the joint resolution extending to the Hungarian congressional greetings by adding a provision to give him a copy of the federal statutes on treason. Giddings noted this symptom of Southern anxiety, checked with Charles Allen and George Julian, and reported to his son that the "free-soilers intend to make Capitol [sic] out of Kossuth, and they will do it." [43]

One perceptive supporter of the compromises quickly sensed the strategy and warned the House that the "shrewd, keen-eyed gentleman from Ohio" had decided to advocate American intervention abroad in order to start "intermeddling with, and revolutionizing the peculiar . . . institutions of a portion of our own complex society." Days of debate on Kossuth followed, in which slavery was on everyone's mind, though it was never directly mentioned. Giddings remained silent. Finally, on January 2, 1852, Edward Stanly of Virginia could no longer bear the strain of hearing so many veiled references to the Southern labor system and committed a bad blunder. He introduced a set of resolutions absolving Kossuth of abolitionist taint and made the unprovoked charge that Giddings, Sumner, Chase, and William Seward were conniving with Kossuth, hoping to make the emigré hero a pawn of their emancipationist schemes. Giddings scoffed at the allegation and announced that since no slaveholder had yet intimidated him "by the crack of the lash," Stanly could expect to hear his full views on foreign policy in a formal speech.[44] His tactic of simple patience had forced the Southerners into the open, and Giddings was free to exploit the situation.

He did so in the House on January 28, 1852, taking fully an hour to put forth most unusual arguments about the obligation of the United States to preach the spirit of the Declaration of Independence in world affairs. The self-evident truths of human equality, he began, "embraced the whole family of man" and were the true "law of nations." The European reactionaries who had crushed Kossuth while keeping millions in ignorance and poverty should be met the world over with America's "moral intervention." The United States must lead global efforts to persuade and exhort "all civilized nations" to end war, oppression, and tyranny and to work for universal brotherhood, social progress, and peace.

The United States possessed "great moral influence among civilized governments," Giddings maintained. Were it to initiate worldwide evangelism in the name of human equality, other nations would soon follow. "The age in which we live is emphatically an age of progress. Men and nations are now taught to rely more upon reason, upon truth, upon justice . . . and less upon the power of arms." As such enlightenment diffused throughout the world, "intelligent, civilized Christian men" would understand if told of war's futility and the immorality of oppressive government. It was the United States' responsibility, he concluded, to bring to other nations the message of God's just demands of peace, freedom, and brotherhood. "Few intelligent men [would] resist . . ." if the United States were to commence the work. "It [would] prove a glorious mission to that nation, inspired by the spirit of Christian benevolence [which] . . . shall move forward in redeeming the world from the crimes and horrors of war." [45]

Such statements must rank high among the most ineffectual ever put forward in a foreign policy debate. But, as was often the case with Giddings, his sincere convictions coincided with his tactical objectives. His speech publicized by implication that slavery was brutal, a distasteful anachronism in the eyes of the Western world. Such innuendos hardly escaped his Southern listeners. But he had chosen an infuriating device, for what congressman would dare reject openly Giddings' endorsement of pacifism,[46] brotherly love, and human charity? [47] At the same time, utopian pleas for worldwide reformation announced an emerging quality of genuine radicalism in Giddings, caused by further changes in his religious thinking. In early 1850 he had begun to alter his personal theology, and by 1852 he was employing a new religious outlook in order to refocus his political perspective.

Young George W. Julian, who shared quarters with Giddings during these years, believed that his friend was becoming "less orthodox but more Christian" by scrapping all formal theology for pure humanitarianism. Giddings' "faith in the fatherhood of God and the brotherhood of man . . ." was compelling him gradually to reject all dogma that stood in the way.[48] Julian's is a fair description, but not a good explanation.

By 1852, Giddings had begun to show his age. He was fifty-seven, white-haired, and had put on a great deal of weight. He had also become deeply intrigued by the Fox sisters, whose "spiritual rappings" had attracted national notice.[49] Perhaps the fear of dying which the advance of years brings with it drew him to this mixture of Swedenborgianism and spiritualism. Giddings' sudden recourse to mystical "conversations" with departed loved ones such as his mother and John Quincy Adams could offer him the comfort of knowing that Heaven was nearby. He enjoyed "looking forward to the future, [for] in looking into the spirit land we bring heaven to us, and at once enter upon its felicity and enjoyment." God became a completely loving entity, and Giddings now anticipated "that state where we shall see and know Him more perfectly than we do now." [50] In mid-1852 he informed his wife that he had absolutely no fear of death and would welcome its arrival.[51] Besides, there was the promise, offered by spiritualism, of continued temporal activity after death. Giddings was, above all, an activist, and he could feel that, if he should die before society had been regenerated, he would still have a hand in the process by communicating with those left behind.

Beyond being soothing to the fears of an aging man, spiritualism also held far deeper meanings for some Americans who had already strayed far from orthodoxy during the "great revival." It was, as utopian social scientist John Humphrey Noyes explained it, "a religion." "The Bible and revivals had made men hungry for something more than social reconstruction," and spiritualism's promise of a "new heaven as well as a new earth met the demand magnificently. . . ." [52]

America in the 1850's could be a bewildering place for a man of Giddings' religious opinions and personal history. The teleological view of human nature, which he had long cherished, was now being challenged by a society increasingly preoccupied by technology. Samuel Morse's telegraph was already transforming the process of communications, and a vast network of railroad lines had begun spreading across the land. The material inventiveness of the human mind was suddenly displaying itself in a manner which the revivalists of the 1820's had never imagined. Concurrently, the people of the North remained unmoved by the cries of antislavery reformers who had warned them, time and again, of the deadly effects of the "slavepower." Since 1839 Giddings had witnessed only one substantial victory—the repeal of the gag rule. Meanwhile, unwilling to question slavery's influence, the North had bowed to the annexation of Texas, the Mexican War, and the Compromise of 1850. An aging Giddings had to account for such confusing developments. The increasing materialism and continued apathy denied all that he had thus far hoped to achieve. The path of adjustment he chose was to incorporate these disturbing developments into his changing theology.

He interpreted new scientific discoveries as an index of society's growing conformity to God's plan for the improvement of mankind. This notion complemented his belief in communication with those in heaven. Both doctrines brought God's will and human endeavor into closer approximation to each other, projecting on earth the highest type of human society. [53] Despite the North's

209

refusal to endorse the reforms of the antislavery crusade, Giddings could feel that society was moving in a positive direction foreordained by God. He now believed that the nation's spiritual destiny had nothing to do with scripture, formal theology, or sectarianism. Doctrinal squabbles, he concluded, had made the United States a "nation of infidels" by distracting citizens from their true task, the perfection of society through the "instruction, the elevation, the unfolding of every human being. . . ." God intended simply that each individual be "morally elevated to the highest level of his powers." Of course, such "elevation" meant that man be relieved of the sins of slavery. The enlightened Christian's duty was to hasten the process by preaching universal freedom and stressing the social implications of the Golden Rule.[54]

Fourteen years earlier William Lloyd Garrison and his followers had reached similar conclusions. Ever since, they had been demanding that Americans disassociate themselves from the political process, which by its very nature impeded perfection by upholding slavery. But Giddings was still a congressman, not a private citizen, and he could not admit either that the Constitution fostered slavery or that politics was hostile to reform. In order to give himself an active role in making earth more like heaven, he had to assign perfectionist responsibilities to the federal government. While still holding to his program of denationalizing slavery without abolishing it, he began demanding that Congress act on a theological interpretation of the Declaration of Independence. The Creator, he concluded, had endowed all men with the right of life, liberty, and pursuit of happiness. The function of the government was to legislate for the promotion and protection of these "Gifts of God." "Every act in harmony with those [God's] laws necessarily elevates the individual and prepares him for higher levels of attainment," Giddings believed. With the help of Christian congressmen each member of society would enjoy the freedom necessary for self-perfection and the eventual consummation of God's plan. On that day, Giddings promised, "false theories and infidelity, love of oppression, violence, polygamy, and slavery shall be overwhelmed." [55]

Giddings had always desired the union of morality and politics. The hope had often led to his confusion and disappointment on witnessing the shifty maneuvers of his associates. Now he was linking perfectionism to the legislative process through his view of the Declaration of Independence. As he crystallized his new theology over the next few years, he moved ever further from the mainstream of American politics and ever closer to the radical mentality of revolutionaries like William Lloyd Garrison. At the same time, Giddings' belief that John Quincy Adams was keeping a critical eye on his actions provided compelling new reasons to expose the "slave power." Giddings drew from his spiritualism and perfectionism renewed determination and a heightened awareness of social injustice, even though his fourteen years of effort had left the nation's conscience placidly accepting the sin of slavery.

In June the Whig and Democratic presidential conventions gave Giddings a clear picture of the "unregenerate" condition of American political morality. The Democrats drafted Franklin Pierce, whom Giddings deemed "an unrelenting partisan of the Hunker stripe," and he judged the Whigs' choice of Winfield Scott as no better. Both parties' platforms upheld the Compromise measures and promised to "resist all attempts at renewing, in Congress or out of it, agitation of the slavery question. . . ." [56]

Giddings, nursing a bad cold, read the platforms and was anxious to speak no matter how miserable he felt.[57] The major parties had hurled a blanket challenge at his reconstructed Free Soilers, and the situation in Washington looked "dark" and "dreary." Sumner remained silent in the Senate, and because of political development in Massachusetts antislavery-minded Whigs like Horace Mann and John Howe did nothing for the cause in the House. The Barnburners endorsed Pierce, ending forever their three-year charade as dedicated antislavery men, and

211

Giddings reported that his general agitation did not "meet the approbation" of many ex-radicals.[58] He was determined to launch the Free Soil campaign, single-handedly if necessary. His speech on the Whig and Democratic platforms, delivered on June 23, did just that—and in the most effective fashion. Giddings seldom enjoyed a more dramatic and courageous moment on the floor of the House.

The Democrats promised to "resist" agitation and the Whigs would "discountenance" it, said Giddings, reading from the platforms and glaring at his audience. "I, sir, am about to agitate this question. I intend to speak plainly of slavery, of its most revolting features. . . . I am now agitating this subject and what will you do about it?" Congressmen fidgeted in embarrassed silence. No one said a word in protest. Giddings, triumphant, announced to the nation, "They dare not do it. . . . They have not the moral power to effect that object." Such doctrines represented no more than a "ridiculous attempt to ape the despotisms of Europe" by suppressing free speech. Instead of attending conventions, the platforms' authors would have been better off at "some Sabbath school, gaining intelligence and qualifying themselves for useful employment." Antislavery appeals would continue, Giddings promised, and the major parties were powerless to stop them.

Giddings went on to assail the Whigs and Democrats for jointly supporting the Compromises, especially the fugitive law, with its "baying of bloodhounds, clanking of chains and shrieks of slaves." No Free Soiler would agree to "supinely become tributary to Southern taskmasters." Instead, the third party would dwell on the questions of slavery until the people reacted *en masse* to "hurl from power the men who thus condemn popular feeling." The law made the antislavery movement unstoppable, and the Free Soil party would emerge triumphant. "For thousands of years" the instruction and elevation of mankind had been carried forward by disruptive leaders "who had driven tyrants from thrones and regained the people's liberties." Samuel Adams and Thomas Jefferson had played such roles during the Revolution, and the Free Soilers would follow in their tradition. Stop agitation, Giddings warned, and America would soon succumb to "frauds, abuses, and corruptions" which would "putrify the vital blood of the nation." Against these Whig and Democratic attempts to destroy the United States, the Free Soilers would place their "unceasing, unyielding, undying hostility" until the federal government was "totally redeemed from the foul stain of chattel slavery." The Free Soilers' aim was to uplift the entire human community, Giddings concluded: "The political and moral regeneration of our country; the entire reformation of this Government from . . . oppression, slavery and crime, is our object." [59]

Giddings' spirited defense of the moral reformer sent a thrill through the antislavery community. William Lloyd Garrison, doubtless noting Giddings' emphasis on social regeneration, which closely approximated some of his own perfectionist thinking, praised the speech for its "sublime, defiant tone," which "surpasses every effort that has been made on the floor of Congress." Back on the Reserve, antislavery voters never felt prouder of their representative. "The old Ajax towers up well . . . ," said the *True Democrat*, recommending that printed copies "be scattered far and near. . . ." [60]

Giddings, sensing the impact of his speech, increased his activities as the National Free Soil Convention, scheduled for August 11, drew closer. After a quick trip to Worcester, where he spoke to the state meeting,[61] he returned to the House and attacked the government policy of enslaving free Negroes who had been accused of rape. "I wish that gentlemen would learn to treat colored people as *men*," Giddings thundered as he argued for judicial equality. When Negroes committed such crimes, "let them be punished as others are." Soon after, he castigated the government's repressive treatment of Indians, saying that benevolence would turn them into allies: "I do not believe in Christianizing Indians by whipping them, by shooting them, by cutting their throats." [62] Giddings' new concern for a total restructuring of society to fit the Declaration of Independence and the Golden Rule was becoming ever more apparent. If his protests were ineffectual, politically impotent, he was using his new religion to see the injus-

213

tices of American society far more inclusively than he ever had before. He no longer aimed just at changing political parties in order to implement antislavery measures. Now all of American society needed revamping, with the help of Giddings and the federal government.

The National Free Soil Convention opened on August 11 in Pittsburgh's Masonic Hall. Giddings' efforts of the previous summer were unmistakable to all, for Samuel Lewis chaired the convention and Ohio's delegates set the tone by carrying around an enormous banner proclaiming "No Compromise with Slaveholders or Doughfaces." Giddings, as chairman of the Platform Committee, reported resolutions which denounced the Compromises, endorsed a complete denationalization of slavery, and called for the recognition of Haiti as the first step toward "moral intervention" in foreign affairs. Some of Giddings' more radical associates from the Cleveland convention, F. Julius LeMoyne and William Goodell, protested the platform as too conservative and followed Gerrit Smith back to the Liberty League. Lewis Tappan, however, chose to endorse Free Soil nominees John P. Hale and George W. Julian, although he did little to help in the campaign. Giddings had been unable to make permanent his alliance with the emancipationists, but from his own point of view it was fortunate that the Liberty Leaguers had refused to compromise their doctrines. Had they accepted John P. Hale's leadership, they would not again have been able to encourage more moderate antislavery politicians in the adoption of higher principles. Partly because Goodell, LeMoyne, Tappan, and others had been willing to give Giddings their moral support, the third party banner was now far less sullied by expediency than it had been in 1848. The delegates adjourned the Pittsburgh convention in high spirits, determined to make a strong showing.[63]

Back in Ohio, no one was betting on Giddings to succeed himself, for again his district had been drastically gerrymandered. Cuyahoga, Lake, and Geauga counties, in which he had always polled majorities, had been replaced by Trumbull and Mahon-

THE CONSERVATIVE ASCENDANCY

ing counties. Mahoning had gone consistently Democratic since the 1830's, and antislavery sentiment in Trumbull County had decreased markedly after the Free Soilers bolted in 1848.[64] Giddings, for once, was worried. He exhorted his son Joseph to "cast aside the God of indolence" and to organize the district with utmost vigor. He also published an open letter telling the *True Democrat* to stop assailing Chase. Chase had again returned to the Free Soil fold when Pierce obtained the Democratic nomination, and Giddings was far more interested in party unity than in dwelling on past grievances. His own political future and all his rebuilding efforts depended on a concerted Free Soil effort. The *True Democrat* duly apologized to Chase and turned its attentions to helping Giddings in his struggle for survival.[65]

Giddings, for the first time in his life, called on his associates to help him. He certainly needed any and all aid. Ben Wade's Conneaut *Reporter* rejoiced that "for the first time in fourteen years there will be a contest . . . to determine whether the people are ready to surrender themselves to the one man power." Wade and Elisha Whittlesey joined to accuse Giddings falsely of mileage fraud, while the Cleveland *Herald* ran editorials announcing that "the cloven hoof of the perpetual member from Ashtabula is at last exposed. . . ." [66] Giddings sent out appeals to the nation's leading Free Soilers, and they responded by arranging a lavish "Giddings Festival," which took place in Painesville two weeks before the polls opened. The Painesville, Ohio, brass band supplied the music, and dinner consisted of "products of the free soil of Lake County," spread out on four tables, each an incredible thirty yards long.

Chase, Edward Wade, Edward S. Hamlin, and John P. Hale himself all gave glowing speeches about Giddings. A rousing toast praising him as "a noble specimen of American manhood" brought deafening cheers from the well-fed guests. Letters were read from Cassius Clay, William Jay, Gerrit Smith, Elizur Wright, Theodore Parker, Samuel Lewis, Adams, Palfrey and Sumner—men who represented nearly every imaginable position within the larger crusade against slavery. Each message thanked Giddings for his devoted service to the cause of humanity and pleaded for his re-election.[67]

On the strength of this display, Giddings carried his new district, even though he had to settle for a second place in Mahoning County and an overall plurality. Nearby, in Cleveland, Edward Wade used Giddings' momentum to frustrate his brother Ben by capturing a seat in Congress. Ironically, the gerrymander returned two Free Soil representatives, whereas before there had been only one.[68] Giddings with justifiable pride noted how "astounded" the "old hunkers" were at his re-election. "Nothing," he judged, "has occurred better calculated to commend the respect of both parties. . . ." [69]

When the votes were tallied in the national contest, Franklin Pierce had scored an unparalleled victory. Scott's control of only forty-two electoral votes foreshadowed the demise of the national Whig party. Hale's total of 156,000 looked unimpressive on first inspection, slightly more than half of Van Buren's 1848 figure. But the statistics were deceptive, for Barnburners, who now supported Pierce, had furnished the bulk of the Free Soilers' 1848 total.[70] If Whiggery was slowly expiring, at least an unequivocally antislavery political party was still alive, and Giddings would be present in Washington to testify to this fact.

NOTES

[1] Smith, *Liberty and Free Soil Parties*, 182–83; JRG to Albert Gallatin Riddle, March 29, 1850, Albert Gallatin Riddle MSS, cited by permission of The Henry E. Huntington Library, San Marino, California (hereinafter HHL) ; JRG to JAG, July 1, 1850, Giddings MSS.

[2] Smith, *Liberty and Free Soil Parties*, 182–83, 185–86, 220–24.

[3] JRG to "Molly" [LMG], December 8, 1850, Giddings-Julian MSS, LC (quotation) ; Patrick Riddleburger, *George Washington Julian: A Study in Nineteenth Century Reform and Politics* (Indianapolis, 1966), 41–42, 52, 57, 67.

[4] JRG to JAG, December 16, 1850, Giddings MSS.

[5] U.S. *Congressional Globe,* 1st Cong., 2d Sess., XX, Appendix, 252–56.

[6] JRG to [n/a], December 16, 1850, Giddings-Julian MSS, LC.

[7] JRG to JAG, December 16, 1850, Giddings MSS.

[8] Washington *Globe,* December 12, 1850, Boston *Atlas,* December 12, 1850, JRG Scrapbook, 1850, Giddings MSS; Cleveland *Herald,* December 20, 1850; JRG to JAG, January 20, 1851, Giddings MSS; Ashtabula *Sentinel,* February 1, 1851.

[9] JRG to JAG, December 30, 1850, Giddings MSS; JRG to John G. Palfrey, December 28, 1850, Palfrey MSS, HL.

[10] U.S. *Congressional Globe,* 31st Cong., 2d Sess., XX, 705.

[11] *Ibid.,* 596–97.

[12] *Ibid.,* 705–6.

[13] The *Republic* (Washington) , December 11, 1850, JRG Scrapbook, 1850, Giddings MSS.

[14] Salmon P. Chase to Edward S. Hamlin, December 9, 1850, Chase MSS, LC.

15 JRG to Thomas Bolton, December 17, 1850, Giddings Miscellaneous MSS, NYHS; JRG to Albert Gallatin Riddle, December 28, 1850, Riddle MSS, HHL; JRG to JAG, December 16, 1850, Giddings MSS. The friend to whom Giddings confided was Albert Gallatin Riddle. Riddle, years later, was to write the laudatory and useful *Life of Benjamin Wade* (Cleveland, 1888).

16 Giddings wrote Chase that Wade's election would do "little good to our cause," even though the new senator was "now strongly with us, and bitterly opposed to the [Fillmore] administration." Giddings feared that Wade's "sort of semi-free-soil Sewardism" would cause him to value party over principle. "Yet," Giddings promised, "we shall all do what we can to encourage him, to maintain his integrity." JRG to Salmon P. Chase, April 3, 1851, Chase MSS, HSP.

17 Smith, *Liberty and Free Soil Parties,* 226–27; *National Era,* February 20, 1851.

18 Ashtabula *Sentinel,* April 26, April 5, 1851 (both issues quoted).

19 "Pacificus [pseud. JRG] to a Citizen of Kentucky," December 2, 1843, and "Essays on the Van Zandt Case," August 19, August 26, September 2, September 9, 1843, all in Ashtabula *Sentinel.*

20 JRG to Salmon P. Chase, April 3, 1851, Chase MSS, HSP. This letter also gives the details of Giddings' strategy meetings and the rejection of Chase's plans.

21 Painesville *Telegraph,* May 7, May 14, 1851; Cleveland *True Democrat,* May 10, 1851.

22 Cleveland *True Democrat,* May 13, May 18, 1851.

23 *Ibid.,* June 27, June 30, 1851.

24 Ashtabula *Sentinel,* June 28, 1851; Salmon P. Chase to Charles Sumner, June 28, 1851, Chase MSS, LC.

25 Ashtabula *Sentinel,* July 12, 1851.

26 Cleveland *True Democrat,* August 25, 1851 (quotation); Ashtabula *Sentinel,* August 30, 1851 (quotation of resolutions).

27 JRG to George W. Julian, August 27, 1851, Giddings-Julian MSS, LC.

28 Ashtabula *Sentinel,* September 6, October 14, 1851.

29 Salmon P. Chase to C. R. Miller, reprinted in the *National Era,* September 11, 1851.

NOTES TO CHAPTER 10

[30] Smith, *Liberty and Free Soil Parties,* 239; Sewell, *John P. Hale,* 145.

[31] *National Era,* September 11, 1851.

[32] Ashtabula *Sentinel,* October 25, 1851.

[33] Giddings limited his efforts to an exhaustive canvass of the Reserve, presumably to solidify his party where it was most practical to do so. See the Ashtabula *Sentinel,* September 20, September 27, October 4, 1851.

[34] JRG to George W. Julian, August 27, 1851, Giddings-Julian MSS, LC.

[35] *National Era,* October 2, October 9, 1851; Ralph Volney Harlow, *Gerrit Smith: Philanthropist and Reformer* (New York, 1939), *passim.*; Bertram Wyatt-Brown, *Lewis Tappan and the Evangelical War Against Slavery* (Cleveland, 1969), 269–87, 331–32; Filler, *Crusade Against Slavery,* 152, 156; Smiley, *Cassius M. Clay,* 221–33; David L. Smiley, "Cassius Clay and John G. Fee, A Study in Southern Antislavery Thought," *Journal of Negro History,* XLII (July, 1957), 201–13.

[36] Gerrit Smith to JRG, August 30, 1851, Gerrit Smith to Cassius M. Clay, August 16, 1851, Cassius Clay to JRG, September 3, 1851, Charles Sumner to JRG, September 11, 1851, Giddings MSS.

[37] Ashtabula *Sentinel,* September 27, October 4, 1851; *National Era,* October 2, October 9, 1851; Cleveland *True Democrat,* September 25, 1851; Wyatt-Brown, *Lewis Tappan,* 331.

[38] For Giddings' trip to Massachusetts, see the Boston *Commonwealth,* reprinted in the Ashtabula *Sentinel,* November 15, November 29, 1851. Historians who have denigrated the roles of radical reformers during the 1840's and 1850's while emphasizing the "practical politicians'" activities are led by Barnes, *Antislavery Impulse,* 161–97. John Thomas develops a slightly different criticism of radical reformers, charging them with failure to provide politicians with "practical" guidelines for the solution of racial issues. Both views, however, overlook the multitude of connections between moral reform and radical politics. See *The Liberator, William Lloyd Garrison,* 452–59. A noteworthy exception to these standard views is Filler, *Crusade Against Slavery, passim.,* wherein the relationships between reformers and politicians are subtly drawn and arbitrary divisions avoided.

[39] U.S. *Congressional Globe,* 32d Cong., 1st Sess., XXI, 9–10.

[40] Ashtabula *Sentinel,* December 13, 1851.

219

[41] Benjamin F. Wade to Caroline Wade, February 8, 1852, Wade MSS, LC.

[42] Reinhard Luthin, "A Visitor from Hungary," *South Atlantic Quarterly,* XLVII (January, 1948), 29–34.

[43] U.S. *Congressional Globe,* 32d Cong., 1st Sess., XXI, 58; JRG to JAG, December 29, 1851, Giddings MSS.

[44] U.S. *Congressional Globe,* 32d Cong., 1st Sess., XXI, 160–82, 187–96, 200.

[45] *Ibid.,* Appendix, 143–45.

[46] Although he often sounded like a pacifist, Giddings hardly opposed violence. After this speech, he spelled out his thinking clearly but with tongue in cheek to Julian: "I go for non-resistence [sic] in all cases except in self-defense or in the defense of . . . the rights of others. I think those that kill tyrants and negro catchers do God's will, and man's duty: Now dont [sic] laugh at my non-resistence [sic] doctrine. It is sincere. . . ." JRG to George W. Julian, February 21, 1852, Giddings-Julian MSS, LC.

[47] After a "safe" three weeks had elapsed, Edward Stanly did attack Giddings with exceptional viciousness for his foreign policy doctrines and their relation to slavery. The brutality of Stanly's remarks indicates how deeply Giddings' innuendos had been felt. See U.S. *Congressional Globe,* 32d Cong., 1st Sess., XXI, 531–35.

[48] Julian, *Giddings,* 402.

[49] JRG to GRG, January 26, February 9, 1850, B. W. Richards (presumably a spiritualist medium from Jefferson) to JRG, January 29, 1852, Giddings MSS; JRG to LAG, January 26, 1852, Giddings-Julian MSS, LC.

[50] JRG to LMG, February 3, 1855 (quotation), JRG to George W. Julian, March 2, 1852, Giddings-Julian MSS, LC; JRG to LWG, January 23, 1853 (quotation), March 23, 1856, Giddings MSS.

[51] JRG to LWG, June 20, 1852, Giddings-Julian MSS, LC.

[52] John Humphrey Noyes, quoted in Cross, *Burnt-Over District,* 343.

[53] *Ibid.,* 342–43.

[54] JRG to Lewis Tappan, December 31, 1859, Lewis Tappan MSS, LC (quotation); JRG to Editor, *National Anti-Slavery Standard,* undated clipping, JRG Scrapbook, 1857, Giddings MSS (quotation).

55 *Ibid.*

56 JRG to Editor, Ashtabula *Sentinel,* June 19, 1852 (quotation); Julian, *Giddings,* 302 (quotation).

57 Giddings later remarked: "I was anxious to speak though I had been on my death bed." JRG to JAG, June 30, 1852, Giddings MSS.

58 Donald, *Sumner,* 223–27; JRG to George W. Julian, June 30, 1852, Giddings-Julian MSS, LC (quotations).

59 U.S. *Congressional Globe,* 32d Cong., 1st Sess., XXI, Appendix, 738–42.

60 *Liberator,* June 30, 1852; Cleveland *True Democrat,* July 3, 1852.

61 JRG to H. C. Gray, July 9, 1852, Giddings Miscellaneous MSS, NYHS.

62 U.S. *Congressional Globe,* 32d Cong., 1st Sess., XXI, 1815 (quotation), 1910 (quotation), 1918.

63 *National Era,* August 19, 1852; Ashtabula *Sentinel,* August 21, 1852; Sewell, *John P. Hale,* 146–147; Wyatt-Brown, *Lewis Tappan,* 331–32; Filler, *Crusade Against Slavery,* 213.

64 *National Era,* April 7, 1852; Ashtabula *Sentinel,* May 8, 1852.

65 JRG to JAG, June 30, 1852, Giddings MSS (quotation). Cleveland *True Democrat,* August 21, 1852.

66 Conneaut *Reporter,* undated clipping, JRG Scrapbook, 1852, Giddings MSS; Cleveland *Herald,* October 6, 1852; Ashtabula *Sentinel,* September 25, 1852.

67 Ashtabula *Sentinel,* September 25, 1852; Painesville *Telegraph,* September 22, September 29, 1852; Cleveland *True Democrat,* September 21, 1852.

68 Election results reported in the Cleveland *True Democrat,* October 16, 1852.

69 JRG to JAG, January 11, 1853, Giddings MSS.

70 Julian, *Giddings,* 306; *Ohio State Journal,* November 23, 1852.

Chapter 11

THE
AGING
WARRIOR

·❀ ❀·

1853-1857

In December, 1853, the Free Soil party's resurgence appeared to matter little, for the political atmosphere was placid, unclouded by sectional turbulence. Antislavery issues, it seemed, had been effectively buried, and the number of congressional agitators was greatly diminished. Charles Durkee, Charles Allen, and George W. Julian had all failed to obtain re-election in 1852, and Giddings counted only two reliable allies, his neighbor Edward Wade and Gerrit Smith, the famous political abolitionist. The voters of Genesee County, New York, had elected Smith on his Liberty League platform of legislative emancipation, and, for the only time in American history, a self-confessed "friend of the slave" took part in congressional debate. Because of his sensitivity to compromising his principles, Smith was never able to reconcile himself to the day-to-day tactics which Giddings had long employed. For example, planned boycotts of legislative sessions in order to prevent quorums struck Smith as being abridgments of free speech.[1]

Despite their differing views on such matters, Giddings and Smith quickly established both a lasting friendship and a close political collaboration which was to benefit both men in later years. They shared a belief in spiritualism and human perfection, and they quickly began holding long discussions about how best to promote the elevation of the human community. Smith seemed to Giddings to be "an abler man" than most people suspected. Mrs. Smith, with whom Giddings was fascinated, seemed "a most estimable lady." [2] But what first impressed Giddings about Gerrit Smith was his courage. As soon as Pierce had released his annual message, Smith was on his feet condemning the President's espousal of the Compromises. "Never before did a *new* member lead off in that important discussion at the commencement of his service," Giddings noted in awe.[3] Not to be outdone by a neophyte, the Ohioan mounted an attack of his own upon the President's recommendation that Congress pay a slave claim to the Spanish government that had been outstanding since 1841.[4] "You see Smith and I let 'em have [it] . . . on the President's message," he confided proudly. "Some hunkers awoke from their sleep with perfect astonishment at finding free soil was not dead. . . ." [5]

As it turned out, the free soil issue was about to explode, not expire. While Giddings and Smith were arraigning Pierce in the House, the Senate was considering bills to organize territorial governments in Kansas and Nebraska. Initially, the sight of such activity had cheered Giddings a good bit, for both territories lay about 36°30′, the demarcation line between freedom and slavery within the Louisiana Purchase lands set by the Missouri Compromise. As eventual free states, Kansas and Nebraska would "at no distant day, give a heavy preponderance to freedom" in national politics, Giddings predicted. Southern men knew this, but he was sure that they could "discover no escape" from the "death below." [6]

His overoptimistic analysis was never laden with more brutal, if unintentional, irony. In early January, 1854, Illinois' Stephen A. Douglas announced his intention to present a bill to repeal the Missouri Compromise and throw Kansas and Nebraska open to

223

popular sovereignty. In theory at least, slavery would then have vast new areas for expansion. Stephen Douglas somehow never sympathized with the volatile passions which surrounded the issue of slavery in the territories. Personally, he cared little whether slavery was "voted up or down" in Kansas and Nebraska and thus had given in to Southern pressure for opening these areas to popular sovereignty.[7] Salmon Chase immediately got wind of Douglas' plan and was able momentarily to forestall its presentation. Fully intent on proving Douglas correct when he promised that his bill would raise a "hell of a storm," Chase rushed off to consult with Charles Sumner and Giddings.[8] By January 22 the three Free Soilers had finished composing an "Appeal of the Independent Democrats in Congress to the People of the United States," designed to mobilize the North against this sudden incursion of the "slave power." [9]

The "Appeal" was a model of sectional propaganda, for its authors were experienced hands at such business. Giddings furnished the rough draft, Chase edited it, and Sumner revised it to fit his high literary standards.[10] Doubtless its writers had private political ends in mind, for a sectionally aroused North meant the solidification of the shaky coalitions which kept both Chase and Sumner in Washington. Giddings, for his part, harbored less hardheaded motives. He had noted the plummeting fortunes of Ohio's Whigs in 1852 and 1853, and for the previous six months his *Sentinel* had been editorializing that they should disband completely. Giddings had invited them to join a revived reform party which would never attack the South physically but would "war" upon slavery through agitation, "aiming always at the heart of the monster" and not stopping "short of its total extinction." [11] Awakening the North to the evils of the Kansas-Nebraska Act undoubtedly looked to Giddings like a perfect way to further such radical plans.

The "Appeal" indicted the Act as a "gross violation of a sacred pledge," which would convert free territory "into a dreary despotism inhabited by masters and slaves." It was undoubtedly unfair to Douglas. Given his sectional astigmatism, he felt innocent of any "monsterous plot" to sacrifice the nation's freedom.[12] Yet, it was Douglas' Kansas-Nebraska Act, not the Free Soilers' "Appeal," which touched off the Northern upheaval. The signers of the "Appeal," Giddings, Chase, Sumner, Gerrit Smith, Edward Wade, and Alexander DeWitt, were simply the first to react in a typically Northern fashion. Across the North citizens rose up in united protest against what they judged the most brazen encroachment of the slave power" yet seen. Public opinion took seriously the "Appeal's" warnings, which were, indeed, real ones. Many people began for the first time to question seriously some of the anomalies implicit in a "free" society which condoned slavery. Others feared that Southern masters and their black chattel were about to make off with homesteads reserved by God and the Constitution for the white settler. Vociferous "indignation meetings" swept every free state as Douglas, with the full support of Pierce's administration, passed his measure in the Senate after three months of vituperative discussion.[13] Douglas and his cohorts, not the Free Soilers, were ultimately responsible for the rebirth of sectional hostility.

In the House and Senate the Whig party totally dissolved, its Northern branch uniting with the Free Soilers against the Kansas-Nebraska Act. A splinter group of Democrats, led by Maine's Hannibal Hamlin and New York's Preston King, also decided to place sectional loyalty over party allegiance. Giddings, excited by the coalition, welcomed conservative William Seward, his old foe Benjamin Wade, and Hamlin's Democrats as they "came into the very position which they have so long condemned." As sectionally moderate political professionals quickly assumed leadership within the anti-Nebraska ranks, Giddings rejoiced over the "enviable" position he foresaw for the Free Soilers. "We head the hosts of freedom," he wrote excitedly to his son.[14] He could not admit that he, Gerrit Smith, and Edward Wade stood no possible chance of directing a movement which included the North's most influential politicians. Moreover, he had waited sixteen years for the "moral revolution" to begin, and countless times he had predicted its arrival, only to be sorely disappointed. At this late stage of his career he was not given to analyzing critically the sudden zeal for "Northern rights." Instead, he judged it initially to be the beginning of the millennium. Outrage though there was at the Kansas-Nebraska Act, Giddings remained far in advance of majority opinion on questions of slavery. As in 1850, the Northern political spectrum had again contracted. Joshua Giddings now stood further to the left of center than ever on antislavery issues.

While the Kansas bill continued to inflame passions in the Senate, Giddings' change of position became very clear to the Ohioan's new allies, for he spent his time attacking a Negro exclusion amendment to the Homestead Act. Hoping to broaden Northerners' antislavery interests in a time of crisis, he criticized the measure as illiberal. But, instead of enlightening anti-Nebraska men, his remarks caused snickers from all parts of the hall and he became furious. "I intend to create no laughter," Giddings stormed. "We have brought these people from their native land, and are we to persecute them and trample them into the dust? On behalf of that class of men, I protest against it here and everywhere." His motion to strike out the anti-Negro amendment was crushed, with nearly every new "free soiler" voting nay.[15]

The same pattern occurred when Giddings, Edward Wade, and Gerrit Smith composed the only Northern opposition to New Mexico's territorial constitution, which contained a clause outlawing the migration of free Negroes. Giddings declared such racial exclusion "cruel, inhuman, and unjust," for legislators should act on "the principles of justice and righteousness, rather than low, unworthy prejudices." Northern Whigs, far preferring frontier territory without Negroes to Giddings' humanitarian vision, united to pass the measure.[16] From the outset, it was clear that the rising insistence on free soil among Northerners was in no way linked with Joshua Giddings' commitment to civil equality.[17] His emphasis on justice had little influence on men who shared more fully than he the nation's belief in Negro inferiority and who also realized that espousals of social equity would cost them votes.[18]

On March 4 the Kansas-Nebraska Act was sent to the House.

Giddings had confided earlier to his old friend John G. Palfrey that he had "seen the power of the Executive prevail" too often in the past. He felt "great dangers, even more than I dare express to my associates whom I would not discourage." [19] Giddings' fears were well grounded, for Stephen A. Douglas and Franklin Pierce had planned their strategy carefully. Southern Whigs supported the measure, and Pierce put irresistible pressure upon the Northern Democrats as two weeks of impassioned speechmaking began.[20]

Giddings, of course, added his voice to the debate and on May 16 addressed the House on the "Moral Responsibilities of Statesmen." His remarks included not only variations on the "Appeal" but also a typically direct assault upon slavery which described to the Northerners the horrors of the institution which they were being called upon to promote. He also warned that applying "popular sovereignty" to Kansas and Nebraska would mark only the beginning of slavery's march. Next the South would demand equal access to a conquered Cuba, to Oregon, and to Minnesota. Besides, he maintained that "popular soverignty's" emphasis on democracy was a sham; principles of free self-government did not include the right of enslaving powerless humans, and the slaves themselves would have no vote in determining their condition. Were the bill to pass, Northern resistance would assume violent dimensions, Giddings warned. "We shall not wait long to witness bloodshed in our own country. . . . The remedy for these things rests with the people of the North." [21] Giddings' predictions of violence did not come true for about a year, but he was correct about initiative shifting away from the South. On May 22, amidst groans and cheers, the Kansas-Nebraska Act passed the House.[22] Northern politics immediately began a dramatic, confusing transformation from which the Republican party was finally to emerge.

In Ohio a complicated series of conventions which paralleled those in other states had already prepared the way for a massive free soil fusion attempt. Benjamin Wade had called on all Whigs to dissolve their party, and the Democrats had even found some members deserting their ranks. A statewide nonpartisan meeting

227

held in Columbus during mid-March had set the tone of the movement. Thomas Ewing, a luminary of Ohio's "hunker" Whigs, had sent his warmest endorsement, as had Charles Reemelin, spokesman for Ohio's strongly anti-Negro German minority. The enthusiastic participants unanimously approved resolutions condemning the Kansas-Nebraska Act and endorsed the Compromise of 1850, Fugitive Slave Law and all, as the "final solution" to sectional quarrels. The *Sentinel*'s fear that ex-Whig delegates would fall prey to "the same old timid apprehensions of doing something too strong . . ." had been borne out completely.[23] The anti-Kansas-Nebraska enterprise had begun in a very conservative manner.

Nevertheless, Giddings was unable to follow Gerrit Smith's refreshing example of refusing to associate with a political situation which denied his antislavery principles.[24] Too much of Giddings' career had been based on reforming society through whatever party he had belonged to, and old habits were impossible to break. Then too, any massive awakening of the Northern conscience was a welcome sign, perhaps a prelude to the total regeneration he believed inevitable. Understandably, Giddings threw himself into the spreading coalition, unworried by the limited doctrines and timorous positions of most of his associates. As always, he placed his own, more radical interpretation upon the creeds of his emerging party, acting as a lobbyist for advanced positions instead of compromising himself by becoming a regular politician. After 1854 Giddings remained as much an unreconstructed maverick as ever. In mid-May he traveled to Massachusetts, Rhode Island, and New Hampshire to speak before state anti-Kansas-Nebraska conventions. On each occasion he exhorted his listeners not only to denationalize slavery forever but to broaden coalitionist aims to include the complete renovation of American society. Late in the month he agreed to sponsor Chase's, Thomas Corwin's, and Benjamin Wade's call for a July fusionist meeting in Ohio which would set up a permanent party and nominate a complete slate of candidates.[25] "Ohio must exterminate the whole race of doughfaces . . . ," Giddings told his constituents, for 1856 would see the election of "a *Northern man* who will adhere to the political faith of 1776, that *all* men are created equal in their right to life and liberty." [26] But, as Giddings soon discovered, there were many in Ohio, even in his own district, who did not approve of such a sweeping objective.

Chase's anti-Nebraska nominating convention assembled in Columbus on July 13. The delegates nominated a complete slate of state candidates, endorsed the idea of a national convention, and again assured the public that the Compromise of 1850 offered the best solution to the slavery question. "Had I penned the resolutions, . . . I would have used other language," Giddings announced to his constituents bluntly. He felt that the emerging party should have committed itself at once to a full denationalization of slavery "and the total employment of our energies to the protection of liberty." Reluctantly, he gave the convention his approval just as the electors gathered in the Twentieth District to pick a fusionist candidate for Congress.[27]

It took five ballots and a bitter behind-the-scenes struggle to secure Giddings' renomination. On the final vote he barely scraped by, 43–40, and the closeness of the contest was an excellent barometer of his tenuous place in the emerging party. Giddings' militant opinions and independent organization had confounded and infuriated conservatives for years, and now many of these "old hunkers" were exerting their leadership in the largest antislavery movement to date. Somehow, Ben Wade's post-convention endorsement of Giddings' candidacy and his promise to forget all old animosities sounded hollow.[28] The conservatives had nearly mustered Giddings out of the Republican party just as it was forming.

With the perils of the nomination behind him, Giddings' reelection was a certainty. Sensing the need to force the fusionists into a more radical posture, he completely neglected his district, joined with the most unabashed antislavery men he could find, and ventured into Illinois to confront Stephen A. Douglas. In addition to Chase and Cassius M. Clay, his speaking partners included two root-and-branch abolitionists, Frederick Douglass and Ichabod Codding, adherents of Gerrit Smith's Liberty League. This brigade of "ultraists" stalked the senator from town to town, even when Stephen Douglas canvassed Illinois' southern districts, nationally known for their Negrophobia. Then, parting company with his friends, Giddings traveled on to Michigan and Indiana to complete his extensive tour.[29]

By October the voters had rejected the Democrats in all Northern states except Illinois. Every district in Ohio elected a fusionist candidate for Congress and the anti-Kansas-Nebraska nominees for state offices secured 75,000 vote majorities. Of the 159 congressmen who put through the Kansas-Nebraska Act, all but 75 would now serve out their "lame-duck" sessions.[30] Stephen A. Douglas had all but destroyed the Northern branch of his own party.

The Democrats were thunderstruck, and Giddings never felt better. "After fighting so long against . . . spiritual wickedness in high places, . . ." he found it fulfilling to forget about his narrow escape in the district nominating convention and to believe instead that after "so long a time" the public was finally endorsing his ideas. The need to savor a national victory was especially compelling to one who had numbered among "despised minorities" for seventeen years, and Giddings was understandably sure that he had "never stood higher in the political world. . . ."[31]

Following this renewal of self-confidence, however, Giddings found the second session of Congress unresponsive to his reform appeals. He castigated the proslavery aspects of Franklin Pierce's annual message and tried, without success, to amend the District of Columbia's laws to protect free Negroes.[32] Holdover Democrats sullenly ignored his speeches, and Northern coalitionist congressmen paid no attention either, for most were increasingly preoccupied with disturbing political changes in their districts. The year 1855 witnessed the rise of an ominous new party in American politics, which threatened to eclipse the still unstable anti-Kansas-Nebraska movement. Soon, Giddings also began worrying about the future of the fusion effort. By the time Congress adjourned in May, his mood of complacency had vanished.

In 1854 America's deep streak of anti-immigrant and anti-

Catholic bigotry erupted with unusual virulence, taking the form of a tasteless political crusade which spread rapidly to nearly every state. The "Know-Nothing" party, as it was called, attracted many followers, for it provided an outlet for intolerance while acting as a political haven for displaced conservative Whigs.[33] Though the nascent party had been completely overshadowed by Ohio's 1854 free soil upheaval, by early 1855 it was starting to draw a statewide following. In Massachusetts Know-Nothings were already absorbing the anti-Kansas-Nebraska movement, and Giddings was hardly alone in fearing for Ohio's fragile fusion group. Besides, his humanitarian beliefs never let him condone a movement which injected "new and unconsciencable [sic] elements of oppression" into American politics.[34] Giddings had but two objectives as he left early for Jefferson before Congress ended its stagnant session. He hoped to draw the fusionists away from nativism, and from their disturbing habit of endorsing the Compromise of 1850.

The 1855 gubernatorial race promised to be another turning point in Ohio politics, and the complexity of the situation would have delighted a Renaissance prince. The fusionist movement contained a mass of contradictions, for "hunkers" typified by Thomas Ewing and Thomas Corwin claimed allegiance to the same party as did Giddings and his equally radical friend, Edward Wade. Between these extreme positions resided ambitious, cautious young politicians like John Armour Bingham and John Sherman, violently anti-Negro free soil immigrants, and other anti-Kansas-Nebraska men who hated foreigners. None could say that this unstable mixture would not dissolve into its components, since the Kansas-Nebraska bill had been irrevocably enacted. In fact, the 130,000 Know-Nothings in Ohio were counting on just such a fragmentation.[35]

Salmon Chase had long been considered the most acceptable fusionist choice for governor. Giddings repressed his understandable misgivings and promised Chase his support after the Know-Nothings had announced they were planning a state nominating convention of their own in Cleveland. With the obvious intention of coercing the fusionists by endorsing Chase first, the nativists had scheduled their gathering for late June, only two weeks before the anti-Nebraska men were due to assemble in Columbus for the same purpose. Giddings felt he had no choice but to pre-empt the Know-Nothings by backing Chase as quickly and emphatically as possible.[36]

Giddings had a simple, effective strategy in mind. He knew that the Know-Nothings had begun to split on sectional lines over the Kansas-Nebraska question, and he was certain that the best policy was to "drive the wedge of division home." Fusionists, he decided, must "stand firmly and unmoveably" upon their doctrines, letting the nativists know that "we have no terms to make with slavery, or slaveholding aspirants. . . ." Giddings also told Chase bluntly that he planned to bolt the Columbus convention if even the slightest bargain was made with the nativists. "I will leave the convention, proclaim my protest to the people and call on them to act for themselves." He made it clear that there was already too little humanitarianism in the anti-Kansas-Nebraska organization and that he did not intend to let it be diluted further with bigoted "Know-Nothingism." [37]

Throughout the spring and early summer the *Sentinel* issued one tirade after another against the idea of restricting immigrants while the nation was threatened by a ravenous, conspiring "slave power." Soon, radical and moderate anti-Kansas-Nebraska presses all over the state picked up the theme, as Giddings released a glowing endorsement of Chase. The tempo of the attacks quickened and the Know-Nothings grew ever more unsure of themselves. When the nativist convention assembled on June 20, the delegates quickly vetoed independent nominations, adopted a strong anti-Kansas-Nebraska platform, and made clear their desire to work closely with the Columbus meeting scheduled for July 13. [38] So far, Giddings' tactics had worked quite well. "Our strongest K.N. [Know-Nothing] papers appear to have surrendered," he announced with satisfaction to John G. Palfrey. "I think the K.N.s will give us no more trouble in this state." [39]

Giddings' prediction to Palfrey was only partially accurate, for the Columbus convention was certainly not all he had hoped for, even though concessions to the nativists were held to a minimum. Chase received a unanimous nomination for governor, and the rest of the slate was filled with conservative fusionists acceptable to the Know-Nothings. Most of the nativists were now completely fused with the Free Soil political machine, and all factions within the anti-Kansas-Nebraska complex felt partially mollified. Ohio's Republican party had finally come into being.[40]

The least satisfied delegate at the convention was Joshua Giddings, member of the platform committee. The resolutions merely condemned the Kansas-Nebraska Act, insisted on free soil, and endorsed the idea of a Republican presidential convention to meet the following year. It was the most restricted antislavery program yet put forward in Ohio. Giddings seized the floor and announced that, although he would not object to the resolutions, they certainly did not go far enough. In the platform committee meeting he had pressed for a statement asserting the duty of the federal government to denationalize slavery and legislate to protect man's God-given right to human freedom. The others had overruled him, but he still wished to make his own position clear. In the moment of decision, Giddings failed to make good his threat of bolting, for the dilemmas of the politician as social reformer had not been solved by the passage of time. The contradictions were now just as bedeviling as in 1839, when Giddings had tried to reconcile antislavery activity with membership in the Whig party. In this case Giddings acquiesced to the will of the delegates, overlooked the resolutions, and assumed that he could best improve Republicanism by remaining associated with it. He thereupon offered a resolution calling on all members of the convention to vow perpetual allegiance to Republican creeds and never to return to their old parties. His proposal was voted down, *viva voce,* and the enthusiastic delegates headed off to campaign for Chase.[41] While Giddings had worked hard to keep the

233

Republicans from falling prey to nativism, his services were far less recognized by his colleagues than his radicalism, which was placing him beyond the pale of party regularity.

Since the state Central Committee refused Giddings' request to speak in conservative areas of southern Ohio, he decided to campaign out of state. He broached this idea to other Republicans, who were only too glad to send the "ultra" old man off to the east coast.[42] The Republican managers' strategy was quite sound, for, although they believed Giddings constituted a liability at home, his general presence within the party had great political value. Giddings' name had long been associated with courage, earnestness, and an unflinching devotion to principle. It would scarcely do for the new party to reject this vigorous warrior whose tireless agitation had made him an institution in American politics. Republicans soon began calling him "Father Giddings," and there was accuracy in the title, for he gave the party a high-minded historical justification, a connecting link with John Quincy Adams himself. Giddings' preachments of human freedom and governmental perfectionism might evoke wry grins or nervous looks from other politicians, but his name would always attract a large audience. The Northern public could not help but like a man of integrity. His endorsements would usually help more than hurt, and the Republicans were glad to keep a hold on him, at least for the time being.

Giddings accepted this situation rather easily, for it provided him with a role which he had often held in the past. By retaining his Republican ties he could push the party toward his own views, and none could deny that his national reputation gave him moral leverage. After completing an arduous tour of Massachusetts, Maine, New Hampshire, and New York,[43] Giddings wrote to Chase. He pleaded that the newly elected governor attack the District of Columbia slave trade in his inaugural address. "Our people," he explained, "are not conscious that the party now in power protects the revolting practice of rearing boys and girls for market. . . ."[44] Advancing age and partial political ostracism had not caused Joshua Giddings to compromise his independence of party or sense of moral purpose.

During the summer of 1855 the nation's attention shifted from state elections to the frontier, for a crisis was developing in Kansas. Once that territory had been opened by Douglas' bill, the Northern and Southern settlers had begun a sectional footrace to the frontier, and the stakes were free soil or slavery. By 1855 Northern immigrants clearly outnumbered their Southern foes, but through coercion a bogus proslavery legislature was chosen, the Missouri slave codes were enacted, "abolitionism" was made a capital offense, and political office was limited to slaveholders. The infuriated Northerners set up a rival legislature, drew up a free soil constitution, elected a governor, and petitioned Congress for admission to the Union.[45] By late 1855 Kansas teetered on the brink of civil war, and Giddings' earlier warning of "bloodshed in our own country"[46] promised to be distressingly accurate unless Congress took quick action.

The new House of Representatives, however, was hardly equipped for such work, being composed of 108 Republicans, 83 Democrats, and 43 Know-Nothings. No party had a majority, and the contest for Speaker promised to be the most chaotic in history.[47] Even Giddings momentarily toyed with the idea of competing, which indicated dramatically just how confused the situation was when Congress opened on December 3.[48]

The Democrats refused to cooperate with the nativists. Meanwhile, Giddings organized a small number of Republicans who agreed to vote only for candidates pledged to appointing committees that would have majorities favorable to the denationalization of slavery. Other Republicans tried a round of fruitless negotiations with the Know-Nothings, and two months of legislative bedlam began as the first ballot was totaled.[49] After a second phlegmatic effort to unite with Northern Know-Nothings, the mass of Republicans decided to drop their pledge to Giddings and put their votes behind dapper Nathaniel Banks of Massachusetts, who had recently cast off his nativist affiliations to assume a conservative Republican position. Banks, one of the most antisectional individuals in the North, had only the remotest connection with Giddings and his radical thinking. It was among such leaders that the old Ohioan had to pick and choose as he made his way through the labyrinth of Republican politics. But Giddings hoped that Banks' earlier nativism would appeal to Northern Know-Nothings and induce them into a permanent fusion on Republican terms. For this reason he announced his support of the Massachusetts congressman's candidacy. The nativists, however, remained intransigent as the balloting dragged on through weeks of caucuses, speeches, motions, and violent outbursts of temper.[50]

As in 1849, Giddings was completely caught up in the frenzied stalemate. "I have been active, vigilint [sic] and almost unceasing in my efforts to keep our troops in order . . . ," he confided to his daughter. Without a moment's regard to consistency, he offered resolutions demanding the adoption of the same plurality rule which he had opposed in 1849, for now it was Nathaniel Banks, a "friend of freedom," not Howell Cobb or Robert C. Winthrop, who had control of the most votes.[51] His predictions alternated between cosmic optimism and profound despair, but one fact constantly cheered him: the Republicans refused to barter with anyone. Whether or not Banks won was of secondary importance to him, for the party was continually "becoming more and more consolidated": "The lines of demarcation that separate us from the South . . . and from the Democrats are becoming more and more distinctly marked. . . ." Such maturing augured well for a strong Republican showing in the 1856 presidential race.[52]

Finally, on February 2, 1856, the stalemate ended. The House invoked the plurality rule, and, despite "gloomy apprehensions of defeat," an exhausted Giddings joined in the shouting as Banks won by two votes over William Aiken of South Carolina. Giddings, completely overwhelmed by the thrill of victory, rationalized Banks' conservatism by telling his constituents that the new speaker had been chosen "upon the identical doctrines, for the utterance of which I was driven from my seat in this body fourteen years since." And when the result was announced, all the Republicans rushed up to his seat and shook his hand.[53]

The Clerk picked Giddings, as the oldest member of unbroken service, to administer the oath to the new Speaker, and white-haired "Father Giddings" performed his symbolic task with dignity and solemnity. That night he held a modest open house to celebrate the triumph and was astounded when nearly every Republican made a point of stopping in. It seemed far different from the days when Edward Black had told Giddings that no self-respecting congressman would resist a chance to knock him down. "I have reached the highest point of my ambition. *I am satisfied,*" Giddings told his daughter.[54] It was of no matter that Nathaniel Banks' opportunism and willingness to compromise soon led him to accept a temporary Know-Nothing nomination for the presidency. The friendly handshakes were in themselves some sign of "moral revolution," and Giddings' grasp of political reality melted as he finally enjoyed the warm smiles of fellow congressmen.

The House spent the rest of the session squabbling with the Senate and the President over the Kansas question, and the crisis remained without solution.[55] In the midst of the tumult, Giddings never worked harder, for Banks appointed him chairman of the Claims Committee and second ranking Republican on the crucial Committee on Territories. Giddings dropped his duties in Washington only long enough to appear at a preliminary Republican convention held in Pittsburgh. There he delivered a militant speech humiliating poor Horace Greeley for his mild stance on the Kansas question. During the same period, Giddings wrote long editorials for the *Sentinel* which endorsed Chase for president and declared that issues in the 1856 election should rest solely on "the final establishment of slavery in every state of the Union; or its final extinction from all." [56] Even during the gag-rule struggles fifteen years before Giddings had not been so active.

Finally, on May 8, he rose to deliver a speech against an

237

administration-sponsored bill to increase the number of federal marshals. Giddings had "labored hard and thought intently" while composing his remarks, and he began by charging Franklin Pierce with planning to intervene forcibly with the new marshals in Kansas. Lewis D. Campbell, an Ohio Know-Nothing, interposed several questions, adding to Giddings' "high pressure of excitement." Suddenly, Giddings stopped speaking, his head fell forward, and he toppled over unconscious. After several minutes he opened his eyes, and, feeling "totally unable to account for what was going on," he was escorted to the Speaker's chambers. After an hour of rest, the House was thunderstruck as he reappeared on the floor and delivered the balance of his speech.[57]

Medical men diagnosed the seizure as heart trouble, advising Giddings to recuperate at home, and the Ohioan finally returned to Jefferson on May 22. He stayed just long enough to establish some sort of record for abbreviated convalescence. The very day he left Washington Charles Sumner fell bloodied and unconscious in the Senate. Giddings' friend had been caned by Representative Preston Brooks, a hothead from South Carolina. On May 24 Giddings had heard the news and was again in transit between Jefferson and the Capitol.[58]

Sumner had delivered a speech entitled "The Crime Against Kansas," an elaborate philippic studded with unwarranted slanders of Senator Andrew P. Butler, Preston Brooks' uncle. But the violence of Brooks' retribution far outstripped the excesses of Sumner's speech. Giddings, like the rest of the North, was shocked at the outrage. Henry Wilson and Ben Wade stalked the halls of Congress with handguns bulging under their coats, fully intent on dispatching the first Southerner who attacked them.

Typically, Giddings tried to act as Christian pacifier. He reminded Wilson and Wade that the Republican cause was "one of high moral character" and did not include Mosaic law, pointing out that, if violence were repaid in kind, "the political death of the victor would be as certain as the physical death of the other. . . ." His speech on the assault, delivered on July 11, was equally calm and charitable, reflecting little of the anguish Giddings felt at the hurt done to his Massachusetts friend.[59] On this occasion Ohio's radical representative appreciated the value of muting agitation. The thought of Sumner's vacant seat was sufficient in itself to keep Northern pulses beating at a rapid rate as men contemplated this latest atrocity of the "slave power."

As the presidential convention drew closer, the Republicans began dwelling on "Bleeding Kansas" as well as "Bleeding Sumner." During the summer, Washington newspapers began receiving reports of lawlessness and violence, as Northern and Southern men contested for control of the territory. Proslavery forces sacked the city of Lawrence, and fanatical free soilers responded by murdering several Southern settlers at Pottawattomie Creek. Over-zealous Yankees began organizing the New England Immigrant Aid Society, the aim of which was to supply Northern pioneers with arms. Giddings' youngest son, Grotius, made plans to strike out for the frontier, rifle in hand, to aid the free soilers. This project his father promptly vetoed.[60] Giddings' hopes for a United States governed by Christian charity and divine law were rapidly being dashed by the violence of sectional passion. Needless to say, there was material aplenty for Republicans to stress in the impending presidential election.

Giddings' preferences for the Republican standard-bearer lay with his few associates in the party's high councils, John C. McLean and Salmon Chase. But dashing John C. Frémont had a reputation for being acceptable to the Know-Nothings, and he was the fore-ordained nominee when the Republican National Convention met at Philadelphia in June. Giddings secured a spot on the platform committee, but, even if his hand was evident in the resolutions, the doctrines hardly measured up to those of the Free Soilers in 1848. Instead of even mentioning slavery or the slave trade within the District of Columbia, the platform merely put forward a four-point program for free soil which also denounced Southern expansionist efforts in Cuba. The committee humored Giddings by letting him include a resolution which simply upheld the Constitution and the federal government's duty to enforce the "self-evident truth" of man's equal rights.[61]

It was fortunate for Giddings that the convention agreed to his motion to affirm Jefferson's sentiments. Without such assent he could not have continued to act in an uncompromised fashion within the party, for he seized upon this endorsement in order to make his perfectionism compatible with Republicanism. Even if the platform remained mute regarding the slave trades and the Fugitive Slave Law, he argued that it had "no limitation to Kansas or restriction to locality." The party stood by implication for the regeneration of all society and was pledged to use every constitutional means to defeat the "slave power." After making this mighty rationalization he wrote to George W. Julian expressing his pleasure over the Philadelphia platform. "I think it is ahead of all other platforms ever adopted," he reported with complete sincerity.[62] Convinced that Republicans would legislate God's obvious designs after electing John C. Frémont, Joshua Giddings had preserved his independence in the usual way. He had misdefined his party to accommodate his vision of a more just, more humane society.

Giddings' attempts to style himself a good Republican while accounting to his conscience were taking on ever greater tinges of unreality. Even so, he felt deeply proud that the delegates gave him nine rousing cheers and affirmed his adamant motion to reject all concessions to a splinter group of Northern Know-Nothings. But even this victory was less meaningful than the old man thought. Most Republicans had long been planning to force dissident Know-Nothings to drop their nominee, the same Nathaniel Banks whom Giddings had recently hailed as an antislavery hero. Nevertheless, Giddings judged that "never were wireworkers knocked in the head more completely and in a shorter time than they were by my motion." He left Philadelphia certain that he had played a most constructive role in shaping the Republican cause.[63] The belief allowed him to campaign with equanimity for John C. Frémont and to stand again for re-election.

This time Giddings received the unanimous endorsement of the district convention. In his speech on the Sumner assault he had

240

announced his desire to retire because of poor health, and he had confirmed privately that he longed to "get out of sight and live in private life." But the influential *Ohio State Journal* had applauded his speech for its "temperate" tone, had praised his integrity, and for these reasons had suggested his reelection. The delegates, perhaps hoping that Giddings was learning moderation, could do little but comply, and he retained his seat with ease.[64]

The new, still unsteady Republican party showed heartening strength in the presidential election. Frémont carried eleven northern states, while the Democratic nominee, James M. Buchanan, took nineteen states with 174 electoral votes. "This is the first instance since the revolution in which self-evident truths . . . have been put in issue," announced a gratified Giddings. The "higher law" had begun to operate, and the day was fast arriving when "piracy, outrage and murder shall cease to be authorized by human enactments." [65] With full heart and beclouded political vision Giddings returned to Congress, soon to be told by his Republican colleagues that he did not speak for the party.

NOTES

1 Filler, *Crusade Against Slavery*, 255.

2 JRG to John G. Palfrey, January 26, 1854, Palfrey MSS, HL (quotation) ; JRG to LMG, July 5, 1854, Giddings-Julian MSS, LC (quotation) .

3 JRG to Editor, Ashtabula *Sentinel*, January 5, 1854.

4 U.S. *Congressional Globe*, 33d Cong., 1st Sess., XXIII, Appendix, 52–54.

5 JRG to GRG, December 30, 1853, Giddings MSS.

6 JRG to Editor, Ashtabula *Sentinel*, February 17, 1853.

7 For the best review of the Kansas-Nebraska Act, Douglas' motives, and the meaning of the bill for American politics, see Roy Franklin Nichols, "The Kansas-Nebraska Act: A Century of Historiography," *Mississippi Valley Historical Review*, XLIII (September, 1956) , 621–47.

8 Nevins, *Ordeal*, II, 93–159.

9 JRG to GRG, January 22, 1854, Giddings MSS; James C. Malin, *The Nebraska Question: 1852–1854* (Lawrence, 1953) , 300–302.

10 Julian, *Giddings*, 311.

11 Ashtabula *Sentinel*, September 29, December 22, 1853, January 12, 1854 (quotation) ; Luthin, "Chase," 517–40; Donald, *Sumner*, 249–52.

12 *National Era*, January 24, 1854; George Fort Milton, *The Eve of the Conflict: Stephen A. Douglas and the Needless War* (Boston and New York, 1934) , 117; Nevins, *Ordeal*, II, 102–7.

13 Nevins, *Ordeal*, II, 122–32.

14 JRG to GRG, February 12, 1854, Giddings-Julian MSS, LC.

15 U.S. *Congressional Globe*, 33d Cong., 1st Sess., XXIII, 504.

16 *Ibid.*, 1073–75.

[17] *Ibid.*, 504.

[18] See Litwack, *North of Slavery*, 214–80; and Robert F. Durden, *James Shepherd Pike: Republicanism and the American Negro, 1850–1882* (Durham, 1957), Chaps. 1 and 2.

[19] JRG to John G. Palfrey, January 26, 1854, Palfrey MSS, HL. See also JRG to GRG, February 12, 1854, Giddings-Julian MSS, LC; JRG to GRG, March 3, 1854, Giddings MSS.

[20] Milton, *Stephen A. Douglas*, 141–42; Thompson, *Robert Toombs*, 99.

[21] U.S. *Congressional Globe*, 33d Cong., 1st Sess., XXIII, Appendix, 986–89.

[22] *Ibid.*, (text), 1240–54.

[23] *Ohio State Journal*, March 23, March 24, 1854; Ashtabula *Sentinel*, March 9, 1854.

[24] Filler, *Crusade Against Slavery*, 225–26.

[25] JRG to GRG, May 21, 1854, Giddings MSS; JRG to Readers, Ashtabula *Sentinel*, June 8, June 15, 1854; Providence *Daily Tribune*, July 11, 1854, JRG Scrapbook, 1854, Giddings MSS; Luthin, "Chase," 523–25; *National Era*, June 22, 1854.

[26] JRG to Readers, Ashtabula *Sentinel*, June 15, 1854.

[27] JRG "To the People of the Twentieth Congressional District of Ohio," *National Era*, July 27, 1854, and in the Ashtabula *Sentinel*, August 10, 1854. It is instructive to note that Giddings released his protest to a national paper before giving it to his own district organ. Clearly he was concerned already over the national tendency of fusion movements to take conservative postures.

[28] Ashtabula *Sentinel*, August 17, August 31, 1854.

[29] Milton, *Stephen A. Douglas*, 173; Ashtabula *Sentinel*, September 14, September 21, 1854; *National Era*, October 22, 1854. For Codding, see Filler, *Crusade Against Slavery*, 152, 232, 247.

[30] *National Era*, October 10, 1854; Ashtabula *Sentinel*, September 28, October 19, November 9, 1854; Ralph V. Harlow and Nelson M. Blake, *The United States From Wilderness to World Power*, 4th edition (New York, 1964), 312.

[31] JRG to JAG, January 22, 1855, Giddings MSS.

[32] U.S. *Congressional Globe*, 33d Cong., 2d Sess., XXIV, Appendix, 31–35, text, 84–85.

[33] Ray Allen Billington, *The Protestant Crusade, 1800–1860: A Study of the Origins of American Nativism* (New York, 1938), 322–430.

[34] Eugene H. Roseboom, *The Civil War Era, 1850–1873*, vol. 4 of *The History of Ohio*, ed. Carl Wittke (Columbus, 1944), 286–99; JRG to John G. Palfrey, December 30, 1854, Palfrey MSS, HL; JRG "To the People of the Twentieth Congressional District of Ohio," Ashtabula *Sentinel*, March 22, 1855 (quotation).

[35] Roseboom, *The Civil War Era*, 296–97.

[36] *Ibid.*, 304; JRG to Salmon P. Chase, April 18, 1855, Chase MSS, HSP; JRG to Readers, Ashtabula *Sentinel*, February 1, 1855.

[37] JRG to Salmon P. Chase, April 18, May 1, 1855, Chase MSS, HSP (both letters quoted) ; JRG to George W. Julian, May 30, 1855, Giddings-Julian MSS, LC.

[38] Ashtabula *Sentinel*, February 8, March 8, April 19, 1855; Roseboom, *The Civil War Era*, 302.

[39] JRG to John G. Palfrey, June 29, 1855, Palfrey MSS, HL.

[40] Roseboom, *The Civil War Era*, 303–5.

[41] Ashtabula *Sentinel*, July 19, 1855.

[42] JRG to Salmon P. Chase, September 7, 1855, Chase MSS, HSP.

[43] JRG to LWG, November 11, 1855, JRG to LMG, November 17, 1855, Giddings-Julian MSS, LC; JRG to JAG, September 17, 1855, Giddings MSS; Ashtabula *Sentinel*, October 11, 1855.

[44] JRG to Salmon P. Chase, November 2, 1855, Giddings MSS.

[45] Nevins, *Ordeal*, II, 380–93.

[46] U.S. *Congressional Globe*, 33rd Cong., 1st Sess., XXIII, Appendix, 986–89.

[47] Nevins, *Ordeal*, II, 413–14.

[48] JRG Memoir Fragment, Julian MSS, ISL; JRG to Gamaliel Bailey, November 11, 1855, Giddings-Julian MSS, LC; JRG to Salmon P. Chase, November 2, 1855, Chase MSS, HSP.

[49] JRG Memoir Fragment, Julian MSS, ISL; Nevins, *Ordeal*, II, 413–14; U.S. *Congressional Globe*, 34th Cong., 1st Sess., XXV, 45–46.

[50] *Ibid.*, 45–245; JRG to Readers, Ashtabula *Sentinel*, January 10, 1856; JRG to JAG, January 12, 1856, Giddings MSS. For a complete treatment of Banks' career see Fred H. Harrington, *Fighting Politician: Major General N. P. Banks* (Philadelphia, 1948), *passim*.

[51] JRG to LMG, February 1, 1856, Giddings-Julian MSS, LC (quotation) ; U.S. *Congressional Globe,* 34th Cong., 1st Sess., XXV, 251–55.

[52] JRG to Gerrit Smith, January 21, 1856, Gerrit Smith-Miller MSS, SUL (quotation) ; JRG to JAG, January 12, 1856, Giddings MSS (quotation) ; JRG to LWG, January 27, 1856, Giddings-Julian MSS, LC; JRG to LMG, February 1, 1856, Giddings-Julian MSS, LC.

[53] JRG "To the People of the Twentieth Congressional District of Ohio," *National Era,* February 14, 1856; JRG to Daughter, February 3, 1856, Giddings-Julian MSS, LC.

[54] *Ibid.*

[55] Nevins, *Ordeal,* II, 416–28.

[56] U.S. *Congressional Globe,* 34th Cong., 1st Sess., XXV, 412; Ashtabula *Sentinel,* February 28, April 24, 1856 (quotation) .

[57] U.S. *Congressional Globe,* 34th Cong., 1st Sess., XXV, Appendix, 526–29, text, 1159; JRG to LMG, May 9, 1856, Giddings-Julian MSS, LC (quotation) .

[58] JRG to LAG, May 27, 1856, Giddings-Julian MSS, LC.

[59] *Ibid.;* Donald, *Sumner,* 278–82; JRG to Charles Sumner, July 24, 1856, Sumner MSS, HL (quotation) ; JRG to Daughter, May 28, 1856, Giddings-Julian MSS, LC; U.S. *Congressional Globe,* 34th Cong., 1st Sess., XXV, Appendix, 1117–21.

[60] Milton, *Stephen A. Douglas,* 198–200. Giddings did not object to Grotius' excursion to Kansas on the basis of principle but rather because he had reservations about James Lane, leader of the Kansas free soilers. "I should not object to his going," Giddings wrote, "but would prefer him to have better company. I have no confidence in neither [sic] Lane's judgment nor his courage. I fear he will make a *faux pas* and embarrass the free states." JRG to JAG, July 4, 1856, Giddings MSS.

[61] Ruhl Jacob Bartlett, "John C. Fremont and the Republican Party," in *Ohio State University Studies in History and Political Science,* XIII (Columbus, 1930) , 11–17; Julian, *Giddings,* 335; JRG to JAG, July 2, July 20, 1856, Giddings MSS; Ashtabula *Sentinel,* June 19, June 26, 1856.

[62] JRG to George W. Julian, June 24, 1856, Giddings-Julian MSS, LC.

[63] Ashtabula *Sentinel,* June 26, 1856; Charles W. Johnson, *Proceedings of the First Three Republican National Conventions . . .* (Minneapolis, 1893) , 53, 63; Nevins, *Ordeal,* II, 467–71; JRG Memoir Fragment,

Julian MSS, ISL; JRG to JAG, July 2, 1856, Giddings MSS (quotation);
JRG to LMG, June 18, 1856, Giddings-Julian MSS, LC.

64 JRG to GRG, August 10, 1856, Giddings MSS (quotation); *Ohio
State Journal,* quoted in the Ashtabula *Sentinel,* July 24, 1856; Ashtabula
Sentinel, August 13, 1856.

65 Sewell, *John P. Hale,* 173; JRG "To the People of the Twentieth
Congressional District of Ohio," Ashtabula *Sentinel,* November 20, 1856
(quotation).

Chapter 12

ASCENT
INTO
"ULTRAISM"

·⟨ ⟩·

1857-1859

Franklin Pierce felt deeply embittered by the Republican triumphs. Four years earlier he had been elected on a platform pledging sectional peace. Now, as a disgraced outgoing president he was leaving behind him a dividing nation. The 1856 election amounted to a blanket repudiation of his tenure by the North, a stark challenge to the South, and perhaps a prelude to disunion. Disillusioned, Pierce gave vent to every bit of his petulance in his last annual message. In it he indicted the Republican party as a collection of hypocritical abolitionists anxious to wreak bloody violence upon the South. Under the guise of "pretending to seek only to prevent the spread of . . . slavery," he asserted, the Republicans were really "enflamed with the desire to change the domestic institutions of the existing states." After reading the president's message, Joshua Giddings rightly judged it "disgraceful to his official position." [1]

The president's charges instantly evoked impassioned sectional debate in the House, and to prove Pierce's case Southern speak-

247

ers dredged up passages from old speeches by Giddings, especially the one delivered in 1846 on the Oregon question. At that time, it will be remembered, Giddings had painted frightening scenes of slave insurrections which he had predicted would accompany Anglo-American war.[2]

Giddings chafed at hearing himself quoted out of context, while his nervous Republican colleagues tried their best to keep him quiet; they feared, with good reason, that he was not the proper man to argue the moderate nature of the party. As he heard one colleague after another protest the antisectional aims of Republicanism, Giddings felt "constrained to speak and must do so. The great work of reform is going forward, but too slowly for my desire . . . ; all around me young men are holding back and begging me to be *cautious* and *prudent*. The old songs are repeated until I am sick at heart. . . ." Despite the increased number of new free soilers, Congress' "moral sentiment" seemed "so corrupted by oppression that regeneration appears almost hopeless." Suddenly, he perceived the brutal truth of his party's conservatism. His rationalizations were momentarily swept away, and he discovered that no large political organization could possibly pledge itself to perfectionism. "I feel an intellectual lassitude that almost disqualifies me from speaking my own sentiments," he confessed pathetically to his daughter.[3]

On December 8, the day after Giddings had unburdened his soul in private, moderate Ohio Republican John Sherman stood to rebuke the Southern charges of abolitionism. He did so by making a detailed analysis of the antislavery movement, and in the process he shattered any of Giddings' remaining illusions. There were two types of antislavery men with whom the Republicans had nothing to do, Sherman explained, Garrisonian abolitionists and slightly less "ultra" men like Joshua Giddings. Giddings' opinions, said Sherman reassuringly, were "no more engrafted upon the Republican platform than the recent doctrines of Governor Adams of South Carolina in favor of reopening the slave trade." To be sure, Republicans regarded the venerable agitator with "great respect," but hardly considered him a legitimate member of the party.⁴ Giddings was being disavowed on the floor of the House by the very men who called him "Father."

The agony of hearing Sherman's speech only dictated more vigorous action to one who had spent a lifetime trying to reverse the mainstream of opinion rather than being swept along by events. John Sherman denied Giddings' definition of Republicanism, so Giddings attempted to create a place for himself by changing the party's mind. His recognition that Republicans refused to embrace social transformation was quickly obscured by his need for party identification and his faith in the power of moral truths. On December 10 Giddings rose to inform his colleagues of what they *really* believed.

His message was that all Republicans stood on the "self-evident truths" of the Declaration of Independence, for had not his resolution affirming that creed been accepted by the Philadelphia convention? Although the party did not endorse abolitionism, it did, or should, have an undying commitment to Jefferson's phrases. This meant ceaseless effort to promote the elevation of *"all men,* embracing high and low, rich and poor . . . of light complexion, of dark complexion, of mixed complexion. . . ." No Republican would promote slave revolts, Giddings asserted, but were any bondsman to break through his mental oppression and realize the extent of his suffering, Republicans should not impede his attempts to free himself. "On this rock we build our political church, and neither the gates of Hell nor the Democrats shall prevail against it." Republicans would "stand by their oath pledged to God, to Christianity and to the civilized world . . ." to uphold "self-evident truths." According to Giddings, the party would work to repeal the Fugitive Slave Law, to abolish slavery in the District of Columbia and the slave trades along the coasts, and to preserve the territories for freedom.⁵

The next day Sherman again obtained the floor to remind the Southern members that none should take Giddings seriously. Virginia's John Letcher had just quoted another of Giddings' torrid passages while crying "black Republicanism." Sherman in reply cautioned that "when the gentleman quotes the language of a particular member . . . let him not attribute that language to a party." ⁶ Giddings' forensic efforts had created no impact whatever.

Desperate, Giddings turned to Salmon Chase, one of the "few" men left to whom he felt he could speak his whole mind. The debate over Pierce's accusations was still raging, and many Southerners had promised to secede were the Republicans to capture the presidency in 1860. Giddings decided that Southern militancy provided a way to stimulate the moral sensibilities of Northern congressmen who acted "gentlemanly" and sought "quiet and friendship instead of contention." Mutual hostility between the two sections was "increasing daily, growing stronger, more determined at all times." Fire-eaters were preaching disunion and would soon "bring others up to that point."

To counter the Southern threat and arouse the Republicans, Giddings suggested a plan to Chase which he felt "any honest and conservative man must acknowledge as just and reasonable." Chase should join him in opening a campaign for a national Republican convention. Such a convention would "not . . . promote dissolution," Giddings explained, but would announce that "our union should be maintained for the purposes of *freedom*" while fully asserting the "higher laws" of the Declaration of Independence. "Indeed I deny the right of any man . . . to change our position until a national convention shall do it," he vowed hotly. "One thing appears to be settled. That is Northern liberty or Southern slavery must fall." ⁷

Congressional rejection had driven Giddings to try an appeal to the nation, and his dilemma was excruciating. As his position put him out of phase with the Republican party, he could only act on conscience and habit, for he had always believed in the regenerative powers of confrontation. Such faith had led him to his most fruitful achievements: the censure, the quarrels with Winthrop, the Speakership bolts, and the work for the Free Soil party. Now, when most politicians in the North were leery of his radicalism, his natural tendency was again to speak freely.

Chase vetoed adamantly Giddings' proposal. With "impaired

250

morale" and tenuous organization Republicans were "in no position to hold . . . advanced ground." [8] Giddings undoubtedly puz-
zled over what Chase found so "advanced" about "self-evident
truths," but it was also clear to him that his final attempt to promote political perfectionism and to return himself to the center
of party affairs had been an unmitigated failure. Three days after
his correspondence with Chase, on January 17, Giddings collapsed
on the floor of the House.

He was in the midst of a twenty-minute speech on a routine
private bill when he suddenly fell unconscious. Speaker Banks
adjourned the House at once, and Giddings was carried into the
lobby, where doctors tried to restore his circulation by covering
him with mustard plasters, bruising his flesh, and bathing him
in warm water. Over seventy-five minutes elapsed before Giddings
opened his eyes, but his memory had temporarily escaped him,
and it took him five days to regain his ability to write. "It was a
terrible blow," he told his daughter, "my last battle has been
fought. I have laid aside my armor and shall no more mingle in
those conflicts which twenty years have rendered familiar to me."
After nine days' recuperation, the doctors judged Giddings fit
enough to survive a trip to Jefferson.[9]

Laura Giddings spent many hours seated beside her husband's
bed, reading aloud the condolences which arrived daily from
every part of the North. Old friends like John G. Palfrey, Amos
Tuck, Charles Sumner, and John P. Hale joined a multitude of
common farmers and tradesmen in expressing their hopes for Giddings' full recovery. Most significant, however, was the concern
shown by William Lloyd Garrison's circle of radical abolitionists.
Henry C. Wright, one of the oldest and most fervent exponents of
the Garrisonian program, sent along warm wishes not only in his
own behalf, but also for Parker Pillsbury and Oliver Johnson,
two longstanding warriors of the American Anti-Slavery Society.
Wright also told Giddings that he spoke for Garrison himself in
saying that "of all politicians, you are the most consecrated &
respected in the hearts of those . . . in the *moral* conflict with oppression." [10]

JOSHUA R. GIDDINGS

Ever since 1840, when the Liberty party had departed from the American Anti-Slavery Society, the Garrisonians had remained constant in their insistence on immediate emancipation. Unhampered by political association of any kind, they had long preached disunion while demanding the overthrow of all sinful institutions which impeded human regeneration. Giddings' own developing perfectionism had already been noted and duly praised by Garrison's *Liberator,* and he had occasionally enjoyed the moral support of these true radicals of American reform. During his period of recuperation, Giddings began taking further steps toward "ultraism" and also started channeling the radicals' sentiments toward his all-too-conservative Republican party.

Giddings now had time to deal with difficult questions, since he felt convinced that he would never return to Congress,[11] and certainly things did seem confusing. Even if John Sherman had read him out of the party, Republicans did testify to the existence of a huge antislavery enterprise. Giddings had to admit that progress, at least in one sense of his definition, was perhaps being achieved. But was there really a moral revolution stirring the North? Republicans seemed stubbornly unwilling to grasp the sweeping reforms which Giddings' spiritualism demanded and to which he clung with increasing ferocity after suffering two strokes. Judging from his experiences of the past two years, the old man could not honestly say that the Republican party had done much except violence his perfectionist convictions.

He tried to adjust by taking a step to the left, squarely into the camp of millennial radicalism.[12] Here was a position which freed him from his frustrating inability to come to terms with the Republican version of antislavery politics. At the same time, if reform was by some chance headed in the direction that Giddings desired, it behooved him to speed up the process. Many old institutions, he now decided, needed a complete redoing, and new personal statements on antislavery issues were in order.

As usual, religious thinking provided the basis of Giddings' decisions, for, although he already had come far with spiritual-

252

ism since abandoning orthodoxy in 1852, he now carried the belief to its ultimate conclusions. The old Calvinism of his youth, even as softened by the evangelical creeds of revivalist Charles Grandison Finney, now filled him with shivers of revulsion—especially the dogma of predestined damnation to a literal hell: "What terrible thoughts of the dangers of eternal fires!" he exclaimed to his daughter. He thought back on jeremiads he had heard years earlier, which "if uttered now would cause any hearer to recoil from them." Now he was sure that humanity needed "a higher, purer theology" to guide governments and churches as they "cast aside" institutions which were "inert, inefficient and worn out." He was convinced that an atmosphere must be developed which would promote "a union of hearts" upon the "great and vital truths" of human freedom and personal elevation.[13] With such religious purposes completely framed, it was easy for Giddings to assume a far more radical posture on slavery. While the need to retain his political identity kept him from adopting outright abolitionism, he came as close to this position as was humanly possible.

Giddings found no lack of issues on which to expound his newly developed opinions. Just after he arrived home in Jefferson, the United States Supreme Court handed down the Dred Scott decision, which invalidated every law prohibiting the spread of slavery. Even a popular sovereignty vote for free soil now carried no legal weight. This sweeping decision, if enforced, literally nationalized the "peculiar institution." It also made racial inequality the basis of all legislation. Chief Justice Roger B. Taney appended to the ruling the gratuitous statement that no Negro was entitled to legal protection anywhere in the country or had any rights that white men were compelled to uphold.[14] The decision was one which even extremely conservative free soilers could not endorse. Most Northern men now looked beyond the rule of law for other weapons with which to impede the spread of slavery, and Giddings numbered among the first to demand open defiance of the Dred Scott decision. While espousing civil disobedience in letters to the

Ashtabula *Sentinel,* he also called on the nation to redefine its rapidly eroding sense of values.

To Giddings the Dred Scott decision marked the final stage of transition in the government from "a Christian democracy" to a "tyrannous [sic] oligarchy unsuited to the age in which we live," for Taney had excluded the Negro from all guarantees of the Constitution and Declaration of Independence. In a lengthy series of articles in the *Sentinel* Giddings dwelled exclusively on refuting this aspect of the decision, while paying absolutely no attention to the free soil issue.[15]

Giddings aimed the entire thrust of his argument at Taney's assumption of innate Negro inferiority, for Giddings maintained that nation's history and Christian principles demanded federally sponsored equality for all men, regardless of race, wherever the government possessed the constitutional power to act. The Negroes who served during the Revolution and the War of 1812 "did not sacrifice their lives to establish the revolting proposition that *'black men have no rights that white men were bound to respect.'* " On the contrary, they had died for principles of the Declaration of Independence, "set forth by a Deity which guarantees *equal rights to all* men. . . ." By every usage slaves had always been considered men. Citing Greek practices of bondage and the views of Bartholomé de las Casas, Giddings declared that the African in slavery "has worshipped the same God, trusted in the same salvation and to this day must be regarded as entitled to all the religious rights that whites enjoy." Even granting Taney's belief in Negro inferiority, the government's job was to make laws "for protecting the weak and friendless [rather] than the strong and powerful." Congress should ignore the court's ruling and take special pains to legislate for the Negro's protection rather than abide by laws detrimental to his improvement.[16]

By September, Giddings had completed a second series of essays, this time on the question of compensated emancipation. This solution to the slavery question had been popular in many circles, receiving at various times the endorsements of Ben Wade and Abraham Lincoln. As the sectional crisis deepened, the idea of

Congress' peacefully purchasing and colonizing slaves seemed to many a very alluring, rational alternative to secession. Giddings, however, regarded such proposals as immoral and utopian. Besides, he had now concluded that only through successful slave insurrections could the problems of bondage in America be solved. Southern states would refuse to ratify the constitutional amendment necessary for compensated emancipation, and slaveholders would never sell their chattel, Giddings argued. Back in the Middle Ages, he recalled, Philip the Bold of France had resorted to *"fire and sword"* to attack and destroy Tunisian slavedealers, and America's Stephen Decatur had done the same to the Barbary pirates. These measures Giddings judged "right and just." It would be morally inconsistent for Americans "to pay our slaveholders who are far more worthy of the sword and the bayonet that the slaveholders of Tunis were . . . inasmuch as they were more ignorant." Americans had for years been subsidizing slavery anyway, and Giddings felt it high time that "future donations . . . be made in *powder and ball,* delivered to the slaves to be used as they may deem proper." [17] Giddings had abandoned nonviolence as a solution to the slavery question, and his idea of delivering *"powder and ball"* to the slaves needed only that bloody apostle of abolition, John Brown, to give it reality.[18] Probably unwittingly, Giddings had helped make Northerners more receptive to the idea of violent solutions to the slavery question.

Garrisonians and Liberty Leaguers were quick to act on Giddings' perfectionist emphasis and his increasingly "ultra" antislavery views. To America's outspoken abolitionists the old agitator represented a fruitful liaison between radical abolitionism and the bulk of conservative Republicans. He still insisted that he spoke for the party, but he did so in a reform idiom which the root-and-branch reformers easily understood. Abolitionists as anxious as Giddings for a moral revolution began hoping that by goading him into more advanced positions the tone of Republicanism could be improved. Some even felt that Giddings could be totally converted, for the famous political agitator certainly would have made a handsome addition to the stable of unflinching abolitionists. Gerrit Smith often tried to convince Giddings of the emancipationists' logic.[19]

Parker Pillsbury, one of the Garrisonians' most hardworking agents, was the first to attempt influencing the Republican party through the Ohio congressman. In a series of abrasive letters addressed to Giddings and published in the *Sentinel*, Pillsbury made a sweeping indictment of Republican conservatism. He charged the party with moral timidity, for its goals were fragile and half-hearted. According to Pillsbury, all the party cared about was free soil. It utterly lacked the moral power to overcome the sins of slavery, for Republicans did not endorse complete equality and the right of suffrage for the Negro. Pillsbury's tactic was a realistic one, for Giddings had long been a foe of voting restriction in Ohio, and he might argue that the party endorsed political equality all over the nation. Giddings was only too happy to reply, for in so doing he could try to make his own sweeping commitments for the party. He disappointed Pillsbury, but only partially.

Giddings denied the Negro's national right to vote, saying that Republicans saw it as a question of a political "privilege" rather than a "natural right." But, at the same time, he assured Pillsbury that the Republicans maintained the "right of the negro *to live, to that liberty* which is necessary to sustain and cherish life, to attain knowledge and enjoy happiness." Republicans would be glad to hang any white who murdered a Negro, for "we protect the negro just as we protect our wives, our children, ourselves. . . ." Pillsbury undoubtedly was not completely satisfied with the response, yet he had enabled Giddings to put his party on paper as advocating far more humanitarianism than most were willing to do. Giddings, for his part, felt pleased about committing Republicans to everything but direct emancipation and unqualified Negro equality. Contrary to the opinions of several historians, Pillsbury and the other radicals were exercising an important influence on political parties in the 1850's.[20]

The old congresssman recovered his strength with surprising rapidity as the summer wore on, and he even felt strong enough to campaign for Chase's successful re-election as governor. He attended the Republican state convention and after some impassioned pleading he convinced the delegates to resolve to oppose the Fugitive Slave Law. He also used this occasion to announce that he would return to the House for the next session. By August he informed George W. Julian that he had taken the stump, "not for myself or for anybody in particular, but 'for all the world and the rest of *mankind*," including the 'niggers.' " [21]

He also took time to attend and criticize a "compensated emancipation" meeting held in Cleveland which pacifist Elihu Burritt had organized. Oliver Johnson, one of Garrison's most trusted lieutenants, and Gerrit Smith tried to infiltrate and disrupt the meeting through Giddings by urging him to become a radical abolitionist. "It would be a bold act," Johnson argued, "striking terror into the hearts of the slave-mongers and rebuking the timidity of men who are doing their worst to keep the Republican party on the lowest platform of principles." [22] Although Giddings refused to be swayed, he certainly had become the political darling of "non-political" abolitionists. Still, he remained unwilling to confront slavery in the South and deny the Constitution, for if he did so he could hardly return to his congressional seat and agitate for the millennium. [23]

The national crisis over Kansas had scarcely subsided in Giddings' absence. In January, 1858, President Buchanan endorsed the fraudulently ratified Lecompton Constitution, a product of Kansas' bogus proslavery legislature. After Giddings had arrived in the Capitol, the Senate approved the document. The House then rejected the constitution and the issue was finally settled by a compromise, the English Bill. Giddings assented to this measure only at the last minute, after agonizing misgivings, a physical threat from Mississippian Lucius Q. C. Lamar, and another very mild stroke. Kansas finally became a peaceful place, but sectional discord was hardly muted by the volcanic debate which occupied Congress from January to mid-June. [24]

257

On February 26, Giddings added his very weak voice to those opposing the Lecompton Constitution. His remarks were nearly inaudible to most,[25] a not displeasing situation from a conservative Republican's point of view, for he had decided to unveil his new radicalism in the House. His speech was based on ideas found in his articles of the previous summer and sounded very much as if its author had decided to appoint himself chaplain of the House. Giddings spoke of universal freedom, the moral elevation of all mankind, and the need for Congress to create a totally benevolent, reconstructed government. "If there be a class of men on earth who ought to be religious . . . members of this body ought to sustain that character. . . ." Government should work solely to promote God's gift of human freedom, which is essential if each individual, white or Negro, is to be brought "into harmony with God's law, and [to] enjoy the happiness resulting therefrom. . . ."

The "primal issue" in America, he intoned, rested between congressmen who were willing to act upon such "self-evident truths" and the "slave power," whose "heathenism" had driven Southern men to assert that "black men have no rights which white men are bound to respect." Giddings pleaded that "this conspiracy may be defeated . . ." by the acts of a "Christian government." He called for "the final eradication of . . . infidelity from the earth . . ." through the enactment of legislation following "the laws of our common Father . . . for the progress, the moral elevation of our [human] race. . . ." Were the Congress to vote for God's precepts, all mankind would soon "attain that happiness that constitutes the ultimate object of human existence." [26]

Predictably, his sermon had no effect at all upon the Republicans. Instead, they began making it a point to avoid him. "I cannot consult with men in whom I can[not] confide, who are all distant from me, and almost every man of experience here is opposed to me . . . ," Giddings complained privately.[27] But the radicals were overjoyed upon reading his remarks and hoped that his speech signaled a rapid moral advancement in Northern politics. "I love and venerate you for what you have done . . . ," wrote Oliver Johnson.[28] The aging Quaker abolitionist, Arnold Buffum, told his daughter, "I would like to go into the future or spirit world in Joshua R. Giddings [sic] carpet bag. I felt [sic] undoubting assurance that I would be safe." Gerrit Smith congratulated Giddings for successfully promoting advanced principles within the party, and William Lloyd Garrison himself thanked the old Ohioan profusely in a long private letter. Garrison felt that Giddings' efforts marked the first political step toward Christian government in America, and Oliver Johnson's *National Anti-Slavery Standard* saw hope for Republicanism at last. But Marius Robinson, who had manned a lonely outpost of Garrisonian support in the Western Reserve for nearly twenty years, showed the most perception of all. "There are not many men left . . . of the stamp of Mr. Giddings," said Robinson, fully appreciating the congressman's uniqueness in American politics. Robinson knew that Giddings had now adopted the radical reform mentality of an earlier era. "It almost seems," the abolitionist observed, "as if the mold has been broken in which such souls were shaped." [29]

Arnold Buffum, Oliver Johnson, Marius Robinson, Gerrit Smith, and William Lloyd Garrison had led the antislavery crusade's first generation, just as Giddings had directed the earliest congressional agitators. Now, as the issue of free soil forced Northern opinion toward a unified, but extremely qualified, anti-Southern position, Giddings and these older abolitionists found themselves in similar situations, despite their doctrinal differences. Giddings, Gerrit Smith, and the Garrisonians could not possibly hope to lead the Republicans. But together they could criticize, interject moral issues, and demand advanced positions. Giddings' unusual relationship with the uncompromising abolitionists had now been fully cemented. This alliance proved crucial, not in improving the party, but in keeping Republicans from abandoning their principles completely.

The congressional convention which met in August at Jefferson passed over Joshua Giddings for renomination. Even though he wanted to run again, his radicalism had far outdistanced the party's opinions, and his fragile health also counted against him. It proved easy for John Hutchins, the man chosen to run, to change the minds of several precommitted delegates. The veteran took the decision in stride, telling the convention: "I leave you today with a lighter heart than ever before. . . . The quiet gratifications and joys of social life now seem within my reach . . . and they beckon me on." Defeat after eleven straight re-elections bothered Giddings little. At least he did not complain openly.[30]

Charles Sumner, John G. Palfrey, William Seward, and Henry Wilson all told Giddings how bad they felt about his retirement, but Giddings was not thinking of a placid summer.[31] Instead, he was worried that the Republican party was lapsing into a condition of compromise. Conservative politicians like William Seward and John C. McLean ranked high among the party's leadership. Never did such men mention the Fugitive Slave Law or any other sectional issue, save that of the territories. Important Republican presses began emphasizing other points, like the benefits of high tariffs and homestead laws, which Giddings judged irrelevant "dodges." He rightly suspected that an "extensive effort" was afoot to make the Republican party palatable to the conservative Northerner and moderate Southerner. Anxious to combat this trend, he wrote to Gerrit Smith, asking for help: "I am desirous of bringing the authors out before the public and with the aid of yourself and others I hope to do it. . . . Your position may save us from such folly." [32] Giddings had decided to use his popularity with the radicals to prod the Republican party, and Smith through his Liberty League publications made himself a willing ally.

As soon as the 1858 campaign commenced, harsh letters from Smith, which castigated the Republicans for being reactionary, timid politicians who were bankrupting themselves by their limited doctrines, began appearing in the *Sentinel*. True antislavery voters, they asserted, should support Smith's emancipationist Liberty League. Giddings issued a blistering reply which argued that the party endorsed the revealed truth of the Declaration of Independence and thus stood pledged to denationalize slavery and promote human improvement throughout the nation. Streams of vitriol poured from both men's pens well into November, as Giddings continued to insist upon the radical nature of Republicanism. At the same time, Giddings wrote with tongue in cheek to his "antagonist": "I would not permit it to be said that I entered into any arrangement with you or anyone to bring our doughfaces . . . out to public view. I trust you have done that in your answer to my letter." [33] The opinion of some historians, that the Republican party threatened the roles of abolitionists, causing them to attack it irrationally, certainly falls down in the case of Gerrit Smith.[34] To Smith, the party constituted a challenge, not a threat.

Meanwhile, Giddings pursued the second line of his strategy by criticizing the conservatives. Thomas Corwin provided a choice target by campaigning as a Republican while endorsing the Fugitive Slave Law and telling his audiences to beware of any form of anti-Southern "radicalism." By October Corwin had read in his local newspaper a lengthy public letter from Giddings which charged him with moral turpitude and "doughfacery." [35] Giddings also went to slaveholding Missouri to promote reform politics by speaking before the most timid species of antislavery men in America, the border-state Republican and Douglas Democrat. The New York *Post* observed that "a fat juicy Englishman would be as safe among a tribe of cannibals . . ." as Giddings in Missouri, but he emerged alive and even drew applause.[36]

When the campaign ended, the Republicans had scored substantial gains on the strength of the Lecompton Constitution and Dred Scott decision. Giddings congratulated Gerrit Smith, who had run for governor in New York, and complimented him on his efforts to help the Republicans: "I am of the opinion you never did better service to the cause. . . . The efforts to induce the Republican Party to modify its doctrines . . . seem to be given up." [37] With improved spirits Giddings returned to Washington to sit out his last session. On the way, he attended a dinner given in his honor by his old Boston friends and "was most eloquently praised by all present." [38] The prospect of retirement might be frustrating, but moments like this helped to make up for it.

In early January, Giddings delivered his farewell speech, enti-

tled "The Spirit of Compromise Within the Republican Party."
By now, Republicans had adjusted themselves to his insistence on
"Christian government" and "higher law," so they took his preachments in stride. But Giddings also refused to vote for Oregon's
free soil constitution, since it excluded Negroes. This intransi-
gence worried many Republicans and so did a heated debate between Giddings and Ohio Democrat Samuel S. Cox over Negro
suffrage. Even though Giddings "dodged" the voting issue and was
certainly bested in the encounter, he was leaving Congress as he
had entered it twenty years earlier, as much a maverick as ever.[39]

Still, most Republicans had to admit they admired Giddings
greatly, though preferring to do so from a safe distance. His rug-
ged earnestness commanded respect, even if few understood him.
Toward the end of the session, 104 senators and representatives
agreed to John A. Bingham's suggestion and presented him with
an ornately decorated solid silver tea set. The engraving read "To
Joshua R. Giddings, as a token of respect for his Moral Worth
and Personal Integrity." Soon after, he received a gold watch and
family Bible, fittingly enough, from the congregation of abolitionist Henry Highland Garnet's Negro church in New York City. The
gifts were offered by "The Colored People of New York and Brook-
lyn," in recognition of Giddings as the "Champion of American
Freedom." [40] The American Negro and the Republican party were
yet quite estranged from each other, but gestures from both groups
did justice to a man whose conscience had given him the strength
to begin bringing the two together. Joshua Giddings had been
given full symbolic recognition for his congressional career.

NOTES

[1] JRG to LMG, December 7, 1856, Giddings-Julian MSS, LC (quotation) ; U.S. *Congressional Globe,* 34th Cong., 3d Sess., XXVI, Appendix, 1–3 (quotation).

[2] *Ibid.* (text), 56, 68, 71; for Giddings' 1846 statements and the circumstances surrounding them, see Chap. 6, notes 19–23 and corresponding text.

[3] JRG to LMG, December 7, 1856, Giddings-Julian MSS, LC.

[4] U.S. *Congressional Globe,* 34th Cong., 3d Sess., XXVI, 53–56.

[5] *Ibid.,* 78–80.

[6] *Ibid.,* 105.

[7] JRG to Salmon P. Chase, December 18, 1856 (quotation), January 14, 1857 (quotation), Chase MSS, HSP.

[8] Salmon P. Chase to JRG, January 7, 1857, Giddings MSS.

[9] U.S. *Congressional Globe,* 34th Cong., 3d Sess., XXVI, 362–63; Ashtabula *Sentinel,* February 5, 1857; JRG to LAG, January 25, 1857, Giddings-Julian MSS, LC.

[10] Henry C. Wright to JRG, February 4, 1857, Giddings MSS.

[11] JRG to John G. Palfrey, April 30, 1857, Palfrey MSS, HL.

[12] For the tendency of certain segments of the antislavery movement to lean in a violent direction during the 1850's and for a persuasive view that William Lloyd Garrison muted this trend while keeping abolitionists unified see Bertram Wyatt-Brown, "William Lloyd Garrison and Antislavery Unity: A Reappraisal," *Civil War History,* XIII (March, 1967), 5–24.

[13] JRG to LMG, March 14, 1856, quoted in Julian, *Giddings,* 406, JRG to Editor, *National Anti-Slavery Standard,* undated clipping, JRG Scrapbook, 1857, Giddings MSS (quotation).

14 Allan Nevins, *The Emergence of Lincoln* (New York, 1950), I, 90–118.

15 "The Truth of History Vindicated," articles in the Ashtabula *Sentinel*, March 26, April 2, April 9, April 16, 1857.

16 *Ibid.*

17 "Compensated Emancipation," in the Ashtabula *Sentinel*, September 3, 1857.

18 Mary Bright Land, "John Brown's Ohio Environment," *Ohio Archaeological and Historical Quarterly*, LVII (January, 1948), 24–48. This was not Giddings' only statement of violent sentiments. See also his article "Democratic Morality," in the Ashtabula *Sentinel*, September 24, 1857.

19 Gerrit Smith to JRG, July 21, 1857, Giddings MSS.

20 Ashtabula *Sentinel*, September 12, September 19, September 26, October 3, 1857. The judgments of Barnes in his *Antislavery Impulse* and of Dwight L. Dumond in his *Antislavery: The Crusade for Freedom in America* (Ann Arbor, 1961), that radical abolitionism had no effective role to play after the rise of political antislavery, seem controverted in this case and in others to be described.

21 JRG to Salmon P. Chase, April 29, July 17, 1857, Chase MSS, HSP; Ashtabula *Sentinel*, August 20, 1857; JRG to George W. Julian, August 27, 1857, Giddings-Julian MSS, LC (quotation).

22 "The Christian Antislavery Convention," article by JRG in the Ashtabula *Sentinel*, August 27, 1857; Cleveland Herald, August 26, 1857; JRG to Salmon P. Chase, August 29, 1857, Chase MSS, HSP; Oliver Johnson to JRG, August 8, 1857, Giddings MSS (quotation).

23 JRG to the editor of the *Ohio Statesman*, reprinted in the Ashtabula *Sentinel*, December 3, 1857.

24 Roy Franklin Nichols, *The Disruption of American Democracy* (New York, 1948), 125–201; U.S. *Congressional Globe*, 35th Cong., 1st Sess., XXVII, 1435–37; Ashtabula *Sentinel*, May 6, 1858; JRG to Salmon P. Chase, April 14, May 2, 1858, Chase MSS, HSP; JRG to LMG, April 30, 1858, Giddings-Julian MSS, LC; JRG to LMG, January 29, 1858, Julian MSS, ISL; JRG to GRG, April 21, 1858, Giddings MSS.

25 New York *Tribune*, March 2, 1858, JRG Scrapbook, 1858, Giddings MSS.

26 U.S. *Congressional Globe*, 35th Cong., 1st Sess., XXVII, 894–98.

[27] JRG to Salmon P. Chase, May 10, 1858, Chase MSS, HSP.

[28] Oliver Johnson to JRG, March 6, 1858, Giddings MSS.

[29] Arnold Buffum to JRG, April [?], 1858, Gerrit Smith to JRG, March 25, 1858, William Lloyd Garrison to JRG, April 4, 1858, Giddings MSS; JRG to William Lloyd Garrison, April 27, 1858, William Lloyd Garrison MSS, BPL; *National Anti-Slavery Standard,* March 20, 1858; *Anti-Slavery Bulge,* March 20, 1858, JRG Scrapbook, 1858, Giddings MSS.

[30] Ashtabula *Sentinel,* August 19, September 2, 1858 (quotation) ; JAG to George W. Julian, April 2, 1891, Julian MSS, ISL.

[31] Charles Sumner to JRG, February 1, 1859, John G. Palfrey to JRG, [?], 1858, William Seward to JRG [?], 1858, Henry Wilson to JRG, [?], 1858, all in Julian, *Giddings,* 356–57.

[32] JRG to Gerrit Smith, September 20, October 15, 1858 (quotation), September 2, 1858, Gerrit Smith-Miller MSS, SUL.

[33] Gerrit Smith to JRG, JRG to Gerrit Smith, in the Ashtabula *Sentinel,* October 28, 1858, Gerrit Smith to JRG, clipping from the *Gerrit Smith Banner,* November 12, 1858, JRG Scrapbook, 1858, Giddings MSS; JRG to Gerrit Smith, October 15, 1858, Gerrit Smith-Miller MSS, SUL.

[34] The idea that Republicanism destroyed the abolitionists' identity, impelling them to unwarranted attacks upon the party, is put forward by David Donald, "Toward a Reconsideration of the Abolitionists," in *Lincoln Reconsidered: Essays on the Civil War,* 2d ed., enlarged (New York, 1961) , 19–36. As far as my own research indicates, this view is open to serious question, for the abolitionists were simply acting as they always had, employing time-honored tactics to push a conservative society and political structure toward humanitarianism. These men had spent lifetimes at such work, and the Republican party certainly gave them little reason to change their habits. Only by assuming that their agitation was inherently unwise can one interpret as hostile the abolitionist vehemence toward the Republican party.

[35] Roseboom, *The Civil War Era,* 377–78; JRG to Thomas Corwin, in the Ashtabula *Sentinel,* October 14, 1858.

[36] St. Louis *Daily Democrat,* November 9, 1858. New York *Evening Post,* undated clipping, both in JRG Scrapbook, 1858, Giddings MSS.

[37] JRG to Gerrit Smith, January 21, 1859, Gerrit Smith-Miller MSS, SUL.

[38] JRG to GRG, December 3, 1858, Giddings-Julian MSS, LC.

[39] U.S. *Congressional Globe,* 35th Cong., 2d Sess., XXVIII, 343–46, 395– 97; JRG to Salmon P. Chase, February 14, 1859, Giddings Miscellaneous MSS, NYHS.

[40] Julian, *Giddings,* 363; John A. Bingham to JRG, March 4, 1859, Giddings MSS.

Chapter 13

A
VIGOROUS
EXIT

◄ ❡ ►

1859-1864

Giddings now had no source of income. He could hardly return to law after a twenty-one-year absence, so he took to the lyceum circuit, lecturing on the "Trial of John Quincy Adams" and the "Higher Law." By speaking five times a week he could generally net two hundred dollars, a sum bettering the fees commanded by giants like Theodore Parker, Horace Greeley, and Henry Thoreau.[1] People sometimes came from fifty miles away, and once in Concord, New Hampshire, an old gentleman of ninety years hiked six miles through a snowstorm just to hear him. "I meet with warm hearts and devoted friends wherever I go," he told his wife, "and the business *pays*, which you know in these days is the great point." [2]

The schedule was wearying, but Giddings enjoyed traveling from town to town renewing friendships and making acquaintances. John G. Palfrey was again available to instruct him in moral philosophy, and in New York Giddings could meet with "lovely people," radical abolitionists like Theodore Weld, Arnold Buffum, and Oliver Johnson, and have a "grand time." [3]

Royalties from his popular new book, *The Exiles of Florida,* which was published the previous year, also helped him to keep solvent. *The Exiles,* a detailed history of how the South waged the Florida War against escaped slaves, combined painstaking research with voguish sentimentalism and grim exposés of the "slave power's" machinations. The volume received glowing notice in the *Atlantic Monthly* and the New York *Tribune.* Private compliments were sent by Charles Francis Adams, Maria Weston Chapman, Henry Wilson, and, of course, Gerrit Smith, individuals whose opinions typified every sort of antislavery position.[4] The honors, the crowds, and the royalty checks all made the old warrior happy. "I begin to feel somewhat vain and think I am more of a man than I have hitherto thought," he confided with simple candor.[5] Private life treated Joshua Giddings with kindness, and he savored every minute of his good fortune. When Chase asked if he was interested in running for governor, he casually declined the offer.[6]

But if Giddings found retirement enjoyable, it was only because he never relaxed his attention to matters of slavery. By this time, all Republicans had begun to anticipate the 1860 election, and William Seward seemed the logical choice for the nomination. Giddings, who properly judged Seward a most conservative politician, could not abide the thought of the New Yorker's name at the head of the ticket. Soon he began fearing that conniving politicians were simply using Seward as a stalking-horse "to bring down our doctrines to the Filmore [sic] level in order to make Corwin our leader . . ." and a Southern moderate the Republican standard-bearer. Giddings deemed Salmon Chase the only aspirant who had long been associated with the antislavery cause. He therefore put aside all old suspicions and worked hard for the ambitions Ohioan. Often, he tailored his lyceum lectures as thinly veiled stump speeches on behalf of Chase's candidacy.[7]

In April, 1859, federal marshals swept into Oberlin, Ohio, and seized a fugitive slave, who then was promptly spirited away by a mob of irate college students and local citizens. A federal grand jury issued indictments against thirty-seven of the "rescuers." They were arrested and held in Cleveland to stand trial, and the incident touched off waves of protest on the Reserve. Giddings made straightway for the courthouse when the trials opened in May and greeted several of his old Free Soil party friends—Columbus Delano, Edward Wade, Joseph Root, and Leicester King.[8] Together they called a mass protest meeting, and ten thousand turned out on Cleveland's Public Square to listen as Giddings set the tone of the gathering: "We say today *'down with the fugitive slave act; it is unconstitutional and void; it is* PIRATICAL, *and we will not obey it!'* . . . I am aware that the Democratic press, with a holy terror, has represented me as willing to resist this law by violence if necessary. *God knows it is the first time they ever did me justice!"* The crowd roared back its approval.[9]

In the crowd Giddings probably did not notice the presence of John Brown, a gaunt, seedy-looking individual with sunken eyes and thick beard who stood drinking in these heady sentiments. Brown had become a familiar figure to the Reserve's residents and had passed an hour of inconsequential conversation in the Giddings home.[10] Possibly Giddings' advocacy of violent resistance to the Fugitive Slave Law reinforced Brown's revolutionary leanings, for in October he led his band of militant insurrectionists into Harper's Ferry, Virginia, determined to set off massive slave revolts. However, Giddings undoubtedly never had fathomed the bloody intentions and iron will of his one-time guest and certainly had not intended to inspire any such violence; he was at home when news of the raid began to break, and he quickly judged Brown "fool-hardy" and "insane." He regretted that Brown had not simply rescued some slaves "without shedding blood or violating the property rights of anyone," for had Brown remained nonviolent, Giddings felt, he would have "deserved the character of a hero." [11]

But at the same time, Giddings never bothered to chide Gerrit Smith for being one of Brown's financial supporters, and he immediately put the blame for this incident on the South. Brown's "manifestations of dementation" paled in comparison to the "insanity" of President Buchanan and Virginia's governor Henry Wise for becoming frantic over so pitifully few invaders. The Southern men, Giddings decided, were acting "under the infallible law of the American intellect, which causes guilt to shrink before the most distant appearance of justice. . . ." Soon after the raid Giddings made a suggestion to J. Miller McKim, a leader of radical abolitionism in Pennsylvania. Giddings wanted petitions sent to Congress which argued that Brown had been driven mad by the "slave power" while staying in Kansas and had merely returned like for like by invading the South. In adopting the idea that Brown had been unhinged by Southern oppression and was therefore to be condoned, Giddings, like many others, unconsciously cast off his last vestige of nonviolence.[12] He was still convinced that Southerners would never make good their threats of secession and that the "slave power" would be defeated by peaceful legislative measures. Nevertheless, the nation had moved a great deal closer to civil insurrection. Giddings' oft-predicted "moral revolution" was soon to arrive, but accompanied by clashing armies and the smoke of cannon.

For the moment, it looked as if the South were about to move against Giddings personally, since he soon was accused of abetting the Harper's Ferry conspiracy. The New York *Herald* flung out false charges that he, John P. Hale, and Charles Sumner all had a year's foreknowledge of the plan, and a Southern paper quickly put up $5,000 for Giddings' head and $10,000 for the "entire man." This offer alone bore grim witness to the violent paranoia now besetting the Southern mind. Clement Vallandigham, a Democratic congressman notorious for Southern sympathies, tried to implicate his fellow Ohioan while interrogating Brown himself.[13] Giddings promptly and honestly protested in several public letters and in a lengthy speech,[14] but his denials persuaded few in the South, many of whom were fully convinced that the Republican party and John Brown meant one and the same thing. Yankee extremists like Henry Thoreau and Theodore Parker proclaimed Brown a martyr as he was led to the gallows.

But it was the spectre of politicians like Thomas Corwin, not the spirit of John Brown, which haunted Giddings' mind as he surveyed the prospects for 1860, for the Republican party now looked even more conservative than it had in 1858. Seward, the front-running presidential candidate, John C. McLean, and many other Republicans seemed anxious to "debauch our party" by capitulating to the South on every antislavery issue. "If we fail in the next Presidential election, it will be a consequence of this policy. . . ." Republicans must have an "ultra" platform and a president willing to stand boldly on the "doctrines, avowed at Philadelphia in 1776 and repeated in 1856." According to Giddings' radical interpretation, such a stance implied the total denationalization of slavery and the elevation of Salmon Chase as well as American society.[15] Fully intent on achieving these goals, he repaired to Chicago as Jefferson's delegate to the national convention.

Chase's candidacy never advanced very far, for Ohio's large delegation was split, and Benjamin Wade created rancor by also attempting to capture the nomination.[16] Giddings choked down his disappointment as his old messmate Abraham Lincoln was chosen instead. The doughfaces, he reported, had backed Lincoln for reasons of pure geographical expediency and "because his antislavery sentiments have been less prominent." [17] But when the platform was read, Giddings at first felt stupefied, then heart-sick, for all his worst fears of Republican moral bankruptcy were borne out. The resolutions branded secession as treason, called the Dred Scott decision a "dangerous political heresy," and proclaimed the party's resistance to the extension of slavery. The 1856 platform had been difficult for Giddings to rationalize, but this one was impossible. Worst of all, there was only the vaguest mention of the Declaration of Independence. The platform committee had all but severed the one tissue of doctrine which connected

271

Giddings' antislavery radicalism to the political process.

After the delegates gave each plank a joyous ovation, David Cartter of Ohio moved an immediate vote on them. Giddings sprang to his feet in protest. Cartter objected and said sneeringly that he had moved an immediate vote just to make sure that Giddings would be "cut off." Cries of "Giddings! Giddings!" began rising from the delegates, and Cartter's motion was voted down, 301–115. The old man was granted the floor, and he offered an amendment which solemnly reasserted man's inalienable rights to life, liberty, and the pursuit of happiness, affirming "that governments are instituted among men to secure the enjoyment of these rights." The amendment was essential, Giddings pleaded, "because the party was formed on it . . . and when you leave out this truth, you leave out the party." After a short debate, in which Cartter laughed at the amendment as "all gas," it was defeated.

Giddings rose again, turned on his heel, and, after adjusting his hat, stalked out of the convention. For the only time in his life he felt compelled to sacrifice all party affiliation for an idea. When a delegate tried to stop him, Giddings replied, "I see that I am out of place here." [18] As he passed down the center aisle and out the door, George William Curtis, an earnest young delegate from New York, rose and moved to reconsider the amendment while eloquently appealing to the Republican conscience. Giddings decided to wait outside. Dared the Republicans "wince and quail before the assertions of the men in Philadelphia in 1776 . . . ?" Curtis asked. After another brief exchange, the amendment was put to a second vote. This time it passed. Giddings walked back into the hall amidst thunderous applause to enjoy the last dramatic moment of his public life.[19]

Most Republicans were probably neutral about including the Declaration of Independence, and the party's endorsement of it undoubtedly made little difference in the campaign. Nevertheless, Republicans were now on record as favoring an idea which ranked among the most potent in American history and which Southern extremists had denied for years in favor of white supremacy. The resolution had small immediate impact, but it was the germ of a later Republican commitment to the Negro during Reconstruction. Just after the convention, in writing to Gerrit Smith, Giddings overestimated the time span and his foresight was accidental, but he hit th⌣ point squarely when he told Smith, "Our party is progressing and in the course of a half century *may* stand where you and I did twenty years since." [20]

The "half century" prognosis, however, seemed far too long to suit Giddings, so he immediately endorsed Lincoln and began efforts to lead the nominee in a radical direction. As in 1858, a Garrisonian figure, this time Wendell Phillips, gave Giddings his opportunity. Undoubtedly the radicals' most intelligent and talented polemicist, Phillips branded Lincoln a "slavehound," for in 1849 the candidate had offered a bill in Congress upholding the 1793 Fugitive Slave Law. Giddings replied in the *Sentinel* to Phillips' charges. He adamantly defended Lincoln's Christian character and emphasized the nominee's supposed desire to make Republicanism act as God's political agency in the United States. As rebuttal met reply, Phillips gave Giddings the opportunity to make radical promises on behalf of his party, and the correspondence drew national attention. Meanwhile, Giddings began bombarding Lincoln with letters advising him on how to initiate a moral revolution in politics. If Lincoln wished to be a Christian president, Giddings instructed, he should steer clear of all political deals, all "corrupting influences [which] beset our public men. . . ." The executive office had to be kept "pure," so that Lincoln could "exert its constitutional powers to the purposes of truth, justice and the elevation of our [human] race. . . ." Giddings told Lincoln to use John Quincy Adams rather than Henry Clay as his model, for the federal government was "at this time the most corrupt among all the Christian nations of this earth. . . . *Reformation* now invites our incoming President to effort." [21]

Lincoln, the consummate politician, beset with patronage problems and possible cabinet appointments, was aware that Giddings spoke the sentiments of many radical reformers, so he treated such counsels respectfully. "May the Almighty grant that the cause of truth, justice and humanity shall no wise suffer at my hands," [22] he replied in language that undoubtedly made Giddings feel warm inside. After Lincoln had been elected, Giddings continued to pester him by appearing unexpectedly in Springfield, Illinois, the new president's home. He requested that Lincoln appoint three men to the cabinet "who have long contributed their influence to the cause," members of the "old guard" like Charles Sumner, Salmon Chase, and Henry Wilson. For "a few days" Giddings even considered endorsing himself but decided not to, since he did not want to appear selfish. Again Lincoln recognized that the old agitator had much moral support among the abolitionists. His suggestions could not pass unheeded. He told Giddings that his ideas were all worthy of consideration, and reminisced about the days when the two had served together in Congress. The retired radical left Springfield "with more confidence" in Lincoln than ever before.[23] As it turned out, Lincoln made Salmon Chase his Secretary of the Treasury, and Giddings had done much to secure this important appointment.

As the news of Lincoln's election spread, its progress was marked by a growing number of secession conventions in the Southern states. The war for Southern independence was about to start, but frantic efforts immediately began in Washington to forestall it. Giddings' anxiety continued to mount, as he feared that yet another compromise was in the making, one even more odious than that of 1850. He felt only *"somewhat* inclined" to believe the threats of disunion, for he had listened to them since the Missouri debates in 1820 and had always considered such promises mere tactics to coerce the North. While deploring the "many cowards" like William Seward who were sponsoring various attempts at conciliation, he instructed Sumner, who hardly needed encouragement, "to stand firm and unwavering, notwithstanding the threats of dissolution." If the South were not bluffing, Giddings was fully prepared to endorse war in order to end slavery. Unlike William Lloyd Garrison or even Sumner himself, he could not consider seriously the idea of a peaceful separation of states which would purify the North but leave Southern slavery intact. "I am inclined to think your prediction in regard to bloodshed will prove true," he told Gerrit Smith. "I am more than confident that the day of emancipation must come but . . . whether in blood or in peace, *let it come*." 24

Lincoln "stood firm" and the war came. A moral confrontation the size of which Joshua Giddings never dreamed was beginning, but he was sure, as he told Gerrit Smith, that the outcome could be predicted by applying the "great principle of retributive justice. . . ." "The first gun that was fired on Fort Sumpter [sic] wrung [sic] the death-knell of slavery. . . ." "Its final disposition is rapidly hastening," he assured Smith, "and will be complete at no distant day." The nation would purify itself in the flames of war, and Giddings was sure that his hopes for a Christian society would be fulfilled: "We shall emerge from our present difficulties with a better defined government, and better made for liberty and justice than we have ever enjoyed." 25

The onset of war also allowed Giddings to take a step which his religious convictions had long dictated, but which he had stubbornly resisted. He now was willing to publicize an opinion originally rendered by John Quincy Adams that the president had the power to abolish slavery in wartime, by virtue of martial law. In May he so reminded Secretary of the Treasury Salmon Chase, imploring him to lobby for an emancipation proclamation.26 After detesting slavery for nearly twenty-four years, Joshua Giddings had at last become an abolitionist.

The North was no longer in a mood for lyceum speeches; instead it was mobilizing for war and Giddings again needed income. Fortunately, Lincoln had turned over much of his patronage to Charles Sumner, now chairman of the Senate Foreign Relations Committee. The Massachusetts senator was only too glad to help an old friend. In April, 1861, with Lincoln's approval, Giddings gratefully accepted a well-paying, respectable appointment as Consul General to Canada. By the end of the month he had packed his bags and was on his way to Montreal.27

In his new capacity Giddings found himself far removed from the party struggles in Washington which surrounded the fighting. He spent much of his time writing one of the North's first versions of the coming of the war, *A History of the Rebellion: Its Authors and Causes*. Although it was often difficult for him to get a clear picture of what was going on, Giddings never lost interest in politics. The military campaigns fascinated him, and he hotly accused General George B. McClellan of "treason" for dilatory tactics and returning slaves to the enemy. Wringing his hands despairingly, he fretted over various real and imagined "union" movements within the Republican party and heartily endorsed General Benjamin F. Butler's practice of freeing slaves by declaring them contraband of war. Giddings constantly called upon the party to "reorganize" and fight against slavery rather than for union. "Consult members and see that you act," he told Julian. "That must be done or the locofocos will drive you from the Capitol." [28]

But Giddings was not, as one historian has asserted, a private citizen who acted as one with a phalanx of "jacobins" in Washington.[29] In fact, the old man's deepest hatreds were reserved for Benjamin Wade, now one of the most effective radicals in Congress. Giddings believed to his dying day that Wade was ceaselessly intriguing to sacrifice the Negro and the Republicans in order to advance himself. "Whereas McClellan has demoralized the army, Wade had demoralized the Republican party. . . . Thank God neither of these can restore slavery. That is beyond their power."[30] But, like several others in Washington, Giddings feared that President Lincoln would negotiate a premature peace, one which would make the Republican party "fall to pieces," allowing slavery to remain while bringing the Democrats into power. Therefore, he was to endorse Chase as the presidential nominee for 1864.[31]

On January 1, 1863, Lincoln released the Emancipation Proclamation, and Chase wrote bitterly to Giddings, protesting its limited scope: "I wanted some words . . . recognizing . . . the liberation of the slave in the rebel states & the *permanence* of that

276

liberation." [32] Giddings, too, had noted the omission but tried to reassure his correspondent that things would inevitably turn out for the best.

He told Chase that the "unchanging Law that has borne us on thus far" would continue to apply. "The perversity of the South has always supplied a cause for the continued advance of the North," [33] and this same tendency would soon insure Negro equality. The idea made good sense to Giddings, for had not a Southern *faux pas*, his own censure, destroyed the gag rule? Southern demands for an unenforceable fugitive slave law had allowed him to rebuild the Free Soil party in 1852, and the Southerners' insistence of open occupancy for slavery all over America had formed the Republican party, caused the war, and promoted the end of bondage itself. Nearly all of Giddings' musings indicated that the "slave power" had always carried its own destruction with it.

The idea, true, was much oversimplified, but it was one which comforted him, and as such it was worth offering to Chase. Southern "perversity" would not cease after the war ended, Giddings promised. Finally, the exasperated free states would refuse the rebels readmission to the union "until we teach the negroes to protect their own Liberty." Northerners would realize that the rebellion could never really end "until that and *more* shall be done." Southern folly would insure equality for the emancipated slave.[34]

Ten months after tendering Chase this solace, on May 26, 1864, Giddings suffered a fatal stroke at a friend's home in Montreal, while analyzing a difficult three cushion billiard.[35] It was fitting that death came quickly to this man, whose life had been one of ceaseless, selfless activity. But it was almost ironic that Giddings closed his career with an accurate prediction, for too often his romantic optimism had made him a faulty prognosticator. This time, events were to prove Giddings correct. In response to Southern recalcitrance after Appomattox, the Republican party successfully incorporated the Fourteenth and Fifteenth Amendments into the Constitution.[36] Once ratified, these amendments offered the American Negro a first step toward that still unfulfilled something "more" which Joshua Giddings had foreseen. He had

277

met the moral questions of his day courageously, and by serving his conscience he had quickened the sensibilities of his generation to respond to urgent questions. Such accomplishments must border on the heroic, especially since the dilemmas of political morality and racial oppression remain to this day as excruciating as ever.

NOTES

[1] JRG to JAG, December 5, December 10, 1859, Giddings MSS. For the criteria used in weighting Giddings' financial success as a speaker see Sewell, *John P. Hale,* 153.

[2] JRG to LWG, December 4, 1859, Giddings-Julian MSS, LC.

[3] JRG to LMG, March 20, 1859, Giddings MSS (quotation); JRG to LWG, March 20, 1859, Giddings-Julian MSS, LC.

[4] Joshua R. Giddings, *The Exiles of Florida, The History of the Seminole War* (Columbus, 1858), *passim.; Atlantic Monthly* and the New York *Tribune,* reprinted in the Ashtabula *Sentinel,* September 2, 1859; Charles Francis Adams to JRG, August 10, 1858, Maria Weston Chapman to JRG, August 17, 1858, Henry Wilson to JRG, September 15, 1858, Gerrit Smith to JRG, July 20, 1858, Giddings MSS, LC.

[5] JRG to LMG, November 30, 1859, Giddings-Julian MSS.

[6] JRG to Salmon P. Chase, April 9, 1859, Chase MSS, HSP; JRG to Editor, Ashtabula *Sentinel,* April 28, 1859.

[7] JRG to Salmon P. Chase, June 7 (quotation), September 17, September 29, 1859, Chase MSS, HSP.

[8] William Cox Cochran, "The Western Reserve and the Fugitive Slave Law," in *Western Reserve Historical Society Collections* (Cleveland, 1920), 118-204.

[9] Ashtabula *Sentinel,* May 26, June 2, 1859.

[10] Land, "John Brown's Ohio Environment," 24-47; JRG to John Brown, May 26, 1859, a private letter found in John Brown's personal papers, granting Brown's request for an interview, and reprinted in the Ashtabula *Sentinel,* November 3, 1859, along with Giddings' description of the inconsequential nature of their conversation.

[11] JRG to Gerrit Smith, October 20, 1859, Gerrit Smith-Miller MSS,

SUL (quotation); JRG to Salmon P. Chase, October 20, 1859, Chase MSS, HSP.

12 *Ibid.*, JRG to J. Miller McKim, October 29, 1859, Samuel May-J. Miller McKim MSS, The Cornell Antislavery Collection, Cornell University Library, Ithaca, N.Y.; C. Vann Woodward, "John Brown's Private War," in Daniel Aaron (ed.), *Americans in Crisis: Fourteen Crucial Episodes in American History* (New York, 1952), 110–30.

13 Sewell, *John P. Hale,* 182, Richmond *Whig,* reprinted in the Ashtabula *Sentinel,* December 28, 1859; Cincinnati *Gazette,* reprinted in the Ashtabula *Sentinel,* October 27, 1859.

14 *Ibid.;* JRG speech, "On the Riot at Harper's Ferry," reprinted in the Ashtabula *Sentinel,* November 10, 1859.
JRG to Editor, Ashtabula *Sentinel,* March 7, 1860 (quotation); JRG,

15 JRG to Salmon P. Chase, February 5, March 26, 1860, Chase MSS, HSP; JRG to Editor Ashtabula *Sentinel,* February 15, 1860 (quotation); JRG to Editor, Ashtabula *Sentinel,* March 7, 1860 (quotation); "Republican Doctrines," in the Ashtabula *Sentinel,* March 28, 1860.

16 JRG to Salmon P. Chase, May 24, 1860, Chase MSS, HSP; Donnal V. Smith, "Salmon Chase and Civil War Politics," *Publications of the Ohio Historical Society,* No. 17 (Columbus, 1931), 5–20.

17 JRG to George W. Julian, May 25, 1860, Giddings-Julian MSS, LC.

18 Johnson, *First Three Republican Conventions,* 130–36; Julian, *Giddings,* 373; JRG to Gerrit Smith, May 24, 1860, Gerrit Smith-Miller MSS, SUL.

19 Johnson, *First Three Republican Conventions,* 140–42.

20 JRG to Gerrit Smith, May 24, 1860, Gerrit-Miller MSS, SUL.

21 For the Phillips-Giddings exchange see the Ashtabula *Sentinel,* issues for July, 1860; JRG to Abraham Lincoln, May 17, June 19, July 2, October 15, 1860, Robert Todd Lincoln MSS, LC.

22 Abraham Lincoln to JRG, July [?] 19, 1860, Giddings MSS.

23 JRG to George W. Julian, December 14, 1860, Giddings-Julian MSS, LC (quotation); JRG to Salmon P. Chase, December 7, 1860, Chase MSS, HSP; JRG to Gerrit Smith, December 24, 1860, Gerrit Smith-Miller MSS, SUL; JRG to John Allison, December 25, 1860, Robert Todd Lincoln MSS, LC.

[24] JRG to Charles Sumner, December 3, 1860, Sumner MSS, HL (quotation); JRG to Gerrit Smith, December 24, 1860, Gerrit Smith-Miller MSS, SUL (quotation); JRG to Salmon P. Chase, December 18, 1860, Chase MSS, HSP.

[25] JRG to Gerrit Smith, June 17, December 20, 1861, Gerrit Smith-Miller MSS, SUL (both letters quoted).

[26] JRG to Salmon P. Chase, May 4, 1861, Chase MSS, HSP.

[27] Donald, *Sumner,* 344–46; Julian, *Giddings,* 384.

[28] JRG to Editor, Ashtabula *Sentinel,* July 18, July 25, 1861; JRG to JAG, July 3, 1862, Giddings MSS; JRG to George W. Julian, January 18, 1863, Giddings-Julian MSS, LC (quotation).

[29] He is so characterized by T. Harry Williams, in his *Lincoln and the Radicals* (Madison, 1941), 15, 46–47, 188, 312.

[30] JRG to LWG, February 12, 1863, Giddings-Julian MSS, LC (quotation); JRG to George W. Julian, January 18, 1863, Giddings-Julian MSS, LC.

[31] JRG to George W. Julian, March 22, 1863, Giddings-Julian MSS, LC.

[32] Salmon P. Chase to JRG, July 17, 1863, Giddings MSS.

[33] JRG to Salmon P. Chase, July 21, 1863, Chase MSS, HSP.

[34] *Ibid.*

[35] Julian, *Giddings,* 345.

[36] The idea that Southern recalcitrance and the ineptitude of a president surrounded by men of Southern sympathies impelled the North into radical Reconstruction is brilliantly confirmed in Eric L. McKitrick, *Andrew Johnson and Reconstruction* (Chicago, 1960), *passim.,* and LaWanda and John H. Cox, *Politics, Principle, and Prejudice, 1865–1866: The Dilemma of Reconstruction America* (New York, 1963), especially 195–232.

ESSAY
ON
SOURCES

In the following paragraphs I make no pretense at presenting a complete guide to the primary and secondary literature for nineteenth-century America. Included are comments only on the sources I found most useful in this biography.

Manuscripts

The principal manuscript source for this study is the Joshua R. Giddings Papers (OHS). This collection, fertile for many ante-bellum subjects, consists of family letters and correspondence received by Giddings from an extremely wide variety of political and reform figures. This source also contains a valuable scrapbook of newspaper clippings to which Giddings added throughout his career, diaries covering the year 1838–39 and 1848–49, and autograph books. The Joshua R. Giddings-George W. Julian Papers (LC) yielded a mass of informative letters, most of them written by Giddings to his family. The George W. Julian Papers (ISL) contained a good number of Giddings letters and a memoir fragment which he wrote in the late 1850's. Two collections of Joshua R. Giddings Miscellaneous Papers (NYHS and NYPL) were less abundant in useful letters.

The broad scope of Giddings' reform and political activities is confirmed in the many other collections which yielded harvests of the Ohioan's correspondence. The Charles Sumner and John

G. Palfrey Papers (both in HL) revealed a wealth of information about Giddings' friendships, ideas, and activities in national politics during the 1840's and 1850's. So did the Adams Family Papers (MHS, microfilm). The superbly organized Gerrit Smith-Miller Papers, including the correspondence of Seth M. Gates (SUL), were essential in following nearly every phase of Giddings' career and at the same time afforded valuable information about the interrelated aspects of political antislavery and abolition sentiments. Also important in these regards were the two major collections of Salmon P. Chase Papers (HSP and LC), and the David and Lydia Maria Child Papers (BPL).

This biography would have lacked whatever depth it has without the help of documents drawn from less well-known, local sources. The Elisha Whittlesey Papers (WRHS) are a mine of information for many areas of nineteenth-century political and social history. His papers were crucial to my reconstruction of Reserve politics in the 1820's and 1830's and for Giddings' precongressional years. Two collections of the Albert Gallatin Riddle Papers (WRHS and HHL), two repositories of James A. Briggs Papers (WRHS and OHS), and the Ephriam Brown Papers (WRHS) all contained valuable letters revealing Giddings' responses to state and local matters. Less frequently, important insights were obtained from the Edward Fitch Papers (OHS), the James W. Taylor Papers (NYHS), the James Washburn Papers, the Robert S. Pierce Papers, the Peter Hitchcock Papers (WRHS), the Joshua R. Giddings-Milton Sutliffe Papers, Norton Collection (WRHS), and the Benjamin F. Wade-Milton Sutliffe Papers, Norton Collection (WRHS).

The Abraham Lincoln Papers (Robert Todd Lincoln Collection, LC) are one of several manuscript sources which provided information about Giddings' actions and ideas regarding isolated but important issues. The Lincoln Papers, for example, illumined Giddings' behavior during the election and crisis of 1860–61. Other collections which provided such limited but constructive data include the John McLean and the Theodore Dwight Weld

JOSHUA R. GIDDINGS

Papers (both located in the LC). Falling into this same category
are the William Lloyd Garrison Papers (BPL), the Samuel May-
J. Miller McKim Papers, Cornell Antislavery Collection (CUL),
and the Robert C. Winthrop Papers (MHS). The Thaddeus
Stevens Papers, the William Henry Harrison Papers, the Joshua
Leavitt Papers, the Lewis Tappan Papers, and, surprisingly, the
Benjamin F. Wade Papers (all in the LC), added only super-
ficially to this reconstruction of Giddings' career.

Published Correspondence, Collected Writings, Memoirs and Government Documents

Essential to this study was *Letters of Theodore Dwight Weld,
Angelina Grimké Weld, and Sarah Grimké, 1822–1844,* edited by
Gilbert Hobbes Barnes and Dwight Lowell Dumond (2 vols.,
New York, 1934). This work, and Dumond's *Letters of James
Gillespie Birney, 1831–1857* (2 vols., New York, 1938), contain
material essential to understanding the congressional antislavery
insurgency during the early 1840's. Furthermore, the development aims and activities of the entire antislavery movement cannot
be captured fully without reference to these two sources. *A Memoir
of John Quincy Adams, Comprising Portions of his Diary from
1795 to 1848,* edited by Charles Frances Adams (12 vols., Boston,
1874–1877) also sheds light on the insurgency, while presenting
insights into Adams' unique personality. Another very useful
printed source, containing letters written during the early and
mid-1840's by Giddings and others to a powerful Ohio Whig
editor, is "Selections From the [Oran] Follett Papers," edited
by Belle Hamlin, in *Quarterly Publications of the Historical and
Philosophical Society of Ohio, 1915–1917,* vols. X–XII.

Joshua Giddings' own historical writings, *The Exiles of Florida,
The History of the Seminole War* (Columbus, 1858) and *A History
of the Rebellion, Its Authors and Causes* (Cleveland, 1864), are
revealing in two ways. Both works reflect clearly the uniquely
conservative perspective which reinforced so greatly Giddings'
radical actions. These volumes also contributed occasional remi-

284

niscences and observations important to the ongoing narrative. Giddings' *Speeches In Congress* (Boston, 1852) contains little more than polished, expanded revisions of previously delivered public utterances. George W. Julian's *The Life of Joshua R. Giddings* (Chicago, 1892) can best be classified as a primary source. Because the work is a panegyric by one who knew Giddings well, it contains flashes of intuition as well as irrelevant apologia. Julian also reprints (often inaccurately) great amounts of Giddings' personal correspondence.

Several other early biographies fall into the same genre, regarding their subjects, as Julian's attempt to portray Giddings. Such works include Robert Bruce Warden's *An Account of the Private Life and Public Services of Salmon Portland Chase* (Cincinnati, 1874) and Jacob S. Schuckers' *The Life and Public Services of Salmon Portland Chase* (New York, 1874). Unlike Julian, however, Warden and Schuckers found it understandably necessary to make complicated apologies for Chase's devious ways. Chase speaks for himself in "The Diary and Correspondence of Salmon P. Chase," *Annual Report of The American Historical Association,* 1902 (Washington, D.C., 1903). Other memoirs and older biographies proved useful: *A Memoir of Robert C. Winthrop,* edited by Robert Charles Winthrop, Jr. (Boston, 1897) and *Memoir and Letters of Charles Sumner,* edited by Edward L. Pierce (4 vols., Boston, 1877–1893). These two works, when taken together, provide dramatic temperamental contrasts between a "Cotton" and a "Conscience" Whig. Convenient sources which reveal Southerners' opinions of antislavery agitation in Congress include the following: *The Papers of Willie Person Mangum,* edited by Henry Thomas Shanks (5 vols., Raleigh, 1950–1956) which details a moderate's views; and "The Correspondence of John C. Calhoun," edited by J. Franklin Jameson, *Annual Report of the American Historical Association,* 1899 (Washington, D.C., 1900), which indicates the opinions of a "fire-eater" and his followers.

Useful information and description of Free Soil and Republican political conventions can be obtained from several sources. *A*

History of the Republican Party in Ohio, edited by Joseph P. Smith (2 vols., Chicago, 1898), contains useful transcripts of Republican gatherings in Giddings' home state. *Proceedings of the First Three Republican National Conventions . . . ,* edited by Charles W. Johnson (Minneapolis, 1893), recounts all that the title promises, as does *Phonographic Report of the Proceedings of the Free Soil Convention at Buffalo,* edited by Oliver Dyer (Buffalo, 1848). Needless to say, the *Congressional Globe* (46 vols., Washington, D.C., 1833–73) was indispensable to this study. Compilation of the *Messages and Papers of the Presidents,* compiled by James D. Richardson (Washington, D.C., 1896–99), was also consulted when appropriate.

Newspapers

The Ashtabula *Sentinel,* published weekly, was one of the most important single sources for this study. Edited in turn by Henry Fassett, Joseph Addison Giddings, and William C. Howells, the *Sentinel* reported faithfully Joshua Giddings' every opinion and act as he progressed from Whig to Free Soiler to Republican. Whenever Giddings felt moved to write something for the public (a mood which struck him at least twice a week for a quarter century), the *Sentinel* automatically printed the message. The editors were also careful to cover comprehensively all political events in the Reserve.

The Cleveland *Herald* and Conneaut *Reporter* represented conservative and moderate Whig persuasions, respectively, in northeastern Ohio. Neither was particularly kind to Giddings, but the *Reporter* became especially petulant towards him after Ben Wade became its favorite. The Cleveland *Plain Dealer,* poorly edited and badly written during the 1840's and 1850's, stood as the lone guardian of the Democratic party in the Whiggish Reserve. The Painesville *Telegraph* and the *Western Reserve Chronicle* contributed little factually to this study. Yet both papers, when read carefully, reflect accurately the nuances of antislavery opinion in the Reserve's back-country hamlets. But the Cleveland *True*

Democrat, founded in 1847 as an antislavery Whig organ, was comprehensive in its coverage and, along with its chief competitor, the *Herald,* afforded Reserve readers journalistic sophistication lacking in all other papers until the advent of William C. Howells as editor of the *Sentinel.*

On the state level, the Whig *Ohio State Journal* and the Democratic *Ohio Statesman* were useful as barometers of orthodoxy against which to measure the impact of Giddings' activities. Reflecting accurately a moderate Whig and later a moderate Republican stance, the *National Intelligencer* was an indispensable source, amplifying events reported only partially in the *Congressional Globe.* Students of Antimasonry during the 1830's will find instructive both the *Ohio Luminary,* published in Ashtabula, and the *Ohio Republican,* printed in Canfield.

Among Garrisonian journals several titles were especially instructive. William Lloyd Garrison's own *Liberator* (Boston) and the *National Anti-Slavery Standard,* ably edited from New York by Oliver Johnson, are by far the most informative sources for studying radical abolitionism prior to 1861. Marius Robinson's far less famous *Anti-Slavery Bugle,* published in Salem, Ohio, gives a clear picture of Garrisonian projects and opinions in the Reserve.

Several Liberty party journals counted among the most instructive sources for the project. The short-lived (1843–46) Warren *Liberty Herald,* didactic and comprehensive, illuminates the conflicts between antislavery Whigs (especially Giddings) and the Reserve's many third-party partisans. The *Emancipator,* published from 1838 to 1850, first in Boston, then in New York, stands as the articulate voice of eastern Liberty party thinking. Joshua Leavitt, the *Emancipator*'s editor until 1847, was especially sensitive to the dilemmas of principle versus expediency inherent in the third party. Leavitt's successor, Henry B. Stanton, did not share this insight, and the transition of aims from political abolitionism to "free soilism" is documented in the *Emancipator* as a result of this change of editors.

287

The ever-narrowing reform objectives of third-party partisans, however, is best embodied in the editorial career of Gamaliel Bailey. His Cincinnati *Philanthropist,* printed from 1835 to 1848, gradually shifted its stance from immediatism to simple anti-extensionism. Bailey's *National Era* (Washington), founded in 1847, upholds little sectional doctrine other than hostility to extending slavery. Bailey consistently ran a comprehensive newspaper, and for many reasons his journalism is an essential source for any study of Northern politics in the ante-bellum years.

Biographical Works

Besides this study, there are several other treatments of Giddings' career. Walter Buell's *Joshua R. Giddings, A Sketch* (Cleveland, 1882) is shallow and wholly anachronistic. Robert P. Ludlum's "Joshua R. Giddings, Antislavery Radical (1795–1844)" (Ph.D. dissertation, Cornell University, 1935), is incompletely researched, poorly written, and assumes that one had to be mentally disturbed to oppose slavery. The same comments apply to Ludlum's "Joshua R. Giddings, Radical," *Mississippi Valley Historical Review,* XXIII (June, 1936). Byron R. Long's "Joshua Giddings, A Champion of Political Freedom," *Ohio Archaeological and Historical Quarterly,* XXVIII (September, 1929) contains interesting documents, but little else. Richard W. Solberg's "Joshua R. Giddings: Idealist and Politician" (Ph.D. dissertation, University of Chicago, 1952) is adequately researched, extremely lengthy, and reflects older "revisionist" interpretations contested by implication in the present study.

Mary Bright Land's competent "Old Backbone: 'Bluff' Ben Wade" (Ph.D. dissertation, 2 vols., Case Western Reserve University, 1950) is superseded by Hans L. Trefousse's *Benjamin F. Wade: Radical Republican from Ohio* (New York, 1963); so is Albert G. Riddle's *The Life of Benjamin F. Wade* (Cleveland, 1888). The best treatment of John Quincy Adams' antislavery career is Samuel Flagg Bemis' *John Quincy Adams and the Union* (New York, 1956). John G. Palfrey's significant activities are

288

sensitively portrayed in Frank Otto Gatell's *John Gorham Palfrey and the New England Conscience* (Cambridge, 1963). Another of Giddings' closest associates receives brilliant, if sometimes partisan, treatment in David H. Donald's *Charles Sumner and the Coming of the Civil War* (New York, 1960). Richard H. Sewell's *John P. Hale and the Politics of Abolition* (Cambridge, 1965) is a model study of a figure whose reputation ironically remains unrecognized despite the talents of his biographer. A comprehensive study of Salmon P. Chase remains unwritten. Useful but limited inquiries include Donnal V. Smith's "Salmon Chase and Civil War Politics," *Publications of the Ohio Historical Society, No. 17* (Columbus, 1931) and Reinhard Luthin's "Salmon P. Chase: Political Career Before the Civil War," *Mississippi Valley Historical Review*, XXIX (January, 1943). Joseph Rayback's "The Liberty Party Leaders of Ohio, Exponents of Antislavery Coalition," *Ohio Archaeological and Historical Quarterly*, LVII (May, 1948) provides insights into Chase's early career, while elucidating an important phase of transition within political abolitionism. A much-needed study of Henry Wilson is presently under way. Ideally, this monograph will supersede or at least greatly supplement J. Daniel Loubert's "The Orientation of Henry Wilson, 1812–1856" (Ph.D. dissertation, Boston University, 1952).

Patrick Riddleburger's *George Washington Julian: A Study in Nineteenth Century Reform and Politics* (Indianapolis, 1966) presents a competent picture of Giddings' important son-in-law. Reading together Fawn M. Brodie's *Thaddeus Stevens, Scourge of the South* (2d edition, New York, 1966) and Richard Nelson Current's *Old Thad Stevens: A Story of Ambition* (Madison, 1942) reveals the many merits of both studies. Robert F. Durden's *James Shepherd Pike: Republicanism and the American Negro, 1850–1882* (Durham, 1957) is valuable in detailing through Pike the anti-Negro ideology to integral to Northern "free soil" demands. Charles Buxton Going's *David Wilmot, Free Soiler . . .* (New York, 1924) is a cumbersome, outdated book, but is all that Wilmot deserves. An expertly done political and presidential study is Holman Hamilton's *Zachary Taylor, Soldier in the White House*, vol. 2 (Indianapolis and New York, 1951). Equally sensitive portrayals of statesmen used in this study include Glyndon G. Van Deusen's *William Henry Seward, Lincoln's Secretary of State, the Negotiator of the Alaska Purchase* (New York, 1967) and his *Life of Henry Clay* (Boston, 1937). Ruhl J. Bartlett's *John C. Frémont and the Republican Party* (Columbus, 1930) presents faithfully all that the title promises.

Many useful studies of abolitionist figures have appeared within the past two decades. John Thomas' *The Liberator, William Lloyd Garrison: A Biography* (Boston, 1963) and Walter M. Merrill's *Against Wind and Tide: A Biography of William Lloyd Garrison* (Cambridge, 1963) supersede all earlier studies of this pivotal figure. Bertram Wyatt-Brown's *Lewis Tappan and the Evangelical War Against Slavery* (Cleveland, 1969) confirms definitively and in a highly readable way Tappan's centrality to the antislavery movement. The easy reconciliation of racism with abolition is seen in David L. Smiley's *The Lion of Whitehall: The Life of Cassius M. Clay* (Madison, 1962). A long-needed biography of Elizur Wright, Jr., is soon to be completed by David French of Case Western Reserve University.

Adequate, but interpretively prosaic, is Benjamin Platt Thomas' *Theodore Weld, Crusader for Freedom* (New Brunswick, 1950). Betty Fladeland's *James G. Birney, Slaveholder to Abolitionist* (Ithaca, 1955) accurately develops the life of this important Southern-bred antislavery crusader. Ralph V. Harlow's *Gerrit Smith: Philanthropist and Reformer* (New York, 1939) is competent, yet Smith's career could be fruitfully studied in light of current historiography. Samuel Lewis, who deserves full biographical treatment, receives only sketchy notice in Ellis Alston's "Samuel Lewis, Progressive Educator in the Early History of Ohio," *Ohio Archaeological and Historical Quarterly*, XXI (1916). James M. McPherson's "The Fight Against the Gag Rule: Joshua Leavitt and the Antislavery Insurgency in the Whig Party, 1839–1842," *Journal of Negro History*, XLVIII (July, 1963) is extremely useful. Leavitt's much-needed biography, however, remains unwritten. Joel Goldfarb, "The Life of Gameliel Bailey Prior to the Founding of the *National Era:* The Orientation of a Practical Abolitionist" (Ph.D. dissertation, University of Southern California, Los Angeles, 1958) represents a valuable start on a full study of this active antislavery editor. Norman Graebner's "Thomas Corwin and the Election of 1848," *Journal of Southern History,* XVII (February, 1951) summarizes succinctly the behavior and perceptions of an important Northern Whig moderate. William Y. Thompson's *Robert Toombs of Georgia* (Baton Rouge, 1966) is a well-done biography of a leading Southern conservative of the same party.

Monographs, Articles and Other Studies

Valuable information regarding politics and society in Ohio and the Western Reserve has been gleaned from a variety of sources. Harold W. Davis' "The Social and Economic Basis of the Whig Party in Ohio, 1828–1840" (Ph.D. dissertation, Case Western Reserve University, 1932) is a valuable political narrative despite a simplistic class analysis. The same general judgment applies to Edgar Allen Holt's *Party Politics in Ohio, 1840–1850* (Columbus, 1930). Eugene H. Roseboom's *The Civil War Era, 1850–1873,* volume 4 of *The History of Ohio,* edited by Carl Wittke, (Columbus, 1944), offers a comprehensive, detailed view.

Unfortunately, in recent years little scholarly research has been focused upon the Western Reserve. Harlan H. Hatcher's *The Western Reserve: The Story of New Connecticut in Ohio* (Cleveland, 1966) suffers from a uniformly shallow approach. In the absence of any scholarly synthesis, one must rely on antiquated works and little-known specialized studies. In the former category William W. Williams' *A History of Ashtabula County* (Cleveland, 1876) reveals a great deal about society in the rural Reserve. So does Cornelius Udell's *A Condensed History of Jefferson, Ohio* (Jefferson, 1878). A more recent but still antiquated study, William B. Neff's *Bench and Bar of Northern Ohio* (Cleveland, 1921), gives colorful, sometimes deep, glimpses into local legal practice. More helpful in reconstructing Reserve village life and institutions were Page Smith's *As a City Upon a Hill: The Town in American History* (New York, 1966) and Kenneth E. Davison's "Forgotten Ohioan: Elisha Whittlesey, 1782–1863" (Ph.D. dissertation, Case Western Reserve University, 1952).

Of the works dealing with the Reserve's deeply antislavery character, none is wholly satisfactory. Edward C. Reilley's "The Rise of Antislavery Sentiment in the Western Reserve" (Ph.D. dissertation, Case Western Reserve University, 1940) is factually comprehensive but interpretively and structurally weak. Willard D. Loomis' "The Antislavery Movement in Ashtabula County, Ohio, 1834–1854" (M.A. thesis, Case Western Reserve University, 1934) is of marginal value at best. Most informative are reminiscences of an old Reserve Free Soiler and Republican, Albert Gallatin Riddle, in his "The Rise of Antislavery Sentiment in the Western Reserve," *Magazine of Western History*, VI (June, 1887).

For scope and interpretive acuity, best among the broad studies of the antislavery movement is Louis Filler's *The Crusade Against Slavery 1830–1860* (New York, 1960). Gilbert Hobbes Barnes' zestful *The Antislavery Impulse, 1830–1844* (New York, 1933) is flawed with anti-Garrisonian and anti-New England biases but correctly emphasizes the interrelation of religion and reform. So do Whitney R. Cross's *The Burnt-Over District . . .* (Ithaca, 1950) and Alan E. Heimert's *Religion and the American Mind from the Great Awakening to the Revolution* (Cambridge, 1966). Dwight L. Dumond's *Antislavery: The Crusade for Freedom in America* (Ann Arbor, 1961) is a reliable guide to events but is weakened by polemical interpretation. Stanley Elkins in *Slavery: A Problem in American Institutional and Intellectual Life* (Chicago, 1959) is no more successful in explaining the collective motivation of abolitionists than is David Donald in "Toward a Reconsideration of the Abolitionists," in *Lincoln Reconsidered: Essays on the Civil War Era* (New York, 1961).

Russel Blaine Nye in *Fettered Freedom: Civil Liberties and the*

Slavery Controversy, 1830–1860 (Ann Arbor, 1949) views the anti-slavery crusade as a serious struggle for freedom and persuasively analyzes nonabolitionist sources of anti-Southern feeling. Many important perspectives on the antislavery movement are offered by the variety of authors writing in *The Antislavery Vanguard: New Essays on the Abolitionists,* edited by Martin Duberman (Princeton, 1965). Theodore Clarke Smith's *The Liberty and Free Soil Parties in the Northwest* (New York, 1897) is antique and merits immediately a modern replacement. Yet the work is a valuable factual and bibliographic source. Leon F. Litwack's *North of Slavery: The Negro in the Free States, 1790–1860* (Chicago, 1961) is a scholarly, persuasive documentation of the racism which permeated every stratum of ante-bellum Northern society.

Among the plethora of monographic studies dealing with the sectional conflict from 1845 to 1861, Allan Nevins' works are outstanding. His *Ordeal of the Union* (2 vols., New York, 1947) and *The Emergence of Lincoln* (2 vols., New York, 1950) are brilliantly written, magnificent in scope, and factually reliable. Chaplain W. Morrison in *Democratic Politics and Sectionalism, The Wilmot Proviso Controversy* (Chapel Hill, 1967) presents ably the havoc in party allegiance caused by the free soil issue during the years 1845 to 1848. Holman Hamilton's *Prologue to Conflict: The Crisis and Compromise of 1850* (Lexington, 1964) is a convenient, meaty analysis.

The national desire to avoid sectional rupture from 1851 to 1854, as seen in Louis Kossuth's visit to America, is sketched by Reinhard Luthin in "A Visitor from Hungary," *South Atlantic Quarterly,* XLVII (January, 1948). The motives and factors causing the reopening of turmoil over slavery in 1854 are capably examined in Roy Franklin Nichols' "The Kansas-Nebraska Act: A Century of Historiography," *Mississippi Valley Historical Review,* XLIII (September, 1956). Two monographs give highly detailed accounts of the volatile period after 1854, which led ultimately to secession: Roy Franklin Nichols' *The Disruption of American Democracy* (New York, 1948) and George Fort Milton's *The Eve of the Conflict: Stephen A. Douglas and the Needless War* (Boston and New York, 1934). Both of these works interpret the ensuing war as avoidable and censure the "extremist blunderers" like Giddings who failed to forestall it. This interpretation is effectively challenged by Arthur M. Schlesinger, Jr. in "The Causes of the American Civil War: A Note on Historical Sentimentalism," *Partisan Review,* XVI (April, 1949). The onset of the War is recounted well in Kenneth M. Stampp's *And the War Came* (Baton Rouge, 1950).

David Donald's "The Radicals and Lincoln," in *Lincoln Reconsidered,* thoroughly refutes the radical versus conservative congressional dichotomy on wartime issues presented by T. Harry Williams' *Lincoln and the Radicals* (Madison, 1941). Among the best recent studies on Reconstruction are LaWanda and John H. Cox's *Politics, Principle, and Prejudice, 1865–1866: The Dilemma of Reconstruction America* (New York, 1963) ; Eric L. McKitrick's *Andrew Johnson and Reconstruction* (Chicago, 1960) ; and Kenneth Stampp's *The Era of Reconstruction* (New York, 1965).

An important work on the sectional conflict has recently appeared, but unfortunately too late to be consulted in the preparation of this study. Aileen Kraditor, *Means and Ends in American Abolitionism: Garrison and His Critics on Strategy and Tactics, 1834–1850* (New York, 1969), brilliantly analyzes Garrisonian theories of agitation and persuasively argues for the acuity and appropriateness of radical behavior.

BIBLIOGRAPHY

Primary Sources

MANUSCRIPT COLLECTIONS

Adams Family Papers, Massachusetts Historical Society, Boston, Massachusetts. Papers of John Quincy Adams and Charles Francis Adams.

James A. Briggs Papers, Ohio Historical Society, Columbus, Ohio.

James A. Briggs Papers, Western Reserve Historical Society, Cleveland, Ohio.

Ephriam Brown Papers, Western Reserve Historical Society, Cleveland, Ohio.

Salmon P. Chase Papers, Historical Society of Pennsylvania, Philadelphia, Pennsylvania.

Salmon P. Chase Papers, Library of Congress, Washington, D.C.

David Lee and Lydia Maria Child Papers, Boston Public Library, Boston, Massachusetts.

Edward Fitch Papers, Ohio Historical Society, Columbus, Ohio.

William Lloyd Garrison Papers, Boston Public Library, Boston, Massachusetts.

Joshua R. Giddings Papers, Miscellaneous Collections, The New York Historical Society, New York, New York.

Joshua R. Giddings Papers, Miscellanous Collections, Manuscript Division, New York Public Library, Astor, Lenox and Tilden Foundations, New York, New York.

Joshua R. Giddings Papers, Ohio Historical Society, Columbus, Ohio.

Joshua R. Giddings-George W. Julian Papers, Library of Congress, Washington, D.C.

Joshua R. Giddings-Milton Sutliffe Papers, Norton Collection, Western Reserve Historical Society, Cleveland, Ohio.

William Henry Harrison Papers, Library of Congress, Washington, D.C.

Peter Hitchcock Papers, Western Reserve Historical Society, Cleveland, Ohio.

George W. Julian Papers, Indiana State Library, Indianapolis, Indiana.

Joshua Leavitt Papers, Library of Congress, Washington, D.C.

Robert Todd Lincoln Papers, Library of Congress, Washington, D.C.

John McLean Papers, Library of Congress, Washington, D.C.

Samuel May-J. Miller McKim Papers, The Cornell Antislavery Collection, Cornell University Library, Cornell University, Ithaca, New York.

John G. Palfrey Papers, Houghton Library, Harvard University, Cambridge, Massachusetts.

Robert S. Pierce Papers, Western Reserve Historical Society, Cleveland, Ohio.

Albert Gallatin Riddle Papers, Henry E. Huntington Library, San Marino, California.

Albert Gallatin Riddle Papers, Western Reserve Historical Society, Cleveland, Ohio.

Gerrit Smith–Miller Papers, Syracuse University Library, Syracuse, New York.

Thaddeus Stevens Papers, Library of Congress, Washington, D.C.

Charles Sumner Papers, Houghton Library, Harvard University, Cambridge, Massachusetts.

Lewis Tappan Papers, Library of Congress, Washington, D.C.

James W. Taylor Papers, New-York Historical Society, New York, New York.

Benjamin F. Wade Papers, Library of Congress, Washington, D.C.

Benjamin F. Wade–Milton Sutliffe Papers, Norton Collection, Western Reserve Historical Society, Cleveland, Ohio.

James Washburn Papers, Western Reserve Historical Society, Cleveland, Ohio.

Theodore Dwight Weld Papers, Library of Congress, Washington, D.C.

Elisha Whittlesey Papers, Western Reserve Historical Society, Cleveland, Ohio.

Robert C. Winthrop Papers, Massachusetts Historical Society, Boston, Massachusetts.

NEWSPAPERS

The Anti-Slavery Bugle (Salem, Ohio), 1845–1860.

The Emancipator (New York, Boston), 1839–1850.
The Herald (Cleveland), 1838–1859.
The Liberator (Boston), 1840–1860.
The Liberty Herald (Warren, Ohio), 1842–1846.
The National Anti-Slavery Standard (Boston), 1842–1860.
The National Era (Washington), 1847–1860.
The National Intelligencer (tri-weekly, Washington), 1839–1860.
The Ohio Luminary (Ashtabula, Ohio), 1830.
The Ohio Republican (Canfield, Ohio), 1830.
The Ohio State Journal (Columbus), 1838–1859.
The Ohio Statesman (Columbus), 1838–1852.
The Philanthropist (and title variants, Cincinnati), 1838–1847.
The Plain Dealer (Cleveland), 1842–1860.
The Reporter (Conneaut, Ohio), 1842–1860.
The Telegraph (Painesville, Ohio), 1838–1860.
The True Democrat (Cleveland), 1847–1859.
The Sentinel (Ashtabula), 1826–1864.
The Western Reserve Chronicle (Chardon, Ohio), 1838–1860.

U.S. GOVERNMENT PUBLICATIONS

Congressional Globe, 1838–1873. 46 vols. Washington, D.C., 1833–1873.
Richardson, James D., comp. *Compilation of the Messages and Papers of the Presidents.* Washington, D.C., 1896–1899.

PUBLISHED PRIMARY SOURCES

Adams, Charles Francis (ed.). *A Memoir of John Quincy Adams, Comprising Portions of His Diary from 1795 to 1848.* 13 vols. Boston, 1874–1877.
Barnes, Gilbert Hobbes, and Dumond, Dwight Lowell (eds.). *Letters of Theodore Dwight Weld, Angelina Grimké Weld, and Sarah Grimké, 1822–1844.* 2 vols. New York, 1934.
Chase, Salmon P. "The Diary and Correspondence of Salmon P. Chase," *Annual Report of The American Historical Association,* 1902, II. Washington, D.C., 1903.
Dumond, Dwight Lowell (ed.). *Letters of James Gillespie Birney, 1831–1857.* 2 vols. New York, 1938.
Dyer, Oliver (ed.). *Phonographic Report of the Proceedings of the Free Soil Convention at Buffalo.* Buffalo, 1848.

Giddings, Joshua R. *The Exiles of Florida, The History of the Seminole War.* Columbus, 1858.

_____. *A History of the Rebellion, Its Authors and Causes.* Cleveland, 1864.

_____. *Speech of the Hon. J.R. Giddings Delivered in the House of Representatives, Concord, N.H., On the Evening of June 29, 1847.* Concord, 1847.

_____. *Speeches in Congress.* Boston, 1852.

Hamlin, Belle (ed.). "Selections from the Follett Papers," *Quarterly Publications of the Historical and Philosophical Society of Ohio, 1915–1917.* Vols. X–XII.

Jameson, J. Franklin (ed.). "The Correspondence of John C. Calhoun," *Annual Report of The American Historical Association, 1899.* Washton, D.C., 1900.

Johnson, Charles W. *Proceedings of the First Three Republican National Conventions of 1856, 1860 and 1864, With Full Transcripts of Speeches and Resolutions.* Minneapolis, 1893.

Ohio Politics. "Father Giddings" Dodges Under The Bush with his Colored Friends. n.p., n.d.

Pierce, Edward L. (ed.). *Memoir and Letters of Charles Sumner.* 4 vols. Boston and London, 1877–1893.

Shanks, Henry Thomas (ed.). *The Papers of Willie Person Mangum.* 5 vols. Raleigh, 1950–1956.

Schuckers, Jacobs S. *The Life and Public Services of Salmon Portland Chase.* New York, 1874.

Smith, Joseph P. (ed.). *A History of the Republican Party in Ohio.* Chicago, 1898.

Warden, Robert Bruce. *An Account of the Private Life and Public Services of Salmon Portland Chase.* Cincinnati, 1874.

Winthrop, Robert Charles, Jr. (ed.). *A Memoir of Robert C. Winthrop.* Boston 1897.

Secondary Sources

ARTICLES

Alston, Ellis. "Samuel Lewis, Progressive Educator in the Early History of Ohio," *Ohio Achaeological and Historical Quarterly,* XXI (January, 1916), 71–82.

Boucher, Chauncy V. *"In Re* That Aggressive Slaveocracy," *Mississippi Valley Historical Review,* VIII (July, 1921) , 361–82.

Cochran, William C. "The Western Reserve and the Fugitive Slave Law." In *Western Reserve Historical Society Collections* (Cleveland, 1920) , 118–204.

Crowe, Charles. "The Quest for Utopia." In *Main Problems in American History,* ed. Howard Quint, Milton Cantor, and Dean Albertson, I, 217–30, 2 vols. Homewood, Illinois, 1964.

Davis, David Brion. "Some Themes of Counter-Subversion: An Analysis of Anti-Catholic, Anti-Masonic and Anti-Mormon Literature," *Mississippi Valley Historical Review,* XLII (January, 1963) , 205–24.

Davis, Harold W. "Religion in the Western Reserve," *Ohio Archaeological and Historical Quarterly,* XXVIII (May, 1929) , 303–26.

Duberman, Martin. "The Abolitionists and Psychology," *Journal of Negro History,* XLVII (July, 1962) , 183–91.

Gabriel, Ralph. "Evangelical Religion and Popular Romanticism in Early Nineteenth Century America." In *Historical Vistas: Readings in United States History,* ed. Grady McWhiney and Robert Weibe, I, 407–19. 2 vols. Boston, 1963.

Gatell, Frank O. "Palfrey's Vote, the Conscience Whigs, and the Election of Speaker Winthrop," *New England Quarterly,* XXXI (March, 1958) , 218–31.

Graebner, Norman. "Thomas Corwin and the Election of 1848," *Journal of Southern History,* XVII (February, 1951) , 162–79.

Land, Mary Bright. "John Brown's Ohio Environment," *Ohio Archaeological and Historical Quarterly,* LVII (January, 1948) , 24–48.

Long, Byron R. "Joshua Giddings, A Champion of Political Freedom," *Ohio Archaeological and Historical Quarterly,* XXVIII (September, 1929) , 31–53.

Ludlum, Robert P. "Joshua R. Giddings, Radical," *Mississippi Valley Historical Review,* XXIII (June, 1936) , 31–53.

Luthin, Reinhard. "Salmon P. Chase: Political Career Before the Civil War," *Mississippi Valley Historical Review,* XXIX (January, 1943) , 517–40.

————. "A Visitor From Hungary," *South Atlantic Quarterly,* XLVII (January, 1948) , 29–34.

McPherson, James M. "The Fight Against the Gag Rule: Joshua Leavitt and the Antislavery Insurgency in the Whig Party, 1839–1842," *Journal of Negro History,* XLVIII (July, 1963) , 177–95.

Nichols, Roy Franklin. "The Kansas-Nebraska Act: A Century of Historiography," *Mississippi Valley Historical Review,* XLIII (September, 1956), 621–47.

Nye, Russel Blaine. "The Slave Power Conspiracy, 1830–1860," *Science and Society,* X (July, 1946), 262–74.

Porter, Kenneth W. "Negroes and the Seminole War, 1835–1842," *Journal of Southern History,* XXX (November, 1964), 427–40.

Preston, Emmet D. "The Fugitive Slave Acts of Ohio," *Journal of Negro History,* XXVIII (October, 1943), 422–47.

Rayback, Joseph. "The Liberty Party Leaders of Ohio, Exponents of Antislavery Coalition," *Ohio Archaeological and Historical Quarterly,* LVII (May, 1948), 161–78.

Riddle, Albert Gallatin. "The Rise of Antislavery Sentiment in the Western Reserve," *Magazine of Western History,* VI (June, 1887), 145–56.

Savage, Sherman W. "The Origins of the Giddings Resolutions," *Ohio Archaeological and Historical Quarterly,* XLVIII (October, 1938), 20–39.

Schlesinger, Arthur M., Jr. "The Causes of the American Civil War: A Note on Historical Sentimentalism," *Partisan Review* XVI (April, 1949), 968–81.

Smiley, David L. "Cassius Clay and John G. Fee, A Study in Southern Antislavery Thought," *Journal of Negro History,* XLII (July, 1957), 201–13.

Woodward, C. Vann. "The Antislavery Myth," *American Scholar,* XXI (April, 1962), 312–28.

Wyatt-Brown, Bertram. "William Lloyd Garrison and Antislavery Unity: A Reappraisal," *Civil War History,* XIII (March, 1967), 5–24.

_____. "Abolitionism: Its Meaning for Contemporary American Reform," *Midwest Quarterly* VIII, (Autumn, 1966), 41–55.

UNPUBLISHED THESES AND DISSERTATIONS

Bates, Jack W. "John Quincy Adams and the Antislavery Movement." Ph.D. dissertation, University of Southern California, 1953.

Davis, Harold W. "The Social and Economic Basis of the Whig Party in Ohio, 1828–1840." Ph.D. dissertation, Case Western Reserve University, 1932.

Davison, Kenneth E. "Forgotten Ohioan: Elisha Whittlesey, 1782–1863." Ph.D. dissertation, Case Western Reserve University, 1952.

Goldfarb, Joel. "The Life of Gamaliel Bailey Prior to the Founding of the *National Era:* The Orientation of a Practical Abolitionist." Ph.D. dissertation, University of Southern California, Los Angeles, 1958.

Harris, Alfred G. "Emancipation in the District of Columbia, 1801–1862." Ph.D. dissertation, Ohio State University, 1947.

Land, Mary Bright. "Old Backbone: 'Bluff' Ben Wade." Ph.D. dissertation, Case Western Reserve University, 1950, 2 vols.

Loomis, Willard D. "The Antislavery Movement in Ashtabula County, Ohio, 1834–1854." M.A. thesis, Case Western Reserve University, 1934.

Loubert, J. Daniel. "The Orientation of Henry Wilson, 1812–1856." Ph.D. dissertation, Boston University, 1952.

Ludlum, Robert P. "Joshua R. Giddings, Antislavery Radical (1795–1844)." Ph.D. dissertation, Cornell University, 1935.

Mandel, Bernard. "The Northern Working Class and the Abolition of Slavery." Ph.D. dissertation, Case Western Reserve University, 1952.

Reilley, Edward C. "The Rise of Antislavery Sentiment in the Western Reserve." Ph.D. dissertation, Case Western Reserve University, 1940.

Solberg, Richard W. "Joshua R. Giddings: Politician and Idealist." Ph.D. dissertation, University of Chicago, 1952.

Published Secondary Sources

Aaron, Daniel (ed.). *Americans in Crisis: Fourteen Crucial Episodes in American History.* New York, 1952.

Barnes, Gilbert Hobbes. *The Antislavery Impulse, 1830–1844.* New York, 1933.

Bartlett, Irving. *Wendell Phillips, Brahmin Radical.* Boston, 1961.

Bartlett, Ruhl Jacob, *John C. Frémont and the Republican Party.* Columbus, 1930.

Bemis, Samuel Flagg. *John Quincy Adams and the Union.* New York, 1956.

Benson, Lee. *The Concept of Jacksonian Democracy: New York as a Test Case.* Princeton, 1961.

Berwanger, Eugene H. *The Frontier Against Slavery: Western Anti-Negro Prejudice and the Slavery Extension Controversy.* Urbana, 1967.

Billington, Ray Allen. *The Protestant Crusade, 1800–1860: A Study of the Origins of American Nativism.* New York, 1938.

Brodie, Fawn M. *Thaddeus Stevens, Scourge of the South.* 2d edition. New York, 1966.

Buell, Walter. *Joshua R. Giddings, A Sketch.* Cleveland, 1882.

Cochran, William Cox. "The Western Reserve and the Fugitive Slave Law." In *Western Reserve Historical Society Collections.* Cleveland, 1920.

Cox, LaWanda, and Cox, John H. *Politics, Principle, and Prejudice, 1865–1866: The Dilemma of Reconstruction America.* New York, 1963.

Cross, Whitney R. *The Burnt-Over District: The Social and Intellectual History of Enthusiastic Religion in Western New York, 1800–1850.* Ithaca, 1950.

Current, Richard Nelson. *Old Thad Stevens: A Story of Ambition.* Madison, 1942.

Davis, David Brion. *The Problem of Slavery in Western Culture.* Ithaca, 1966.

Donald, David H. *Charles Sumner and the Coming of the Civil War.* New York, 1960.

————. *Lincoln Reconsidered: Essays on the Civil War Era.* 2d edition. New York, 1961.

Duberman, Martin (ed.). *The Antislavery Vanguard: New Essays on the Abolitionists.* Princeton, 1965.

————. *Charles Francis Adams, 1807–1886* (Boston, 1960).

Dumond, Dwight L. *Antislavery Origins of the Civil War of the United States.* Ann Arbor, 1939.

————. *Antislavery: The Crusade for Freedom in America.* Ann Arbor, 1961.

Durden, Robert F. *James Shepherd Pike: Republicanism and the American Negro, 1850–1882.* Durham, 1957.

Elkins, Stanley M. *Slavery: A Problem in American Institutional and Intellectual Life.* Chicago, 1959.

Filler, Louis. *The Crusade Against Slavery, 1830–1860.* New York, 1960.

Fladeland, Betty Lorraine. *James G. Birney, Slaveholder to Abolitionist.* Ithaca, 1955.

Frederickson, George M. *The Inner Civil War: Northern Intellectuals and the Crisis of the Union.* New York, 1965.

Gara, Larry. *The Liberty Line: The Legend of the Underground Railroad.* Lexington, 1961.

Gatell, Frank Otto. *John Gorham Palfrey and the New England Conscience*. Cambridge, 1963.

Going, Charles Buxton. *David Wilmont, Free Soiler: A Biography of the Great Advocate of the Wilmot Proviso*. New York, 1924.

Griffin, Clifford S. *Their Brothers' Keepers: Moral Stewardship in the United States, 1800–1865*. New Brunswick, 1960.

Hamilton, Holman. *Prologue to Conflict: The Crisis and Compromise of 1850*. Lexington, 1964.

_____. *Zachary Taylor, Soldier in the White House*. Vol. 2. Indianapolis and New York, 1951.

Hammond, Jabez D. *The Life and Times of Silas Wright, Late Governor of New York*. Syracuse, 1848.

Harlow, Ralph Volney. *Gerrit Smith: Philanthropist and Reformer*. New York, 1939.

Harlow, Ralph V., and Blake, Nelson M. *The United States From Wilderness to World Power*. 4th edition. New York, 1964.

Harrington, Fred H. *Fighting Politician: Major General N. P. Banks*. Philadelphia, 1948.

Hatcher, Harlan H. *The Western Reserve: The Story of New Connecticut in Ohio*. Cleveland, 1966.

Heimert, Alan E. *Religion and the American Mind from the Great Awakening to the Revolution*. Cambridge, 1966.

Holt, Edgar Allen. *Party Politics in Ohio 1840–1850*. Columbus, 1930.

Jordan, Winthrop. *White Over Black: American Attitudes Toward the Negro, 1550–1812*. Chapel Hill, 1968.

Julian, George W. *The Life of Joshua R. Giddings*. Chicago, 1892.

Litwack, Leon F. *North of Slavery: The Negro in the Free States, 1790–1860*. Chicago, 1961.

McKitrick, Eric L. *Andrew Johnson and Reconstruction*. Chicago, 1960.

McLoughlin, William C., Jr. *Modern Revivalism: Charles Grandison Finney to Billy Graham*. New York, 1959.

McPherson, James M. *The Struggle for Equality: Abolitionists and the Negro in the Civil War and Reconstruction*. Princeton, 1964.

Malin, James C. *John Brown and the Legend of Fifty-Six*. Philadelphia, 1942.

_____. *The Nebraska Question, 1852–1854*. Lawrence, 1953.

Merrill, Walter M. *Against Wind and Tide: A Biography of William Lloyd Garrison*. Cambridge, 1963.

Miller, Perry. *The Life of the Mind in America from the Revolution to the Civil War*. New York, 1965.

Milton, George Fort. *The Eve of the Conflict: Stephen A. Douglas and the Needless War.* Boston and New York, 1934.

Morrison, Chaplain W. *Democratic Politics and Sectionalism, The Wilmot Proviso Controversy.* Chapel Hill, 1967.

Neff, William B. *Bench and Bar of Northern Ohio.* Cleveland, 1921.

Nevins, Allan. *The Emergence of Lincoln.* 2 vols. New York, 1950.

_____. *The Ordeal of the Union.* 2 vols. New York, 1947.

Nichols, Alice. *Bleeding Kansas.* New York, 1954.

Nichols, Roy Franklin. *The Disruption of American Democracy.* New York, 1948.

Nye, Russel Blaine. *Fettered Freedom: Civil Liberties and the Slavery Controversy, 1830–1860.* Ann Arbor, 1949.

Pressley, Thomas J. *Americans Interpret Their Civil War.* Princeton, 1954.

Riddle, Albert G. *The Life of Benjamin F. Wade.* Cleveland, 1888.

Riddleburger, Patrick, *George Washington Julian: A Study in Nineteenth Century Reform and Politics.* Indianapolis, 1966.

Roseboom, Eugene H. *The Civil War Era, 1850–1873.* Vol. 4 of *The History of Ohio,* edited by Carl Wittke. Columbus, 1944.

Schlesinger, Arthur M., Jr. *The Age of Jackson.* Boston, 1950.

Sewell, Richard H. *John P. Hale and the Politics of Abolition.* Cambridge, 1965.

Smiley, David L. *The Lion of Whitehall: The Life of Cassius M. Clay.* Madison, 1962.

Smith, Donnal V. "Salmon Chase and Civil War Politics," *Publications of the Ohio Historical Society, No. 17.* Columbus, 1931.

Smith, Page. *As a City Upon a Hill: The Town in American History.* New York, 1966.

Smith, Theodore Clarke. *The Liberty and Free Soil Parties in the Northwest.* New York, 1897.

Stampp, Kenneth M. *And The War Came.* Baton Rouge, 1950.

_____. *The Era of Reconstruction.* New York, 1965.

_____. *The Peculiar Institution.* New York, 1956.

Thomas, Benjamin Platt. *Theodore Weld, Crusader for Freedom.* New Brunswick, 1950.

Thomas, John. *The Liberator, William Lloyd Garrison: A Biography.* Boston, 1963.

Thompson, William Y. *Robert Toombs of Georgia.* Baton Rouge, 1966.

BIBLIOGRAPHY

Trefousse, Hans L. *Benjamin Franklin Wade: Radical Republican from Ohio.* New York, 1963.

Udell, Cornelius, *A Condensed History of Jefferson, Ohio.* Jefferson 1878.

Van Deusen, Glyndon G. *The Life of Henry Clay.* Boston, 1937.

————. *William Henry Seward, Lincoln's Secretary of State, the Negotiator of the Alaska Purchase.* New York, 1967.

Williams, T. Harry. *Lincoln and the Radicals.* Madison, 1941.

Williams, William W. *A History of Ashtabula County.* Cleveland, 1876.

Wyatt-Brown, Bertram. *Lewis Tappan and the Evangelical War Against Slavery.* Cleveland, 1969.

INDEX

52–53, 55–56, 66–67, 84–87, 95–97, 98; and election of 1840, 54–56; and the insurgency (1841–42), 69–71; and *Creole* case, 70–71; and J. Q. Adams' censure, 70–71; opposes slave claims, 72; censured, 73–74; reelected after censure, 75–76; reasserts *Creole* resolutions, 77–78; and "Pacificus" essays, 84–86; tries improving lot of D.C. Negroes, 89–90, 147, 185, 192n56, 230; leader of insurgency (1843), 90; attacks naval appropriation, 91; protests treatment of Indians, 91, 213; and Texas annexation, 92–94, 103–5, 107; supports Clay (1844), 94–97; reelected (1844), 97; praises Hale and Brinckerhoff, 104; dislike of Winthrop, 107, 125, 183; speaks against slave claim, 108; attacked by Black, 108–9; and Oregon question, 109–13; opposes Mexican War, 113–15, 124, 125, 147–48; issues "dissolution letter," 115–16; travels to New Hampshire, 116–17; reelected (1846), 118; and Wilmot Proviso, 118, 128–31; and Corwin as nominee (1848), 128, 132–33, 134; distrusts Barnburners, 135; and election of Speaker (1847), 135–36, 141–42; friendship with Palfrey, 136, 143, 146, 163n27; controversy with Winthrop, 143, 145–46, 147, 150–51, 155; opposes resolutions of thanks for Taylor and Scott, 147; mollifies Liberty party, 148–49; polarizes northern Whigs, 151; and formation of Free Soil party, 151–52, 154–59; loses Ohio antislavery leadership to Chase, 152; and *"Pearl"* affair, 152–53; trip to Massachusetts, 154–55; suspicious of Van Buren, 156; reelected (1848), 159; organizes con-

gressional antislavery, 167–68; contrasted with typical free soilers, 169; and Gott's resolutions, 169–70; and Calhoun's "Address," 171–72; fails election to Senate, 173–75; opposes Free Soil-Democratic fusion, 175–79; disillusioned with Chase, 179; and election of Speaker (1849), 180–82; hurt by partisan attacks, 182–83; and Compromise of 1850, 184, 185, 186–87; and non-compliance with Fugitive Slave Law, 187, 196, 197, 269; preserves political independence, 194–95; reelected (1850), 195; rebuilds Free Soil party, 197–205; and senatorial election (1851), 198–99, 220n46; attempts fusion of Free Soil party and Liberty League, 200–205; renews agitation in Congress, 205–6; and "Kossuth affair", 206–7; views on pacifism, 208, 220n46; speech opposing major parties, 212–13; election of 1852, 214–16; reelected (1852), 216, opposes slave claim, 223; friendship with Gerrit Smith, 223; and Kansas-Nebraska Act, 224–25, 227, 245n60; on fringe of Republican party, 226, 229, 233–34, 243n27, 245n60; reelected (1854), 229; campaigns in Illinois, 229–30; opposes Know-Nothings, 231–33; and election of Banks as Speaker (1855), 235–37; on Committee on Territories, 237; suffers strokes, 238, 251, 257; and assault on Sumner, 238–39; and Republican party platform (1856), 239–40; wishes to retire, 240–41; reelected (1856), 241; rejected by Republicans, 247–51; promotes anti-disunion conventions, 250–51; and Dred Scott decisions, 253–54; rejects compensated emancipation, 255; cooperates with "radi-

cal abolitionists," 255–57; campaigns for Chase, 257; and Lecompton Constitution, 257–58; not renominated (1858), 259–60; final speech in Congress, 261–62; and lecture tours, 267–68; and John Brown's raid, 269–70; and Republican convention (1860), 271–73; editorial exchange wiith Wendell Phillips, 273; advises Lincoln, 273, 274; on secession crisis and Civil War, 274–75; as U.S. Consul General to Canada, 275–76; opposes McClellan, 276; as "radical Republican," 276; on Emancipation Proclamation, 276–77; death of, 277
—character and antislavery principles of: elitism of, 10–11; ambition of, 10, 11, 15, 20–21n46; conservatism of, 12–14, 20n36; 115–17, 133, 158; religious views of, 24–25, 26–27, 70–72, 208–11, 252–53, 258; antislavery doctrines of, 32–33, 46–49, 84–86, 115–16, 171, 187, 197, 199, 200, 255, 269; and rights of Negroes, 32, 131, 168–69, 197, 199, 226, 262; antislavery strategy and tactics of, 43–46, 62–65, 109–13, 115–16, 131, 135–36, 141–42, 186, 207–8, 256, 260–61, 273; sectionalism of, 45–46; evangelism of, 86–87, 106–7, 177, 197–98; opinions of institutions, 86–87, 252–53; optimism of, 107, 108, 113, 151, 183; bravery of, 109, 152; naïveté of, 152; view of the Negro, 199–200, 254, 256; on role of agitators, 212–13, 219n33. See also Declaration of Independence.

Giddings, Laura Ann, 51
Giddings, Laura Waters, 7, 50, 251

Giddings, Lura Maria, 7, 22, 26, 50–51
Glasscock, Thomas, 43, 44
Globe (Washington), 197
Goodell, William: rejects Free Soil party, 156, 214; and Liberty League, 203; contributions to Free Soil party, 214
Gott, Daniel: introduces resolutions to abolish D.C. slave trade, 169–70; mentioned, 167
Great Revival: and antislavery, 27–28, 29; mentioned, 25–26
Greeley, Horace, 132, 133, 157, 158–59, 237, 267
Green, Beriah, 28

Hale, John Parker: antislavery convictions of, 104; elected to U.S. Senate, 113, 116; role in *"Pearl"* affair," 153; Liberty party nominee for president, 155, 156; Free Soil nominee for president, 214; aids Giddings' re-election, 215; defeated for president, 216; and John Brown's raid, 270; mentioned, 110, 112, 129, 133, 151, 184, 251
Hamilton, Holman: cited, 192n53
"Hamilton County Question," 173–74, 175–78
Hamlin, Edward S., 117, 169, 215
Hamlin, Hannibal, 184, 225
Harrison, William Henry: elected president (1840), 54–55; promises to purge Giddings from Whig party, 66; mentioned, 51, 52, 53, 124, 158
Hawthorne, Nathaniel, 4
Herald (Cleveland), 74, 95, 117, 143, 158, 197, 215
Herald (New York City), 270
History of the Rebellion, Its Authors and Causes, A (Giddings), 276
Holmes, Isaac, 73, 142